THE TOOTH AND THE TAIL

AN ORAL HISTORY OF AMERICAN SUPPORT TROOPS IN VIETNAM

EDITED BY LAWRENCE ROCK
SGT   USMC (1964 – 1967)

Published through Create Space by Lawrence Rock
October, 2012

Copyright 2012 by Lawrence Rock

All rights reserved

This book is dedicated

To those who served

CONTENTS

PART I: THE EARLY YEARS

1. GOING TO WORK
2. MEETING OUR ALLIES
3. MEETING THE ENEMY
4. FRUSTRATION
5. ADVENTURES ALOFT
6. ON LAND AND SEA
7. GUYS AND DOLLS – ASIA CHAPTER
8. END OF THE EARLY YEARS

PART II: THE MIDDLE YEARS

9. 1967 ARRIVALS: OUR NUMBERS SWELL
10. MIXED REVIEWS ON ALLIES
11. A MOMENT OF JESUS
12. FRUSTRATIONS: WORK IN IT; PLAY IN IT
13. PERSONNEL: HEARING THE LIGHTS
14. "WE'RE NOT GOING TO MAKE IT"

15. 1968 ARRIVALS: CALMS BEFORE STORMS
16. THE ASIAN MELTING POT
17. LOVE FROM NEW JERSEY AND DRAGONS NAMED PUFF
18. REPLACEMENT PARTS AND RAINDROPS
19. TET
20. STRIPES AND MEDALS
21. HELMETS WITH BEER; THIMBLES WITH CHEER

22. 1969 ARRIVALS: THE SNAKE ON A STRING
23. VIETNAMIZATION
24. SITTING ON A MINE
25. FRUSTRATIONS & THE TRADING GAME
26. WALTER CRONKITE SURRENDERS
27. SPARE SOCKS
28. THE END OF THE MIDDLE YEARS

PART III: THE LATE YEARS

29. 1970 ARRIVALS: TOO MANY PEOPLE, NOT ENOUGH WAR
30. VIETNAMIZATION CONTINUES
31. EVIL SPIRITS, POTHEADS AND THE DEATH OF SGT. PEPPER
32. ON TO CAMBODIA
33. 1971 ARRIVALS: THE WELL-OILED MACHINE
34. WORKING WITH THE VIETNAMESE
35. DRUGS
36. THE LAST HURRAH
37. WELCOME HOME
38. PEACE WITH HONOR
39. EPILOGUE

Preface

Residents of London in 1940, or Stalingrad in September of 1942, or Hiroshima on August 6, 1945 knew there was a war going on. They could see it, hear it and smell it. Saigon in the late 1950's and early 1960's did not have the look or feel of a war zone. It was called the Pearl of the Orient and the land of a million beautiful women. Acacia-lined boulevards and bougainvillea-framed villas masked the fact that Vietnam was at war; was always at war.

Saigon: 1965
Courtesy: Harley Brinkley

Saigon at war had a much different look than London, Stalingrad or Hiroshima at war. The French-influenced buildings were intact and the cacophony of explosions and the odor of cordite and rotting corpses that jarred World War II London, Stalingrad or Hiroshima were missing; instead the jangle of bicycle bells and cycalos and the sometimes all-too-human fragrances of the city. War is hell and if it was hell in Saigon, it was hell at a slow, lazy pace, like the labors of an overhead fan working to cool a bamboo-lined room in 110 degree heat. Whatever fighting there was took place in the jungle where it belonged; various coups provided the entertainment in the cities. War is war despite the sheep's clothing, although this was a different war, a war with no front lines, no safe "rear areas;" a war in which support personnel would be more important and numerous, and often more at risk, than ever.

A loud siren pierced the hot August night. The lone light bulb dangling from the center of the tent went dark and sound replaced sight. Everyone jumped; since I had only been in Vietnam about twelve hours, I followed them out of the tent into a foreign, flare-lit scene and jumped into a muddy trench. I was wearing white underwear with a cartridge belt around my waist, a helmet and a useless M-14. They had issued us everything we needed earlier that day except ammunition. "Who's got some ammo?" I yelled. No one responded. I was within earshot of fifty Marines and no one offered anything. "Who's got some rounds?" I persisted. A Marine nearby begrudgingly gave me five rounds. I loaded them into a magazine and popped the magazine into my M-14. A sergeant stood above our trench and ordered everyone to follow him. He led us to a small field between the living area and the office work spaces and told us to lie down. There was no shooting; why the siren? Using my helmet I scooped out a small crater in the sand for my chest cavity and awaited orders. Finally the sergeant had us walk through the flare-lit field elbow to elbow, looking for what? We found nothing and finally went back to our tents, covered with sand and sweat. And uncertainty. We were issued ammo the next day, and I took plenty of it.

LCpl Rock, 1st MAW Motor Pool, Danang

Like seventy percent of those who arrived in Vietnam during 1965 and 1966 I arrived by ship[i] (*MSTS General Daniel I. Sultan*) in late August of 1965, landing on the same Danang beach where the first battalions of Marines splashed ashore in March. I was an Embarkation clerk and jeep driver for my year with the 1st Marine Air Wing. I was a support troop. Support troops were defined as those who, while they may find themselves in combat situations, had a primary mission to provide support for the combat troops. All who served in Vietnam – combat or support troop – received combat pay every month. The ratio of support troops to combat troops during WW II was 4:1. By Vietnam, the ratio had risen to 10:1. Ninety percent of those sent to Vietnam were not sent there to fight.

Combat personnel and support troops were given basic combat training and a brief introduction to hand grenades, machine guns, flame throwers and bazookas. In my case I threw one grenade, fired the flame thrower and one bazooka round. Our M-60 machine gun class was rained out and never rescheduled; I didn't see the M-60 until one night in 1965 at Danang when the sirens were wailing and I was ordered to a machine gun bunker. Two grunts were manning the gun and I watched the back door and prayed that they would not become disabled.

Before the arrival of American ground forces in South Vietnam in March of 1965, there were the advisors, American military personnel either attached to South Vietnamese military units or men serving in some support capacity. On January 1, 1962, South Vietnam authorized the integration of American advisors within their units, apparently a formality since the American "advisors" had been there for over ten years by 1964, the first of them arriving about the time the French were exiting the revolving door that was Vietnam. In the early "advisor" days support was hard to come by. A handful of American troops were integrated within select Vietnamese units and expected to make do while training them. Their numbers had swelled from 800 in April of 1961, to 23,000 by 1964[ii]. President Kennedy, enamored with the concept of fighting a counter-insurgency rather than another world war sought to stop the spread of communism and the falling of Asian dominoes at low cost; advisors instead of armies. And so it began. The "advisors" were there to train and counsel the Vietnamese and only use their weapons when they "felt threatened." Decades later most of these men still maintain their professionalism and talk primarily of their work as "advisors" and not of any offensive actions in which they might have been involved. The term "advisor" was, strictly-speaking, applied to those who worked with and trained South Vietnamese armed forces. In a larger sense, every American in Vietnam up to the mid 60's may have been termed an advisor. Robert McNamara told congress that the advisors were there mainly for "logistical and training support. . . it was a Vietnamese war and by leaving the crutch there too long, we would weaken the Vietnamese rather than strengthen them."[iii]

Vietnam lacked port facilities, railroads, highways, telephone lines[iv] *– things that would be required for our military intervention – and the mobilization of troops and construction costs would be enormous, far larger than for Korea. But to "stop the spread of communism" and the falling of dominoes the decision to intervene was made. Some would argue that we attempted to impose a military solution on a political problem. But Support Troops, like Combat Troops, go where they are sent. In any case, a full-scale American military commitment was made. And with commitment came support; these are the stories of American support troops in Vietnam – America's Hidden Army.*

PART ONE: BUILDING THE TAIL

EARLY YEARS (1958 – 1966)

CHAPTER ONE

GOING TO WORK

"Saigon? Where in the hell is that?"

Bob Hope, his ubiquitous golf club clutched loosely in one hand, glided across the newly constructed stage at Bien Hoa, as he had done many times in previous wars, and grabbed the microphone. It was December, 1964, and this would be the first of his Christmas shows to emanate from Vietnam. Hope was about to utter his opening words to some of the U.S. military anxiously gathered to see the show. He paused for a second, his impeccable timing milking the anticipation of the audience. Finally, he spoke: "Hello advisors," he dead-panned, confirming that he was in on the joke. The audience roared.

Spc4 **Pat Gallagher**, *Engineer, 1st Special Forces Group, Airborne, USA*

I joined the Army for a three-year hitch. I was trained as an engineer and in demolitions. Construction and destruction. We used C4 to blow things up. We trained on Okinawa and I arrived by plane at Nha Trang in 1958. The first thing they did was to take our cameras. There were about a hundred Americans in South Vietnam then and they wanted a low profile.

Courtesy: Pat Gallagher

After a couple of weeks of additional training I went to Ben Het, which is fifty miles northwest of Pleiku near the borders of Laos, Cambodia and Vietnam. We weren't supposed to be in either Laos or Cambodia, but we went into both. The French had left in 1954, the year my unit first arrived. I was part of a team of twelve advisors sent to train the Montagnards, tribal mountain people living in the central highlands of Vietnam. Our team was mostly lifers, career guys from World War II and the Korean War. We had two officers but no formality; we were on a first name basis. We wore no rank or patches. We tried to be inconspicuous.

Our training of the Montagnards included weapons, communications, construction, tactics, etc., and I was the engineering sergeant. I took part in some offensive operations, but those were primarily handled by the operations guys. We also planted sensors in the jungle. They looked like plants, and were designed to detect movement.

We worked about 12/7 and longer when we were out in the field. My training classes on construction and engineering fundamentals usually consisted of ten to twenty tribesmen. When we could we tried to teach them to use things that were readily available to them. I showed them how to build wood bridges and rope bridges; before this, they would walk forty miles around, so a rope bridge was a real help to them. We put up about fifty in my time there. We brought some basic tools with us when we arrived; no power tools, just basic stuff. They already had hammers (made from tree branches and stones) and a two-man saw. In some respects, we learned more from them than they did from us; the way they built their hooches out of trees and things like that.

*AT2 **David Greene**, Aviation Electronics Technician, Patrol Squadron 4, USN*

I graduated from high school on a Friday and was in the Navy on Monday. After basic training I was stationed on Okinawa and was in and out but mostly high above the Vietnam area from 1961 to 1964. We flew a Navy P2H or P2D7 Neptune, 2-engine patrol plane. Our job was to detect enemy radar systems and monitor enemy shipping in the South China Sea. We sometimes hopped the waves at 1,000 feet to monitor shipping, or higher to detect the radar sites. It was an unpressurized aircraft so we couldn't fly too high. We had a crew of about eleven -- four officers and seven enlisted - and the plane was crammed full of radio and electronic equipment. There was so much gear it was tough to walk the length of the plane. In fact there was no place to stand up!

In addition to Okinawa we flew missions out of the Philippines, and Thailand, and Japan; even Saigon. The Neptune had two jet pods to help our twin engines on takeoffs. The jet pods could also help in case we lost an engine. Basically, the plane was built for anti-submarine warfare. When they realized we had all this electronic gear aboard they knew we were perfect for detecting the radar installations, and that is when we started flying those missions. The monsoon managed to find us wherever we were; Okinawa, Thailand, Vietnam. And between all the rain and mud there was the oppressive heat working inside the planes. It must have been 130 degrees inside the plane.

I personally worked all the positions in the rear of the plane including radar, anti-submarine detection, radio and other things. My job required a Top Secret security clearance. Our flights were about evenly divided between day and night missions. I do remember the box lunches they provided were not very tasty. We ate great on the ground. We threw the box lunches into the garbage on Hainan Island and I'm sure those people were happy to get it.

**At the radar panel on the Neptune – May, 1963
Courtesy David Greene**

Our work days were insane. We were on call 24/7 and we usually flew every day. But being on a flight crew we didn't have to stand any guard duty or KP. We could have a flight at 0400 and it could last from eight to sixteen hours. We were in the air a long time. Anything that went down on the plane – electronically, mechanically -- we had to fix ourselves. If we weren't flying we were working on our aircraft.

*Spc4 **Frank H. Voytek**, Quartermaster Supply, USA Support Group Vietnam, USA*

A recruiter talked me into joining the Army. I spent the summer after high school at home and I raised my right hand in August of 1962. After basic training and Quartermaster Supply School they gave me orders to Fort Hood, Texas. I called my mother and told her and she was pleased. Then they told us to check the bulletin board since a few of us had changed orders. I saw I was headed to Saigon. When I notified my mother, she said "Where in the hell is that?"

In April, 1963, I flew Pan Am into Tan Son Nhut and the heat nearly floored me as I deplaned. There was a lot of confusion there and they accidentally sent me to MACV for a few days, but then that was corrected and I reported to USA Support Group, Vietnam. We were located along the Saigon River in some old French and Vietnamese warehouses.

**Frank H. Voytek – Saigon, December, 1963
Courtesy Frank H. Voytek**

My job was to requisition supplies from the Navy since the Army was not in a position to supply the effort at this point. I started out in the office In the morning and the sergeant would tell us what he thought needed to be done that day. I might end up going into the warehouse later that day to drive forklifts and things like that, or spend all day in the office. One way or the other I worked from morning till night. I guess I did the work of two working up requisitions in the morning, then pulling supplies from the warehouse in the afternoon based on the requisition I just filled out. We would have worked more I think, but there was no electricity available. Part of the problem was due to the European (French) influence the power system wouldn't accommodate our equipment very well. We had to buy adapters to get things to run. I also stood guard duty from time to time.

Quartermaster Warehouse Yard – Saigon, 1964
Courtesy Frank H. Voytek

As part of my job I issued helmets, flak jackets and other gear to our pilots. One time we got a box back and one of the helmets that we issued was in there with a bullet hole in the top of the helmet. The man must have been shot under the chin, and the bullet went up through the top of his head. I didn't like seeing that.

We did a lot of guard duty at night around the compound and out on the perimeter. We'd be guarding the fuel dumps and things and always with empty rifles! A Seabee friend of mine had bought himself a pistol somewhere and we would take that with us when we went out to the perimeter. I also strapped a bayonet to my leg. There was a lot of shooting around from time to time; you could hear shooting and see the gun flashes. There were occasional mortars thrown at the helicopters around our army base and at the perimeter of the camp, but nothing came directly at me.

"An army, like a serpent, moves on its' stomach." – Napoleon Bonaparte

General Giap, the commander of the Viet Minh forces that defeated the French at Dien Bien Phu, said "Logistics is as important as tactics."[v]

Vietnam was the first time in our military history that the U.S. Army had to establish logistics bases with all ground under continuous enemy observation and hostile fire; with no terrain completely under friendly control.[vi] Despite the enormity of the challenge, to project and supply an army halfway around the world, we entered Vietnam with a logistic system lacking computers and automation. [vii] The initial logistic effort was built on sixteen different systems, most of them manual.[viii] The initial unit supply needs and ammunition expenditure rates were based, incorrectly, on World War II and Korean War experience. [ix] In fact the incredible expenditure of ammunition led to a worldwide shortage of brass. The combat troop deployment unfolded faster than the development of the logistics base.[x] Ideally, the supply lines and logistics are well-established before combat is joined, but that was not to be the case in Vietnam.

The US Army established the 1st Logistical Command in Saigon on April 1, 1965. Most of the Army logistics functions were run out of Long Binh. The US Navy held logistical responsibilities for the Marines and I Corps with their main activity at Danang.

Supply and logistics includes personnel running the warehouse facilities and the truck drivers delivering the supplies, as well as staff personnel at the S-4 and G-4 levels.

*Spc4 **Jack Stroud**, Teletype Operator, JUSMAG (Joint U.S. Military Advisory Group, USA*

I enlisted back in 1960 and spent 21 years in the Army. After I got out I worked with the Army as a civilian for another 21 years. My aptitude testing at Fort Hood sent me to Signal School at Fort Gordon, GA. After that, I spent eighteen months in Korea. There was a lot of tension there since the Berlin Wall had just gone up. I was a "delaying factor" at the Korean DMZ, known as the 38th Parallel...

From Korea I went to Fort Sill, OK for the Army Artillery Command. I was Signal Corps, but I spent a lot of time in the Army assigned to artillery units. I met my wife at Fort Sill. She worked in the Crypto Room there and we were doing radio tests every Thursday throughout the world.

Wearing civilian clothes, I flew into Bangkok, Thailand, in February, 1964. We had been instructed not to wear uniforms. My qualifications sent me up to Detachment 2B in Ubon, which is near the Laotian border. I spent my tour at Ubon Ratchathani, which means Lawyer Town in Thai. I was an overseer for the artillery training for the Thai Army. We were training the Thais on the 105mm howitzers. There was quite a bit of live firing, always pointed toward Cambodia. The 105's had already been given to the Thais, and we were there to train them on how to use them.

**JUSMAG Staff: Major Alves (my boss) second from left
Courtesy: Jack Stroud**

A U.S. Air Force unit was located right near us as was an RAAF (Australian) unit. The first sorties into Vietnam were emanating from this area. The Australians flew the Sabre jets (F-86's) and the Americans had their super-sonic planes. We had a captain that stayed with us whose job was to train the Thais to fly the T-38 observation planes, and we had infantry trainers as well as the artillery training. We had support from a Signal Company that lived down in town and we had Peace Corps in that area. Major Alves was in charge of the whole MAG operation in that area.

I served in Arizona and Fort Benning, Georgia upon return, but I was in Nha Trang, Vietnam, for my second Asian tour by June of 1966, circuit chasing VHF sites. This work was mainly night duty. After the first couple of months I got involved in profiling. This involved being dropped off in certain spots to determine the viability of using it as a communications site. This was always as a prelude to an upcoming operation. I worked with Captain Thomas and a couple of other men. We tried to pick areas of high elevation where we also determined we would be able to get vehicles in there. When we finished our field work we had to make our way to the pick-up point. When we returned, the captain would write up the After Action Report and I would do the profiling on the map to see if our "shots" (line of sight) would work. I was to be at this work until July, 1967.

Army communications in Vietnam started with a single radio teletype circuit running between Saigon and Clark AFB in the Philippine Islands in the early 1950's, and grew to nearly 14,000 circuits spread over 200+ installations, by 1969.[xi] The 1st Signal Brigade was activated in April 1966 to manage this system. This unit comprised 20,000 personnel by 1967, and contained all signal units not belonging to tactical units.

Smooth logistics operations are dependent upon effective communications. The early limitations of the communications network (circa 1965) resulted in the loss of nearly half of all supply requisitions. [xii] Thus, critical logistic needs ultimately forced the development of improved communications systems, which were in place by the summer of 1968.

Communications support includes men out in the field with infantry or artillery units, or the switchboard operators back with the headquarters units, and the guys running wire and building relay sites holding all that together.

Spc5 **Mike Stockton***, 3rd Radio Relay Unit, Army Security Agency, Saigon*

I graduated from high school in 1962 in Virginia and my parents called the Army recruiter to visit me. The recruiter talked about an elite unit – upper ten percent of men can qualify, etc. – known as the Army Security Agency (ASA) and promised that I would spend all my time in Europe or the Far East, working out of an embassy. My mother was all thrilled.
 I went to Richmond on a Saturday to take the physical and do some testing. By 5:00 that afternoon I was sworn into the Army and on a train to Fort Jackson. I passed the additional tests there and was assigned to ASA and sent to school at Fort Devin, in Massachusetts. I was trained in special radio identification techniques.

My job was to be radio direction finding and fixing the targets. It seemed like it was extremely cold with three feet of snow the whole time I was in Massachusetts. I went from there to Texas where I was in the 330th ASA Company. We went out in the field a lot. I decided I wanted a change, so I applied for OCS. I also applied for TDY to Vietnam. A week later I had orders for Vietnam!

I landed at Tan Son Nhut on January 4, 1964, a week after a coup. Upon arrival our plane was greeted by a tall, black officer wearing a pith helmet. He welcomed us to the Republic of Vietnam. We got off the plane and it was hot as hell. Our camp was there at the air base, and was called Davis Station; this guy Davis, for whom our camp was named, was riding in a jeep on a back road near Bien Hoa and he hit a 155m shell buried in the road. At our orientation they kept saying "don't go downtown," which was the wrong thing to say to me; now I couldn't wait to do it. Later, we boarded a bus and got a few hundred feet out the gate and there was a huge explosion. Somebody had blown up a bar. We had just gone by it. There were several bars blown up as I was in the area.

ASA worked for the National Security Agency (NSA). It was pretty significant work, especially tracking the NVA, the VC and the VC government. We had an operations building in Saigon and we had eight radio direction finding sites around the country. We had a Direction Finder location at Kon Ton Island where they had the infamous tiger cages for prisoners, both political and VC. I flew down there to do something with codebooks. I worked both day and night shifts. We also had an aviation section that did direction finding by air. I'd get the reports from these sites and my job was to plot these locations on the big map we had. Now this is all done by computers, which is infinitely easier. I'd compile a monthly Bearing Report for the NSA. These things could be pretty inaccurate due to atmospherics, terrain, and things, but with aircraft you could plot the site to within twenty feet! We had other people that determined **what** was being said; it was our job to pinpoint the location of the transmission. All messages were in code and were sent on to the NSA.

*Sgt. **Allen Thomas Jr**., Radio Relay Crew Chief, 507th Radio Research Battalion, USA*

I entered the Army on my 18th birthday. After Basic Training I received Signal Corps training at Fort Gordon, Ga. I left the Army briefly in 1960, but rejoined within a month. I was at Fort Huachua (electronic proving grounds) in Arizona when my orders for Thailand arrived.

In May, 1965 I landed at Don Muang Royal Thai Air Force Base, the main AFB in Thailand. I flew in there on a commercial airliner in civilian

**Sgt. Allen Thomas Jr.
Courtesy Allen Thomas Jr.**

clothes, with a civilian passport; we were "advisors." We were supposed to have enough money to take care of ourselves for three days until someone came to take care of us. After a time we were trucked to Korat. Korat was our main base then but it was not entirely built up yet; it had about 1200 – 1500 people. After just a few days at Korat I went to Udorn AFB where I spent four months.

**Looking across the Mekong River from Laos into Thailand
Courtesy Allen Thomas Jr.**

I ended up at a site on some high ground between Udorn AFB and Vientiane, which is in Laos. My job was to build the camp and keep the radio relay system running. I was crew chief of the thirteen guys maintaining the site. We were all technically "advisors".

As a radio relay station we weren't actually sending messages, we just provided a tower to help transmit the messages from one location to another. We were in the jungle in the middle of nowhere; if you went away for two days and came back there might be a tree growing in the middle of your tower. In the first days we used portable equipment. Later, we built a 150' tower.

I also had to go to Saigon once a month, mainly for paperwork issues. For example our codes would change every month and we had to pick up the new codebooks. On these Vietnam trips we also did some radio relay work in Vietnam where I helped some units set up their new radio equipment, which was usually sitting around in unopened boxes. I also had to go to Bangkok to pick up food. We were paid with military certificates and we had to feed ourselves.

Naturally we were on call 24/7. We didn't have a regular work day; we just had to make sure the equipment was running. We could listen to the radio traffic going on around us so we had a good idea of what was going on in the world and in the war.

*LCpl **Don Campbell**, RTO, 2nd Bn., 4th Marines*

I crossed the ocean on the *USS George Clymer APA-27* and was stationed on Okinawa. We left there for Vietnam at the beginning of May, 1965, on the *USS Magoffin APA-199,* and landed in mike boats off the coast of Chu Lai, about 55 miles south of Danang.

**Chu Lai Airstrip – May/June 1965
Courtesy: Don Campbell**

The beach at Chu Lai was named by Marine Lt.Gen. Krulak -- an old China Marine -- for the phonetics of his name in Chinese. They planned to have an airstrip with a catapult, which was ultimately built by the Seabees (Mobile Construction Battalion 10, with help from marine engineers), but it was not built yet. We moved inland on Amtrak's.

At night, my job was to maintain a foxhole and M-60 machine-gun bunker around the perimeter of the Command Post. The day job was supplying field wire communication through the switchboard from the Command Post to forward outposts. I also maintained direct field phone-to-phone situations as required. I supplied wire communications from the switchboard to Supply, Sickbay, Transportation, Message Center and the radio relay site within the compound by land line, overhead construction and helicopter.

**Radio Jeeps and Comm Storage Tent – Chu Lai 1965
Courtesy: Don Campbell**

Switchboard duty was the main part of the day and it included maintaining equipment (clean and service) and run or troubleshooting communications wire during the day. We also ran wire out of a helicopter to the furthest outpost from the CP. This position was located on a hill with a mountain and rice paddy in front. We made the connection by splicing donuts of wire together into a canvas bag and feeding it out the gunner door while flying to the outpost. We knew this process before we deployed to Vietnam but had never practiced it. When the work was completed we radioed for the chopper to return to the CP. This was the older H34 chopper. In our haste to get on the chopper we had all gone to the rear, and we had to move forward quickly to balance the load so the chopper didn't fly back over itself. This line remained in service but we still had to troubleshoot it via foot patrol.

**Marines Skip Zierzow and Don Campbell (right) – Chu Lai in July, 1965
Courtesy: Don Campbell**

Everything was established in tents. There were no permanent structures due to our unit being the first here and initial construction efforts were directed to the Chu Lai airstrip. We did manage to get some runway planks to use as the roof on one of our forward bunkers. For the first month we had no water other than what came from water buffaloes for canteens and to wash and shave out of a helmet. We all smelled the same. Showers became available later down at the beach. I slept under a shelter half stretched over poles and lived out of my sea bag.

LCpl *Doug Garrett*, Communications Center Man, HQ Co., 9th Marines

I didn't know what to do after graduating from high school. I knew the Marine Corps would be a real challenge. I did boot camp at Camp Pendleton and went to Comm School at Delmar, California. Our MGySgt had us running with the Recon guys and then a parachute jump with them. An underwater insertion was discussed but never happened.

I flew from California to Okinawa and did some training at the northern training area, then sailed to Danang in February, 1966, along with some RAT (radio & teletype) Comm equipment. Radio wave was replacing land lines. The new radios were the PRC-6 and PRC-8's and a larger one called the PRC-25. That radio was kept in a large hole in the ground in the Comm Center bunker. I went to HQ Company, 9th Marines, upon arrival. The HQ was on Hill 327 overlooking the Danang airstrip. In the Fall I went to 1/9 (1st Bn., 9th Marines), at Hill 55.

When I first arrived I was low man on the totem pole and I pulled perimeter guard duty at night. By day I worked in the Communications Center -- almost an office setting -- at HQ Company, 9th Marines, at Hill 327, in Danang. We handled communications about SitReps (situation reports), Casualty Reports, Troop movements; things like that. We did this by teletype and by radio. We were using the new RAT technology. We passed the messages from our units on to the 3rd Marine Division by teletype. There would be about six of us working in the Comm Center.

The security equipment was called a Cryptographic Decoder. You needed an 8x6" perforated card that went into a slot that would encode and decode the message. I used to jeep out to the battalions to distribute each mornings Crypt sheets to them. I carried an old .45 grease gun with me and I also had my M-14 modified with a selector switch, for automatic fire.

LCpl Doug Garrett, Danang, 1966

In many ways Vietnam was our strangest war. It is said that the Army had more boats than the Navy and the Navy had more planes than the Air Force. The Marines, as usual, got what was left over, or what they could steal. In Vietnam there were aircraft flown by all five branches of the service. Two Army helicopter companies arrived in Vietnam on 11 December, 1961 and Army aircraft reached 510 by the beginning of 1965.[xiii]

General Westmoreland wanted an airfield within 25 kilometers of every point in South Vietnam.[xiv] Many of the existing airfields were found to be inadequate for our transport aircraft; more work for the Seabees and engineers.

Air support will include those serving on cargo planes and helicopters, observation aircraft, electronic surveillance and rescue planes, air traffic controllers, maintenance personnel and others.

*Spc4 **Bob Janecek**, Crew Chief, US Army Support Command, Saigon*

I was always mechanically inclined and in my last year of high school I enrolled in an aircraft mechanics course at the college back home. I graduated with an aircraft mechanics license but the only one that ever used that was Uncle Sam. When I was drafted I ended up in helicopters at Fort Rucker, AL. Most of the school graduates had orders for Vietnam, but not me. One of those going to Vietnam was married with two kids so he and I switched orders.

I flew Continental Airlines into Tan Son Nhut in November of 1964. We rode in a bus with chicken wired-windows to our barracks. I was assigned to the US Army Support Command for about six months and then the unit designation changed to the 12th Aviation Group.

**Supplies for the Orphanage - Saigon, 1964
Courtesy Bob Janecek**

I was a crew chief on a Huey (UH-1B helicopter). Later, when I joined the 12th Aviation Group, I was given the experimental 540 rotor head helicopter which was capable of more speed. A crew chief was assigned a helicopter and responsibility for all the maintenance, paperwork and inspections. There might be different pilots and different gunners but only one crew chief. When the chopper flew the crew chief was required to be aboard. The crew chief sat behind the pilot and manned one of the two M-60 machine guns. We flew three or four days a week, nearly always during the day. When we weren't flying I was responsible for the maintenance of the Huey.

*Spc5 **Donald "Tip" O'Neill**, 3-Qualified, Detachment C-2, 5th Special Forces, USA*

A friend convinced me and a few others that we should become paratroopers. After jump school I learned that I was going to go to a line outfit like the 82nd Airborne, or the 101st Airborne. That didn't seem like a good life to me living outdoors all the time so I kept volunteering for anything that would get me out of that. That's how I ended up volunteering for Special Forces. I flew into Tan Son Nhut in June of 1965. I then flew to Nha Trang, which was the headquarters of my unit, the 5th Special Forces.

**Spc4 Don "Tip" O'Neill, Nha Trang, 1965
Courtesy: Don O'Neill**

I spent four to six weeks there mostly rigging air drops and going up and kicking bundles. Even when I was at Nha Trang I had to pull patrol duty. Then I was sent to Pleiku to replace their parachute rigger. I was the only parachute rigger in II Corps and also the camp demolitions man. When in camp I always had old munitions to explode or I was asked to consult on rigging for other units. Special Forces were divided into three teams, A, B and C. The B and C teams supported the A team, the combat force.

Because I was the lone rigger I flew 550 combat hours kicking supply bundles out to Special Forces A teams when they came under attack. I did my share of ground operations but did more flying than anything.

*CWO **Norris "Woody" Woodruff**, Pilot, B Co., 229th Assault Helicopters, 1st Air Cavalry Division, USA*

I went over on the *USNS Maurice Rose* with others from the 1st Air Cavalry Division. We left from Charleston, SC and it took us a month to cross the Pacific. We landed at Qui Nhon, in the central part of the South Vietnamese coast in September of 1965, and headed for An Khe where we built our base camp. Our commanding general had requested our base camp be in Thailand to free up the 33% of our force that would have to guard the base camp every day and night. This request was turned down.

Courtesy: Annette Woodruff

The 1st Air Cavalry Division (previously known as the 11th Air Assault Test Division) was the first battle-test for the concept of airmobile warfare. We would be getting soldiers to battle at 110 mph.

Improved medical performance during the Vietnam War greatly increased a wounded man's chances for survival. Wounded men reaching treatment locations died 17% of the time during the Civil War, 8% of the time during World War I, and 4.5% in World War II. By Korea and Vietnam, the odds had improved to 2.5%.[xv] Part of the improvement lies in the use of helicopters, and the courage and determination of those who manned them. The number of patients evacuated from the battlefield by helicopter rose from 11,000 in 1965 to 65,000 in 1966.[xvi]

A high number (83%) of admissions to medical facilities traced primarily to malaria and non-battle injuries.[xvii] In addition to providing medical support for the American military the U.S. carried some of the burden of medical care for other allied forces and the host Vietnamese military and, to some extent, the civilian population. This probably tripled the workload on our medical personnel.

Medical support includes Flight Surgeons, doctors, nurses, dentists, medics and corpsmen.

*Airman 2nd Class **Pat Griffin**, Medic, 3rd Tactical Dispensary, USAF*

I graduated from high school in June, 1965 and arrived for basic training in the first week of July in Texas. I was still seventeen. I volunteered for Vietnam. I knew a guy at Base Ops and I asked him where no one wanted to go. He said Turkey and Vietnam, so I volunteered for both. Two weeks later I had orders to Vietnam.

My plane landed at Tan Son Nhut in January, 1966. I had gone to Nam on orders for Bien Hoa but when I arrived they asked if there were any medics and those who responded were sent to what was supposed to be a 400-bed hospital at Cam Ranh Bay. It wasn't a 400-bed hospital; that was a lie, there were just a handful of tents. Actually we helped build the Cam Ranh Bay Hospital, as well as maintaining what services we could provide until they got it up and running. After we were there awhile they sent us back to Bien Hoa; I stayed there a couple of months and they were actually overstaffed, so two of us were transferred back to Cam Ranh Bay.

When I went back up to the medic's quarters at Bien Hoa there was not much to do. I'd take my turn running the VD clinic (lots of gonorrhea) in this Quonset hut, and every morning there'd be a big line of GI's with a sad look on their face. Every one of them, almost to the last man, had gonorrhea. We'd fill out the lab work; it was boring as hell and of course none of them said they did anything. But gonorrhea doesn't come from toilet seats! Officers didn't catch gonorrhea, although we sometimes dealt with their Unspecified Skin Conditions in some of the back area tents.

We worked ten to sixteen hours a day/6 ½ days a week at Cam Ranh Bay. They tried to get you off Sunday afternoon, but not everyone could be off Sunday since we were running a hospital and didn't have a Closed time. You might get eight to ten hours a day; Cam Ranh was go go. The combat casualties we had there were pretty much on the mend. When the hospital was up and running, on my second time there, it was a 400-bed hospital. It had grown from tents during my tour to Quonset huts and air conditioned surgery, then air-conditioned surgical wards, then the air conditioning reached the psychiatric and medical wards. However I was gone by the time it was finished.

We always had more malaria patients than anything else. Our combat injuries were mostly on the mend. We always had a full psychiatric ward too. We had one psychiatrist who wasn't worth a damn, Dr. Gill, and all he tried to do was keep people sleeping until he was ready to leave. He just knocked them all out with Thorazine. Later we had a psychiatrist who came in and started setting up programs and getting things turned around. It was a full scale hospital. Everything you have here we had there. Typically we dealt with guys with the flu, a lot of dysentery, strange tropical diseases, and the occasional case of local people with cholera.

Hospitalman 3rd Class **Scott Squires**, *2nd LAM Bn., 1st Marine Air Wing, USN*

My father was a 27-year navy veteran, a mustang. I grew up in northern California and was always interested in helping and protecting animals. My father worked in the medical field with the Navy, my sister was a nurse, and I always had an affinity for helping people. I had done a couple of semesters of college but I felt strongly about Vietnam; I knew some who avoided the draft and I'm still friends with them, but I didn't want to go to school anymore.

Training for corpsmen was a six-month program; the other services didn't have anything that comprehensive. I think Army medics went for four weeks or something like that. I joined the Navy not as a Seaman Recruit like most guys, but as a Hospitalman Recruit. When I graduated I was headed for school to become an OR tech but I realized if I did that I'd never get out of the hospital, so I quit and volunteered for Vietnam. I really had a strong feeling that I would be of use there. My dad and I both had a knack for saving lives and that's where I felt I belonged.

I flew into Danang in October, 1966 and spent three days there, but then went down to Chu Lai to be part of the 2nd LAM Battalion, a part of the 1st Marine Air Wing When I landed on that short runway at Chu Lai I don't think the plane ever stopped. It slowed down and out I went. They were real short of corpsmen. I had to walk a mile or two to find my battalion. I didn't have a weapon and I didn't know what I was getting in to. I was the junior corpsman in our battalion so I got every job that nobody wanted or that they thought was dangerous. There is no time clock on sickness or injury so you were on call always. There were many days I would come back to my bunk and collapse with my boots on and then I'd wake up in exactly the same position four or five hours later when reveille sounded.

I also spent a lot of time riding the weekly convoys between Chu Lai and Danang, a fifty-five mile trip up Highway 1. We'd spend a couple of days at Danang and then drive back. There had to be a corpsman every fifth or sixth truck on those trips. We were usually on a truck that had a .50 caliber machine gun and the seats in the back were sandbagged. On those trips, you'd be driving along and everything was quiet, and then a truck would take fire. Everybody was always nervous on those trips.

Another thing corpsmen did was participate in the Rabid Dog Patrol. I didn't like that at all. We rode around Chu Lai with shotguns and a few Marines and whenever we saw a dog we would shoot him. It was just terrible. If you liked dogs, as I did, it was like shooting your best friend.

Units that didn't have an attached corpsman would come and take one of us for their missions. We went out with Recon a number of times and with other specialty units. The grunts had their corpsmen attached but we went a lot with these other units. The helicopters were always short of corpsmen for the Medevac's for instance. You might wake up in the morning and eat chow and then they'd grab you for a Medevac helicopter flight. You'd maybe be flying all day, which isn't as much fun as it sounds with people shooting at you all the while. On my first flight I wondered why all the guys on the chopper were sitting on their helmets. I soon learned why they did this.

Protecting supply lines is critical to the success of any army, but the lack of "secure" rear areas in Vietnam made this a difficult task. The task was complicated by the pilferage perpetrated by our "allies."[xviii] In the Early Days, there was a shortage of ports, which increased the importance of using the roads.

However, the lack of armored vehicles made protecting convoys difficult. Given the lack of security on the roads, truck convoys only operated during day time hours, reducing their effectiveness.

Security support includes MP's (military police -- Army and Marines), AP's (Air Police), SP's (Shore Patrol -- Navy) and personnel charged with base or convoy security.

*Airman1st Class **Mike Tillman**, Air Police, 366th Security Police Sqdn, Phan Rang USAF*

I had trouble finding work after high school. I had no trouble with Basic Training; I thought it was fun and they fed me good. In their infinite wisdom the Air Force thought I should go to Russian language school after basic training. The school was at Syracuse University. After about six months of classes they called me in and told me I was passing, but just barely. I could understand Russian, and I could write it. The biggest problem was my rural Kentucky accent! I was speaking Russian with a hillbilly accent. So they asked me if there was something else I'd like to do. I'd always wanted to be an air policeman. So I left the snowy clime of New York for the snowier clime of the Upper Peninsula of Michigan -- Air Police school. Into my third winter in Michigan I went to Base Ops and volunteered to go anywhere it was warm. Orders came through for me in record time -- two weeks -- for Vietnam. Where was that I wondered.

I flew into Tan Son Nhut in January, 1966, and then I flew to Phan Rang. They had just started the Air Force base there. The place was called Grey Eagle at the time. Most of the Air Police that went to Phan Rang knew each other; they had come over as a unit. I went over as a replacement and didn't know anybody. At this time there were only about twenty security police there and some administrative types.

After they finally built a runway and got some planes into Phan Rang we were responsible for the perimeter security. Since we were such a small base, when I first got there we had to run convoys into Cam Ranh Bay for supplies. This was about a forty mile trip and we used a jeep with an M-60 machine gun and three guys. The jeeps without a machine gun had four guys. The convoy might be twenty or thirty trucks. After a few months, they started unloading supplies on the beach at Phan Rang so the convoys stopped. The beach at Phan Rang was very shallow so they'd offload the LST's or whatever into smaller boats to bring the supplies ashore.

A1C Mike Tillman, Phan Rang, 1966
Courtesy: Mike Tillman

At first I worked a combination of days and nights. But then they formed a group called Panther Flight, which was all night duty. I was very proud to be selected for the Panther Flight duty. They wanted the best guys for this duty and I was picked. We went out an hour before dark and came back an hour before light. We worked about 12/7 with an occasional day off.

*Spc4 **Gary Nunn**, Military Police, 716th MP Battalion, Tan Son Nhut AB, USA*

I flew into Tan Son Nhut in May of 1966. We went to a containment camp for three or four days, which helped get us acclimatized and then my unit came and picked me up in a jeep. We were billeted in an old hotel in the Cholon (Chinese) district of Saigon. We fought over the Beanie Weenies in the C rations; everybody loved them. We did have mess halls too. We were advised not to eat any of the local food and when you saw the absence of sanitation, you understood why.

When I arrived at the 716th MP Battalion they gave us an orientation. A sergeant asked me if I had a girlfriend back in the states. I told him I did. He told me to write and ask her to send us some play money which he hoped to use to buy goods and services. The Vietnamese people caught on to that very fast! It was meant as more of a joke than anything.

Some of my first duties included guarding General Westmoreland, we guarded some facilities, and we did patrols, sometimes up Highway 1. It was interesting because you did something different every day. When we escorted convoys we would have one jeep of MP's in the front, one in the middle and one in the back. The thing I remember most about guarding General Westmoreland is they brought us a hamburger and a Coke and I thought I had died and gone to heaven! Westmoreland had a helluva billet over there.

When we guarded a facility they would provide us with an oval unit called a kiat, which was a small concrete structure with a roof. We'd then place sandbags around it and the guard would have an M-60. We worked days and nights. We had A, B and C platoons, so if A was on days, C would be on nights; and B on second shift; something like that.

In the early 1960's the need for construction capability in support of anticipated combat operations in South Vietnam was discussed and recommended and debated, but not approved until March, 1965.[xix] The construction needs were such that a special command was required and in July, 1965, an engineer brigade was summoned to Vietnam. Upon its arrival engineer construction authority was transferred from the 1st Logistical Command to the Engineer Brigade. $40 million was allocated for construction spending in 1965, but spending for the next two years was over $700 million.

Some engineer detachments were attached directly to combat units, but most were autonomous. Engineer units include surveyors, heavy equipment operators, truck drivers and others; during the Early Years they were primarily tasked with building airfields and other base structures. By the Middle Years they would do more work on the South Vietnamese infrastructure.

The U. S. Army's 46th Engineer Battalion, about 1200 men strong, arrived by ship (the USNS General Leroy Eltinge, T-AP 154) in September, 1965, along with other units. The ship broke down on the way over and was towed into Guam. That added three or four days to the journey. Sleeping conditions were six high on the ship; it was very crowded, at least 50% over-packed. Not a pleasant trip! The Eltinge was scheduled to land at Cam Ranh Bay but pulled into Vung Tau to let another unit get off. The 46th debarked also but was only at Vung Tau about a day and then they trucked up to Bien Hoa air base. After a day there they loaded onto trucks and drove up and down Highway 1 almost to Saigon looking for a suitable base camp. They found a spot that was about five acres and free of major obstacles and that was the birth of Long Binh.

*Spc4 **Louis Kutac**, Heavy Equipment Operator, A Company, 46th Engineer Battalion, USA*

I was primarily a front end loader operator working in the rock quarry. We produced the gravel that would become the road foundations. I did drive a dozer and a truck occasionally; I was even a jeep driver. I worked 12/7. It was just like going to work in the real world. We were mainly building roads, ammo dumps; things like that. I did some work in the evenings, under lights, double-shifting, until 0200. At that time I was operating a water truck and we did some work watering down the dusty roads. With our fleet of dump trucks going down the roads it didn't take long before it was so dusty you couldn't see. The monsoon took care of the dusty roads but it made things very messy. The hard part was when the rain stopped and the humidity hit you.

One of our first projects was to build some roads around the 93rd Evacuation Hospital, just down the road from our camp. We were putting asphalt around the hospital to keep the dust down and all that. A helicopter came in with some dead soldiers and they asked me to help them unload. I still shake when I think of having to carry those dead GI's. I don't know why. I get so emotional about it even today. They were the first casualties I had seen. I couldn't understand how you could have so much blood on the blankets; they were just soaked with blood.

*Spc4 **William Wyrick**, Construction Engineer, A Co., 46th Engr. Bn., USA*

I graduated from high school on my seventeenth birthday and went across the street and joined the Army. I was a Construction Engineer. I arrived in August of 1965 on the *Eltinge* with the rest of the 46th Engineers.

I operated bulldozers, front end loaders and other equipment. We worked at least twelve hours a day. I worked on the roads and we built the ammunition dump at Long Binh. I worked on the 93rd Evac Hospital too. I carried an M1 carbine and a .45.

The First Concrete Poured for the 93rd Evac. Hospital
Courtesy: Harley Brinkley

Forty percent of the tonnage arriving in South Vietnam during 1965 and 1966 was construction materials.[xx]

Striker **Rick Dolinar,** *Fire Control Technician, USS Berkeley DDG-15, USN*

After high school, fourteen of us decided to try the Navy because navy life seemed more appealing to us than what the army offered. We went to boot camp in October, 1964, where I was named the Company Honor Man by my peers and the company commander. Based on the testing that we underwent, I was sent to FT (Fire Technology) School at Great Lakes for eighteen weeks following graduation. From school, I was assigned to the *Berkeley*.

I departed on the *Berkeley*, a guided missile destroyer, from Long Beach, California in August of 1965. Although the trip over was uneventful, it was pretty exciting for me since it was my first time on a ship. We were on station off the North Vietnamese coast about three weeks later. On that tour we would be at sea for about two months, getting replenished every few days from transport ships, then into port (Hong Kong or Subic Bay) for a week or so, then back out for another two months.

My job description was Fire Control Technician. Fire as in gunfire. Our fire control radar had input into an analog computer and our job was to operate and maintain the gunfire control systems (the radar and the analog computer); to synchronize with the guns, basically calculating how much to lead the target in order to hit it. As an E-3, I also had to stand regular watches when off duty. My watch was usually in the after steering compartment.

Courtesy: Rick Dolinar

On this tour, with the *Berkeley* we were assigned to SAR (search and rescue) duty; we were also an early warning for enemy planes that may have taken off from North Vietnam. We also kept an eye on junks and sampans coming out of North Vietnamese waters. They would send these pseudo fishermen out in these small boats, armed with a couple of nets and tons of sophisticated radio equipment. We knew what they were doing. It was our job to screen them and we did destroy a few of them if they didn't heed our warnings. We also did a lot of shore bombardment work, mostly into North Vietnam, but for our last month or so we were mainly in the DMZ area.

The day was four on, eight off, but some days, depending on your shift, and when after duty watches fell, you might be working 12 hours. There was also underway replenishment that required taking on provisions. This was usually done every few days, after dark, since it put both ships in a very vulnerable position when they were tethered together, usually with cables and fuel lines. Both ships would usually be moving along at about eight knots. Underway replenishment usually took a couple of hours.

CHAPTER TWO

MEETING OUR ALLIES

There were two ethnic and/or geographic divisions within South Vietnam. Eighty percent of the population lived along the coast and in the major cities. The remaining twenty percent, including the Montagnards, a primitive but fierce tribal people, lived in the central highlands. These two ethnic groups despised each other; sort of a war within the war.

Part of the American difficulty in working with our Vietnamese allies traced to the language barrier. Vietnamese is a difficult tonal language in which the same word might have six different meanings depending on the pitch. But the problems also traced to the issue of respect. As time went by American soldiers thought less and less of the Vietnamese. [xxi] *Conversely, despite language barriers every bit as difficult, our relationships with the Montagnards were splendid.*

Burial Tomb? -- Chu Lai 1965
Courtesy: Don Campbell

Spc4 **Pat Gallagher**, *Engineer*

We weren't briefed on the Montagnard-Vietnamese relationship before we arrived at Ben Het in 1958. Consequently when I first met the elders, I said something about the Vietnamese through the interpreter that didn't sit well; they got hostile over my remarks but we straightened it out.

We lived with the Montagnards. In our location at Ben Het there were about one hundred of them including their family members. We lived in our own hut in the center of the camp with barbed wire around us; an inner perimeter of the camp. The camp was an abandoned French outpost on a hill strategically overlooking three valleys. The VC probably had it zeroed in for mortar fire.

We ate with the tribe a lot and they had fresh fish and produce. They used a lot of *nuoc naum* sauce made from fermented dead fish, which I avoided. We ate K rations out in the field. I really liked the Montagnard people. And they liked us. They were primitive but hard working and quick learners. They were also fierce warriors. There were five Montagnard tribes in Vietnam and they all spoke a different dialect. We were with the Rhad tribe. Perhaps picking up on the Montagnard enmity toward the ARVN and Vietnamese, I ended up not really caring for those people. Centuries ago the Vietnamese had pushed the tribal people off their land along the Vietnamese coast, away from better land and food. These hard feelings were still very much top of mind.

As a gesture to how much they appreciated what our team leader was doing for them the Montagnard chief arranged for his daughter to marry our boss. The boss was thirty-five and she was about fourteen. The boss was also married and we tried to explain that this could not be done. They were upset but some sort of compromise was reached and a two-day celebration where we ate much native food and drank ox blood went on as planned. But there was no ritualistic throwing of rice! We saved the boss from becoming a bigamist.

Airman 2nd Class **Pat Griffin**, *Medic*

The South Koreans handled the security for Cam Ranh Bay. Based on my interaction with them during my tour they gave me a great farewell party, a bigger affair than my own countrymen provided.

Spc4 **Jack Stroud**, *Teletype Operator*

We had a Thai house lady to clean and two girls who did the laundry. We also had a yardman and two Thai drivers who drove the captains around and did translations for them. The Thai troops we worked with were indecisive most of the time. They were okay as long as they had someone like us around them, but when we weren't there they were panty-waists. They were afraid of their own shadow.

Courtesy: Jack Stroud

*Sgt. **Allen Thomas Jr.**, Radio Relay Crew Chief*

Our tiny camp site was supported by the Thai army. All I had to do was pick up the phone and ask for help. These guys were fantastic. I never had a problem. The Thais were lovely people and very friendly. You could stop anyone on the street and they'd help you. I was very proud that we developed a good relationship with the Thais in the village's right by us. Back in 1965 we didn't receive any fire but we did get a few mortar rounds at the air base in 1966. By late 1966, rebels were beginning to slip across the border into Thailand in an attempt to incite the Thais into converting to their side. It really was an Indochina war – a Second Indochina War -- not just a Vietnam War. Why don't they call it that?

*Spc4 **Jack Stroud**, Teletype Operator*

One of my diversions on my second tour at Nha Trang in 1966 was going over to the Australian compound. We drank and watched movies. The

Australians nicknamed me MAG-Jack. They made a big plaque for me that I still have. I could put that plaque on my jeep and they would just wave me through security at the gate. The major gave me two weeks off and I went to Australia with Mac, the projectionist in the RAAF camp. We flew to down-under backwards, in a Kiwi. I had never flown sitting backwards before. He showed me Australia and the Aussies purported to show me how to catch a kangaroo. They had me out there grabbing this kangaroo's tail and the kangaroo nearly beat me to death. They had a big laugh about that.

Spc5 **Donald "Tip" O'Neill**, *3-Qualified*

We had Filipinos working in our C2 detachment. They kept our trucks, generators and other machinery running. They often had to cannibalize one machine to keep another running. When I got to Pleiku there was a row of deuce-and-a-half's lined up with no front ends on them. This was the result of mines on the road. We didn't own the roads, hence the importance of helicopters.

Spc4 **Frank H. Voytek**, *Quartermaster Supply*

I came into contact with Vietnamese people more than Americans. They drove our trucks and they worked in our warehouses. They were our cab drivers and waitresses. We had three Vietnamese guys who worked in our office. The older guy was known as Papasan. The youngest was known as Babysan. They were all good folks; we got along fine. They tried to teach me Vietnamese; I tried to teach them English. I can't say whether working with us was their daytime job and they were VC at night, I don't know.

Courtesy: Frank H. Voytek

We used to pass out food staples such as rice and flour in large burlap sacks to people. We were feeding the populace. Or so we thought. Then I'd go into the shops in town and see this stuff on the shelf for sale!

*LCpl **Don Campbell**, RTO*

The Marine Corps Mighty Mite
Courtesy: Don Campbell

As a mighty mite (jeep) driver, I drove for a sergeant on village patrol to ensure that no marines were there since it was off limits day and night. I was able to interact with the villagers and take some pictures. Of course we didn't understand them or them us. However, they did know what a dollar was. They wanted to sell hats, wash clothes, sell soap, pop, etc. It was strange to see they kept these drinks cold from ice packed in sawdust. The young boys (8 – 10 years old) were curious. Since they don't have a bridge in their nose they were fascinated by mine. The young girls were shy and kept away. The people were friendly during the day, but this was the same village where our wire was cut and abandoned by us.

Friend or foe? - Chu Lai – May 1965
Courtesy: Don Campbell

*Spc4 **Louis Kutac**, Heavy Equipment Operator*

When we went to Saigon all the people there would just stare at us because we were some of the first Americans they had seen. After we were there a few months they had some kind of government program where we were employing the Vietnamese people. I ended up in charge of about fifty of them down at the rock quarry. I showed them what to do; I was kind of like the foreman. They were hard workers; a real gentle, compassionate people. One time NBC News came down and interviewed us. I should have been on TV but I never heard anything more about it. I don't know if it aired or not.

*Spc4 **William Wyrick**, Construction Engineer*

There wasn't much socializing with the Vietnamese people in 1965, but that started to change by 1966. Rules had been relaxed. You could go into the village at Long Binh/Bien Hoa and when you did you didn't take any weapons.

*Spc4 **Gary Nunn**, Military Police*

We did a lot of interaction with the Vietnamese police and their MP's. I tried to learn some of their language. We also occasionally worked with Korean or Australian MP's. We picked up a word or two from each other. I also spoke a little French from my school days, and all of this helped me do my job. It seemed like the people respected you more if you spoke their language. I felt very sorry for the Vietnamese people. They were living in poverty.

*Airman1st Class **Mike Tillman**, Air Police*

We had Vietnamese people cleaning our hooches and burning the shitters, and eventually they began to work in the mess hall. Some of our base police interacted with the QC (Vietnamese military police) but I didn't. We saw the Vietnamese civilians in town occasionally, and in stores, bars and restaurants. We did eat in the Vietnamese restaurants occasionally and we avoided the *nouc maum* sauce. I mean, taking a dead fish and laying it on a rock to dry is not my idea of something good to eat. You could smell it a mile off. I think the Vietnamese people make good capitalists because they know how to make a buck. I think they have had people in there fighting for centuries and we were just another in a long line of foreigners.

Striker **Rick Dolinar**, *Fire Control Technician*

On the *Berkeley* we berthed once at Danang, but we never went ashore. On the SAR picket line we would see the North Vietnamese "fishermen" as they pulled their junks and sampans up close to our ship. Our captain just loved to go through them and tear up their nets because he knew what they were doing. He would basically play Chicken with them. We had .50 caliber machine guns ready, and in cases where the North Vietnamese showed any kind of weaponry, the captain would cut their ship in half.

Spc4 **Bob Janecek**, *Crew Chief*

We paid the hooch girls in *piasters* since they didn't want to flood the Saigon market with American currency. But there was always somebody looking for greenbacks and they would give you a better return for your money.

Vietnam's currency; they preferred greenbacks
Courtesy: Tom Petersen

We had hooch girls who would come in after we left for work in the morning. They would clean the barracks, do our laundry, and shine our boots and things like that. We paid about 500 *piasters* a month for this work, probably about $8 or $9. I also worked a lot with the Vietnamese military, especially in my early days there. I just didn't sense that they were willing to stand up and fight for their freedom. Some of the farmers and villagers out in the field would provide us with information on the VC, but they started to be killed when they did this, so naturally their help evaporated.

LCpl **Doug Garrett**, *Comm Center*

There were some very large rats down by the river. When we shot them the Vietnamese used to eat them. Since we were a communications center we couldn't have Vietnamese civilians around for security reasons. They did do some laundry for us. The same lady who did our laundry at Hill 327 brought her operation, including her sister, to Hill 55.

Spc5 **Mike Stockton** *Army Security Agency*

One of the corner kiosks in Saigon sold several types of food. Located right next to it was one of the French-built outdoor restrooms where pee from the trough came out a pipe in the back. I was watching the mamasan from this eatery while I had a bunch of kids lined up in front of me begging for money; I told them I wouldn't give them money but I'd buy them something to eat. Anyway I'm watching the mamasan and she has an armload of dirty bowls and she takes them over to this drain where the pee is coming out and she washes the bowls out in that. Sadly, I think I saw worse than that!

Hospitalman 3rd Class **Scott Squires**

At Chu Lai we were going out and doing MedCaps almost every day. I delivered a lot of babies and sewed a lot of Vietnamese people up on these trips. We usually went out to some remote spot via helicopter and sometimes spent several days out there alone, with very little security. Our side pretty much controlled things during the day but things were riskier at night. There would be just three or four of us out there. It never occurred to me that I was in a particularly bad place; I didn't much care for the food though. What bothered me the most was the kids. They were kind of forgotten over there. We did a lot of MedCaps out in the bush and we'd arrive and set up shop. The old people showed up first, with teeth problems or chronic illnesses or wounds that hadn't healed. The wounds were opened up and drained. Our battalion doctor was a surgeon. He had taught all of us how to do surgical procedures. We were all adept at it. We dealt with the stuff their primitive folk medicine couldn't handle. Sometimes the enemy would show up for treatment too and sometimes the enemy would punish the villagers for accepting our help. We couldn't solve the politics; we just treated everyone that sought help.

Courtesy: Tom Petersen

Airman 2nd Class **Pat Griffin**, *Medic*

We did MedCap (Medical Civilian Aid Program) in the villages, which I think was instituted by LBJ; we would take an ambulance and the army would supply us with an escort (a jeep with a machine gun and a couple of armed soldiers), and we were armed. And we also went out with the engineers and they built a little one-room schoolhouse and we worked the village with the medical civilian aid.

On our village Medcaps we determined that the Vietnamese were all vitamin deficient. When we turned the kids eyelids over they were all white, a sure sign of vitamin deficiency. Later we found dead VC with our bottled medicine marked Clark AFB; the VC just came into the village and took it.

*Spc4 **Louis Kutac**, Heavy Equipment Operator*

I had a lot of free time in Saigon; there was a small school or orphanage there. The students were all girls about ten years old. They were trying to learn English. They were real friendly and I was teaching them a little bit. They treated me with great respect and they were picking it up really well. I was so proud of those girls.

*Spc5 **Mike Stockton**, Army Security Agency, Saigon*

I was in the shower by myself at Phu Bai; I heard a sound and there was this Vietnamese girl with a hair lip staring at me. I realized she wanted to have sex with me, so I obliged.

Close to our camp there was a walled compound with five bedrooms, located right next to the only railroad line in Vietnam. Five of us rented this place and lived there for $120 a month, which included our houseboy. There was a curfew at night and they'd shoot you if you were out and about. When the bar girls found out we had this place they rang the bell at our gate. This went on every night. I still kept my bunk at the base and one day I came up to our compound and there was this big sign saying OFF LIMITS TO U.S. PERSONNEL. Hell, I was living there! At one time we also had some water buffalo living at our compound.

We had large beds with foam mattresses and mosquito nets, and the girls would come over and we'd have these outrageous parties. Then the train would go by at 5:00 am, and they had these big tank cars with gun turrets on them and they made a lot of noise. Vietnam had just one railroad track and it had to go right by my bed!

There was an old hag Vietnamese lady with just three teeth left in her mouth, and she worked the street corners in Saigon, close by the Majestic Hotel and the Caravelle looking for customers for oral sex, despite the fact that she was baby-sitting her grandchildren. We called her Sweet Tooth

Annie. I watched her one day and she had to take a leak. She reached into her pajamas and pulled out a 12 ounce Coke bottle, and she crouched over a drain in the street and peed into the bottle. I have to admit she was very accurate.

Another time I was walking to work around 11:00 in the morning, and it's hot as hell, and someone in a shiny, baby-blue Mercedes 220 yells to me. It turned out to be Nguyen Ky, the President of Vietnam, and he picked me up and drove me to work.

When I first got there I was guarding the Saigon PX, and there was an American school behind the PX. This is one huge PX in a walled compound. This place sold 600,000 bottles of hair spray one year, which the guys were trading with in town. I saw a disturbance half a block away. There's a group of Vietnamese rolling around. I walked down there and found a big rectangular package wrapped up and a guy getting ready to poke it with a stick. I stopped him and called the bomb squad. Sure enough, there was enough plastique in there to blow up the whole block.

There was a lieutenant living about a block from our compound near the railroad tracks. The VC came by once and threw a grenade through his window and killed him. It was a dangerous neighborhood. There were a lot of refugees from North Vietnam and undoubtedly some were still on the NVA side. I had that place for five months and then I went home.

Airman 2nd Class **Pat Griffin**, *Medic*

We came across a Montagnard family one time and these people were out of the Stone Age, walking down the road with their crossbows and trident spears; they are black with flat noses and enormous leg muscles. I just froze in my tracks. It looked like an extended family and they were spear fishing in the shallows along the side of the bay. My jaw dropped.

Spc5 **Donald "Tip" O'Neill**, *3-Qualified*

The Montagnards were class people. The women were bare-chested and the men wore loin cloths. The Vietnamese really discriminated against these people. At one point there was an uprising by the Montagnards and they were killing the South Vietnamese. In response the ARVN were executing the educated Montagnards.

The Montagnards would travel to Cambodia to see their religious leader and they'd return with a bag of some secret stuff around their necks. They believed this made them invincible. They were great fighters.

There was a female Montagnard nurse that worked for us. She spoke English so she acted as an interpreter for us also. Her husband was also well educated. We hid them from the South Vietnamese when we could. I did not think the Vietnamese people were half as good as the Montagnards.

CHAPTER THREE

MEETING THE ENEMY

February 1965: Operation Flaming Dart, the bombing of North Vietnam begins.
March 1965: First U.S. air strikes against the Ho Chi Minh Trail.
March 1965: Market Time naval interdiction begins.
April 1965: President Johnson authorizes U.S. ground troops in combat.

Most (76%) veterans experienced rocket or mortar fire directly or indirectly, and half saw men killed or wounded according to a Veterans Administration study.

The first big test for the newly-formed Air Cavalry Division, and indeed the first big battle for the U.S. in Vietnam, was our incursion into the Ia Drang Valley in November, 1965. This valley was at the base of the Chu Pong Mountain and convenient to Cambodia. The 1st Battalion of the 7th Cavalry Regiment (Custer's old outfit) landed literally on top of the 66th PAVN Regiment (North Vietnamese), about 1,600 men. Both sides were looking for a fight. The landing zone was called X-Ray; it would hold about eight Huey helicopters at a time. The first wave of eight choppers, including the battalion commander Lt. Col. Hal Moore, landed unopposed. The second flight of eight Hueys picked up some ground fire. Later flights received fire so heavy they didn't land, they just hovered about six feet off the ground and the troopers jumped out.

Chu Lai - July 1965
Courtesy: Don Campbell

CWO **Norris "Woody" Woodruff**, Pilot

My Huey was shot down twice during the October, 1965 Ia Drang battle. Sometimes fire was so heavy guys that had just landed were wounded and we had them thrown aboard the chopper and flew them back to the base area. The fire became so heavy that the medevac choppers stopped coming in; casualties continued to be placed on the transport Hueys, saving many lives. The battle at LZ X-Ray lasted for over two days and resulted in several thousand enemy casualties. Three Medals of Honor were awarded, two to Huey pilots.

During October and November, 1965, the 1stAirCav lost over 25% of their unit (334 killed, 736 wounded, 364 non-battle injuries and over 2,800 lost to illness, mostly malaria). A hundred helicopters were inoperable due to parts shortages.[xxii]

About forty-three percent of the helicopters used in Vietnam were destroyed. About half of the 2700 Americans killed in helicopters were pilots.

Spc4 **Bob Janecek**, Crew Chief

It didn't take long to get shot at for the first time over there. On my second flight we were going north from Saigon, along the coast. My chopper had the M-60 machine guns. I told them I had been trained on the .30 caliber machine guns (vintage WW II) and I knew how to take those apart, but had never seen the M-60. I asked for a 30-second primer on the M-60. They told me they'd do it later in the week and then we took off.

Minutes later we heard there had been an ambush of a Vietnamese convoy in a rubber plantation. We picked up a couple of wounded Vietnamese guys from the ambush site and took them back to their staging area and went on about our mission. On our return we flew by the site of the morning ambush and the VC was in the process of ambushing the relief force heading to the first ambush, one of their favorite tricks. We approached an artillery position which was in the process of providing furious support fire for the beleaguered ARVN. It was dusk and I could feel the concussion of the 105's as they were firing. We were rotating down to their location and as I looked out the window I saw these red basketballs going past. The pilot said those "basketballs," were .50 caliber rounds aiming for us! He put us down hard and fast and we weren't hit.

Courtesy: Bob Janecek

*LCpl **Don Campbell**, RTO*

When we first arrived and moved inland, I was riding on top of an Amtrac. We think we were shot at and we dismounted and took up a perimeter defense around the Amtrac. However we never confirmed the shooting, and the Lord was with me until my flight out of Danang some months later.

South Vietnam's only railroad – Chu Lai 1965 (Amtrac next to bunker)
Courtesy: Don Campbell

*Spc5 **Mike Stockton**, Army Security Agency, Saigon*

They blew up the Brink's Bachelor Officer's Quarters on the eve of the Bob Hope arrival in December, 1964, in downtown Saigon. Hope's line was "I passed the hotel on the way in here!" Three of us had just received our first drink in a bar behind the Brink's BOQ when it happened.
The VC had put a 750lb bomb in a ¾ ton truck and drove it into the underground parking lot of the BOQ. The explosion knocked me off my bar stool, although I didn't spill my whiskey. On the way across the square to investigate the damage, a gas tank from a nearby truck blew up. We were very close to this and it knocked us off our feet. The hood of the truck flew past my head, missing me by just a few feet.

*Airman 1st Class **Mike Tillman**, Air Police*

When our convoys approached the rubber plantations – the mid-point of the trip to Cam Ranh Bay -- it was always tense. The rubber trees were right up near the road and we were getting sniped at every time we went through there. No one was killed but we had a couple of people grazed. So we finally started bunching up about a mile before the rubber plantation and we'd try to get past the trees at about 45 miles an hour. We were blasting away as we flew through there. We shot down a lot of rubber trees but we quit taking fire.

*Airman 2nd Class **Pat Griffin**, Medic*

I was **told** we were shot at once. We were doing the convoy, the Phan Rang Express, which left Phan Rang, stopped at Cam Ranh Bay, and went north to Nha Trang.

Nha Trang was like a resort; we never had any trouble because both sides took R&R there. Nha Trang had little cabanas on the beach and if you had time off you could catch a ride on the Phan Rang Express once it came through Cam Ranh Bay, ride up to Nha Trang, and then come back that evening. You had to ride past a big stretch of rubber plantations; small arms fire out of the rubber plantation was not uncommon. We returned one time and they showed us the holes in the canvas of our truck. It didn't bother me because I didn't know we were being shot at!

*Spc4 **William Wyrick**, Construction Engineer*

I was in charge of the work crew one night in 1966 and one of the guys on the crew told me they had just seen "Charlie" running across the road with back packs. I reported this to the battalion CO. He said the infantry had just swept that area earlier that day and found nothing. About 7:30 in the morning they blew the ammo dump up.

In 1965 we were mortared at Ben Cat quite a bit. And we ran over a lot of land mines on the road.

*Spc4 **Gary Nunn**, Military Police*

You had to qualify with the M-16 before you could carry it. We also had to qualify with the M-60 machine gun. So we went to the range and our people went the same way to this range every day. On the second day the VC had planted bouncing Betty mines and a guy about 45 feet ahead of me stepped on it. It took him and six other guys out.

*Sgt. **Allen Thomas Jr.**, Radio Relay Crew Chief*

On one of my trips over to Vietnam from Thailand I hit a land mine while driving a deuce-and-a-half from Dak To to Kontum; no one was injured but all of us had some blast damage from that mine. Sore necks, black eyes; I looked like a raccoon because of my eyes. I had a couple of tiny holes in me from hot shrapnel and I thought "I'm dead," but the medic calmed me down and told me it wasn't bad. No Purple Heart; I had seen too many guys with no legs and stuff and I told him I didn't want it. I should have taken it but I didn't know I was going to have health problems later on.

LCpl ***Doug Garrett***, *Comm Center*

We did receive occasional mortar fire at Hill 55. We put sandbags on the roof of our Comm Center. We also started getting probed quite a bit at night. A decision was made to bring in a guy to teach us some of the tricks about being a sniper. I had the crash course and there were nights where I was out in the brush with a spotter and a starlight scope. I had good night vision, which helped. I did have occasion to do some shooting out there.

They also gave us claymore mines and listening devices. The listening stuff was worthless; you'd put on the earphones and all you would hear would be static. The engineers had done a nice job of clearing fields of fire around our perimeter. By sitting out there at night we were able to persuade Charley to leave us alone.

*Airman 2nd Class **Pat Griffin**, Medic*

At Bien Hoa there was a terrible explosion on the flight line. We got two stories; one, that a mortar had hit one of the alert planes and it, in turn, detonated two more alert planes. The second story was that a primer went off on one of the alert planes. All I know is that it was a helluva explosion. Of course we thought the base was under attack. We were issued M-16's which were kept at our HQ shack. We also had 38's.

*Airman1st Class **Mike Tillman**, Air Police*

We didn't take much mortar fire; they probably concentrated that on the 101st down the road, but we did have sappers inside the wire a few times. Since the location of the bunkers was well known to them I always slipped out of the bunker and moved about fifteen yards away after dark. One night there was a couple of guys out there; one of them had a gun. They popped one of our trip flares outside the wire. When they did that the guy with the gun emptied a magazine into the bunker that I had vacated. Then he took off running. I put my M-16 on full automatic and led him like I would a bunny in eastern Kentucky. One round fired and the rifle jammed. I pulled the magazine out and got the jammed round out. The trip flare was still going but the rifle jammed again. By the time the reaction force arrived, responding to my radio calls and the shooting, they could follow the trail of my magazines from the bunker to my current position about a hundred yards away. If I could have found a tree I would have rapped that rifle around it. When my first round went off it obviously expanded in the chamber and the extractor wouldn't extract it. Normally we would have had more than one man in each bunker but we were short of people so we could only use one guy.

Overall the Air Force didn't have as much trouble with the M-16 as the other branches did because we used the regular (Remington, Winchester, or whatever it was) ammunition. The Army insisted on trying to use the wrong kind of powder. They wanted to use some powder they already had on hand. That was the only time I had trouble with the weapon. When I got there I had never seen the M-16. When they handed me one I asked what it was and they told me to talk to some of the newer guys; they might know. The added pressure was in the Air Force only the AP's had weapons. So you knew you had to stop any enemy penetration because if they got past you there was no one behind you to stop them.

*Striker **Rick Dolinar**, Fire Control Technician*

There were two islands maybe ten or fifteen miles outside of the North Vietnamese port of Haiphong, Hon Me and Hon Met. You could see North Vietnam from these islands. We were on our SAR picket station, and we were advised that an F-4 was shot down between North Vietnam and these two islands. The pilot had bailed out between the islands and the mainland, and two ships, including the *Berkeley*, were told to go in and get him. We immediately picked up fire from both islands, and from a gun battery on the mainland. Our return fire was said to be the first rounds fired into North Vietnam. The other ship actually rescued the pilot but we did take fire and had some shrapnel hit our ship. It was an exciting day.

When the *Berkeley* was fired upon rescuing that downed pilot around the islands off Haiphong, I was the range finder operator at general quarters. Our radar would usually give us the exact range to the target but when the target was located on land, the radar would only give us the range to the beach; how far inland the battery was emplaced was not known. I got the range on that gun emplacement and subsequent reconnaissance told us it was totally destroyed. My eighteen weeks at FT school did not go to waste!

*Spc4 **Gary Nunn**, Military Police*

We were on patrol once and some tracer rounds went over the jeep. I bailed out of the jeep in a hurry that time. I was on patrol another time with a QC (Vietnamese MP) and a mortar round came in and blew his leg off. In that case there was nowhere to run because you didn't know where the next round would land.

*Hospitalman 3rd Class **Scott Squires***

There were frequent mortar and rocket attacks at our base at Chu Lai, random small arms fire on the convoys, automatic weapons fire while we rode the choppers, and worries about mines on the road with the convoys.

If they disabled a truck on the road the whole convoy was at risk so they gave the truck thirty seconds or so to get things working. If they could not they just pushed it out of the way and went on.

*Spc4 **Louis Kutac**, Heavy Equipment Operator*

We were mortared at the rubber plantation where I spent thirty days. We were sitting in foxholes. We were not shot at while I was at Long Binh. Once we were going through some little villages up near the rubber plantation and there were rumors of VC in this area. They warned the people that they would burn the village down if there was any trouble. And they did burn it that night. The next morning I was on my roller working and there was this mother nursing her child, sitting on what was left of her porch, just staring. It kind of got to me. I was so ashamed that we would come out there and hurt innocent people. We blew her house up. It stays in my mind.

*LCpl **Doug Garrett**, Comm Center*

In the act of distributing Crypt Sheets we came under fire one time. My jeep driver ("Weasel" Preston) was wounded in the head by our exploding windshield; I got some shrapnel in my hand. He received a Purple Heart but I declined mine. I've cut myself worse opening cans than with that wound and I didn't want to worry my parents. I got some antiseptic and a band aid and went back to work. Preston wasn't hurt too badly but future daily distribution was done by chopper. I enjoyed the chopper rides; you got to see a lot of the countryside.

*Spc4 **Bob Janecek**, Crew Chief*

Another time we were flying to Tay Ninh Mountain, known as the Black Virgin Mountain west of Saigon near Cambodia. There was a Special Forces Camp there and a radio relay tower. We controlled the top of the mountain and the enemy owned the rest. This was a hot landing zone where we could see the tracers in the air.

Once we were flying over a convoy just to keep an eye on them. We picked up ground fire. When we dropped the smoke grenade the convoy opened up on the location. We figured we should just stay out of there since we were liable to get shot by our own guys. That smoke grenade probably started a small war down there!

*CWO **Norris "Woody" Woodruff**, Pilot*

I was shot down five times on my first tour and crash landed two other times. I flew with George quite a bit although he was a reluctant flier. I would give him a mouthful of Chiclets to quiet him down and then strap him into his seat. George was my pet monkey.

CHAPTER FOUR

FRUSTRATION

"That which does not kill me makes me stronger." -- Friedrich Nietzke

*CWO **Norris "Woody" Woodruff**, Pilot*

We were having some difficulty getting chest armor through our supply channels. At one point we were told that we'd be getting them "any day." In the meantime (this was late January of 1966) we were issued one flak jacket per helicopter.

Courtesy: Annette Woodruff

We had a mission into Landing Zone Bird, which Captain Phillips (my best friend) was told was not a hot LZ. He decided not to wear the improved jacket since it was somewhat restrictive on the legs, hampering a pilot's control of the pedals. As co-pilot I wore the new jacket that day. LZ Bird turned out to be a very hot zone. We had eight grunts on our Huey. As we approached the red-hot LZ Phillips took a round through the chest, penetrating his old flak jacket and killing him instantly. We were about twenty feet in the air and came down hard but no one was hurt.

Somehow in the instant of death he must have been able to auto-rotate the chopper down. The grunts went about their work and I was left there by myself. The other Hueys coming in were ordered to do their job and not worry about me. I had my weapon, a sawed-off shotgun, with me. A sniper was shooting at me from eighty yards away; I fired an occasional round from my sawed-off to let him know I was armed. My rounds fell about 75 yards short of him but he got the message. When an M-79 grenadier came along I pointed out the sniper to him and he disposed of the guy with one round from his blooper gun. The next flight in picked me up and I went back to my cot to ponder the loss of a friend and the "any day now" status of body armor.

Air crews during the early years wore the M-1952 flak jacket of fiber-reinforced plastic or aluminum segments woven into a nylon vest which had been developed during the Korean War. These vests were hot and uncomfortable in Vietnam's climate in addition to being heavy and bulky. In 1967 vests were designed to hold ceramic plates capable of stopping rifle rounds. Body armor arrived in 1969 and was known as the Fragmentation Protective Body Armor. It weighed just 8.5 pounds and cost taxpayers $35. By the mid-1970's, Kevlar, a synthetic fiber, was layered into vests. Vests were also produced for the working dogs. These safety devices were effective against flak and shrapnel, but bulletproof would be a stretch; bullet resistant would be more accurate.

Hospitalman 3rd Class **Scott Squires**

My gear was stowed up at Bravo Battery, at Chu Lai. I wasn't up there much what with all the work but when there we would sit outside at night and look at all the shooting going on not more than a half mile away. I'm not sure why there was a need for a LAM Battery at Chu Lai. The North Vietnamese never sent any planes down there to attack us. Most of our people were pulled out to go TAD somewhere else. We were just a manpower pool for other units.

Monsoon mud was terrible. I was always looking for some plastic to wrap my medical gear in. It was always raining, always dark. It was cold too. It was really depressing. But it was the one time you got a decent shower!

The Southeast Asian monsoon is caused by the collision of northern and southern trade winds occurring between northern Australia and southeastern Asia.[xxiii] Even the weather was at war in Vietnam! In the southern (Delta) region of South Vietnam the rains usually begin in late May and continue through September.[xxiv] Conditions in the Mekong Delta permitted two rice harvests in 1964 – enough to feed all of Southeast Asia.[xxv] Along the central coast, including Danang, the rains begin in October and run hard to December, turning to drizzles from January to March. I Corps has the most intense monsoon in Vietnam. The average rainfall in Hue is 128" versus 77" in Saigon.[xxvi] The Australians call the monsoon "the wet."

Spc4 **Frank H. Voytek**, *Quartermaster Supply*

I had a lot of frustrations over there. There was one incident where a ten year-old Vietnamese girl ratted on a French guy who was stealing our supplies at night and selling them to the VC. Our captain placed this guy under surveillance. The French guy found out about it and beat the girl nearly to death. I wanted to get my hands on this guy and kill him but he took off and we never saw him again. It took that girl a long time to heal.

I was fighting a losing battle supplying the troops through the system that was in place when I got there in 1963. Green Berets and other soldiers from the field would come down from the hills and yell at me for not getting them what they needed but we didn't have the system in place to do anything more than we did.

**Unloading trucks from ships in Saigon
Courtesy: Frank H. Voytek**

Spc4 **William Wyrick**, *Construction Engineer*

There was a Merchant Marine strike in 1966, and fresh food stopped coming in. We ate C-rats for six or seven months.

*Sgt. **Allen Thomas Jr.**, Radio Relay Crew Chief*

One of my frustrations was replacement parts. Most of the time we'd just jimmy-rig stuff to keep it working. For some reason the only thing I didn't have problems getting was movies! I got movies every Wednesday; somebody would drop off five movies every Wednesday. I guess the USO or somebody ran that and it really worked. Anything organizational we had a problem with. It's like the guys who sent us out there had gone home and no one else knew we were there. I had a commander I never saw! I talked to him on the radio a few times but he never came out. No one seemed to know who I was supposed to talk to if I had a problem. I had a guy who was due to go home and I couldn't get his orders.

*Spc4 **Louis Kutac**, Heavy Equipment Operator*

My frustration is that I didn't get much mail. Some guys got letters every day and I felt somewhat alone. I hadn't realized that a letter could mean that much. Later on, when I got out, my brother went over there and I wrote him twice a week; just scribbled something on a piece of paper. That really kind of got to me that somebody didn't write to me.

*Striker **Rick Dolinar**, Fire Control Technician*

Being at sea for two months at a time was frustrating. For one thing, it prevented regular mail service. We usually got mail once a week or so, during at-sea replenishment. More than once a bag of mail went into the South China Sea. Two months without a beer was also frustrating.

*Spc5 **Mike Stockton**, Army Security Agency, Saigon*

I did see Buddhist/Catholic riots with school children. They were fighting in the street. And I witnessed a twelve-year old girl stab an eight-year old boy to death with a long knife. I was frustrated by the lack of leadership from the Vietnamese politicians and the incredible corruption.

*Airman 2nd Class **Pat Griffin**, Medic,*

When the monsoon started, you wondered "will it ever stop?" You couldn't get away from the moldy smell. Moisture and heat is an incubator for germs.

Hospital administrators were partially graded on how fast they returned men to their units. The recovering patients became more nervous as their wounds healed and you could see the tension in their eyes, and when they asked if you had heard anything about them. The way I felt about it, they had already done their part.

*Spc4 **Jack Stroud**, Teletype Operator*

We were ready for the monsoon in Thailand. We had large, overhanging roofs and a place underneath the buildings to park our jeeps. We had shutters over the windows to keep the rain out. Training was reduced during the monsoon; some just shifted from live firing to the classroom.

*LCpl **Doug Garrett**, Comm Center*

We were in constant need of Crypto repair parts. They didn't want to store parts in the field so when needed, they were not right at hand.

*AT2 **David Greene**, Aviation Electronics Technician*

One frustration is that repair parts were hard to come by. Mechanical parts, electrical parts, hydraulic parts; all of it was hard to find. We cannibalized a lot of equipment to keep what we needed running. We once spent nine days on Guam waiting for a part. Guam is horrible.

*Spc4 **Pat Gallagher**, Engineer*

The monsoon definitely had an effect on our work. At times a river would rise five feet in ten minutes; it is hard to build a bridge under those conditions.

Some of the Montagnard customs could be very frustrating for us. But you had to respect their ways. There was some issue they had about using either the right hand, or the left, I don't recall it anymore. But the Montagnards were very appreciative of everything we taught them. They said thank you over and over.

*Airman 1st Class **Mike Tillman**, Air Police*

I was well into my tour before the monsoon hit and I had never seen anything like it. It was cold too, not just wet. The temperature dropped from about 110 to about 70. And it was windy. You could not stay dry.

The monsoon was heaviest in northern South Vietnam - Danang, 1965

Spc4 **Bob Janecek**, *Crew Chief*

The monsoon, at least down south where we were, gave us rain twice a day, like at 0600 and 1200. Later in the season it would move from 0700 to 1300. It seemed to be somewhat predictable. You could see the rains approaching from up in the air; it was like a curtain, or three curtains approaching, and you could actually fly between them. And of course we could fly above them. If we could avoid flying in the monsoon, we did.

Courtesy: Bob Janecek

Spc5 **Donald "Tip" O'Neill**, *3-Qualified*

It was sometimes hard to get ammo. It was also tough to get replacement parts. I was in charge of an 81mm mortar pit when I first arrived. I went to the pit but there was no mortar there; when I asked about it I was told the mortars were somewhere between the Philippines and Vietnam.

A friend of mine who succumbed to Agent Orange not long ago worked for Air America, flying out of Vin Chin, Laos, kicking bundles out like I was doing. Air America had their operation at one end of the Vin Chin airstrip and the Russians had an operation at the other end. They were kicking bundles out to their people like my friend was doing to our guys.

During the monsoon everything was covered with dust from the termites eating our wood. You could actually hear the termites eating your hooch.

LCpl **Don Campbell**, *RTO*

I was frustrated by the rumors that we were only to be in-country six months, or less if the situation was brought under control. That never happened!

CHAPTER FIVE

ADVENTURES ALOFT

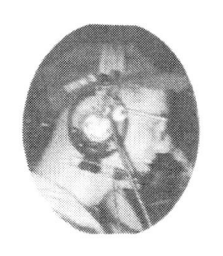

*AT2 **David Greene**, Aviation Electronics Technician*

We had contact with both Russian and Chinese submarines during my three years over there. When we found them we would track them, and we'd spend hours on station following them. Once we left station another plane would come out and relieve us. After I returned home in 1964 some of our squadrons began dropping listening devices along the Ho Chi Minh Trail. We were tracking a submarine once and we had dropped a picket line of sound buoys in the water. We could tell by the engine noise signature it was putting out that it was a Chinese diesel sub. We were only about three hundred feet above the water and I was sitting in my position getting a frequency read on the sub when we lost our starboard engines. We were going down fast but our pilot hit the jet pods and got us safely back to the correct altitude. But because the jets were on we were now in danger of running out of fuel. Our Flight Engineer, an enlisted man, crunched the numbers to see how far we could go; we decided to try to make it back to Okinawa. It looked like it would be a close call and a backup plan was one of the nearby smaller islands of the Ryukus chain, near Okinawa. This smaller island had a crushed coral runway and they used smudge pots to light it at night. The runway there was also pretty short so our pilot really wanted to try and make Okinawa.

When we finally we saw the lights of Okinawa appear in the distance we were really low on gas. The pilot figured we had enough to make just one pass. We went to lower the landing gear and they wouldn't come down; complete hydraulic failure! We were able to lower the wheels manually but the concern then is that you don't get a Locked light. I ran to the radio seat to send the SOS if we didn't make it. The pilot hit the runway on the first pass but we couldn't reverse props and we had no brakes due to the hydraulic failure. We knew from our many previous landings on this field where the runway turnoffs were and we kept flying past them. And the end of the runway was truly the end of the runway; it was ocean and rocks! Our pilot locked the emergency brake which blew a tire. We did a sharp turn and slid onto the grass on one wing. We were safe! We used to have this trailing wire antenna and in the excitement I forgot to reel it in but we were down and safe.

To get from the rear of the Neptune to the flight deck you had to literally crawl under the wing which went completely through the aircraft. We had an electronics technician named Douglas on another flight who snagged his foot on the twelve-man life raft as he crawled over the wing. The life raft proceeded to inflate! This is a monster life raft and as it inflated it began to crush all our electronic equipment. Me and another electronics technician took our flight knives and started to stab the raft. Naturally the raft blew up. The three of us were sitting there covered in talc laughing hysterically at one another. It was funny at the time although it meant we were without a life raft if trouble came. The end result is we had to replace several pieces of our electronic equipment.

Spc4 **Bob Janecek**, *Crew Chief*

We were flying over a Special Forces Camp and the camp commander was swearing that it had been three days and no choppers had landed to evacuate his dead and wounded. The commander saw two choppers, including us, above him and demanded that someone land to help with his wounded. He said their morale was terrible and guys were dying like crazy. It turns out that the commander that was yelling to us was Norman Schwarzkopf.

Our pilot decided to go down and help out and our co-pilot, who was a really good pilot, took over. We flew out about two miles, and came in at treetop level. We could see the VC as we flew over them but we were looking at their backs since they were facing the camp. Our rule was, if someone is shooting at us, we shot back. They probably didn't hear us until we passed them because we were flying so low. We came in over the camp barbed wire and did a flare with the chopper, standing it on its' tail, and then flopped down on the ground.

We were immediately charged by twenty or twenty-five wounded ARVN wanting to get out of there. I was pushing them off the skids. A couple of Special Forces guys came and pushed excess people off the chopper and we started our run across the camp to lift off. Suddenly, an empty body bag flew into our rotor blades, which threw the chopper off balance. I wasn't sure how I was going to die: Would I be thrown out or would the rotors hit me? Finally centrifugal force threw the bag off and we got up.

There were three leper colonies in South Vietnam. Our colonel took it as a challenge to try to support them. They were run by French priests and nuns. We took them supplies when we could. The lepers always wanted to look at the chopper. These people had open sores; their noses would crumble. No one ever came out of there alive. Once we took the priests to Da Lat, where they had a monastery and libraries. It R&R for them.

While I was flying for the 12th Aviation Group later in 1965, we were in the 540 chopper and we had a pilot who preferred to be flying rather than pushing a pencil. He got the best co-pilot he could find and he liked to put himself in harm's way. We were in the area of the Plei Me Special Forces Camp during a siege. The Plei Me ground was littered with multi-colored parachutes which indicating supplies had been dropped to these guys, but most of the chutes were outside their barbed wire. The cargo pilots had probably dropped their loads from too high up.

The helicopters could either fly at 1500 feet, or at 50 feet. The pilots loved flying down low. There was beautiful country to see including many waterfalls and birds, parrots and monkeys. And elephants! We once came across ten or fifteen elephants in a clearing and we flew low by them. They moved and it was almost as if we were herding them. Frustrated, they sat on their haunches and began trumpeting. Finally I guess they decided to ignore us, and it worked. We went away.

Courtesy: Bob Janecek

*Spc5 **Donald "Tip" O'Neill**, 3-Qualified*

The war was really starting to pick up in late 1965 and we had a lot of camps being hit. I was called on a lot to do air drops. At this time the Special Forces camp at Plei Mei was under a fifteen-day siege. I flew supply drops for five days of that siege. It all started with me, a young nineteen-year old guy sitting in our little bar -- we called it the Bamboo Hut --drinking a beer. This place was no bigger than 25' X 25'. Plei Mei had started and we had a lot of aircraft being shot up pretty good. They couldn't get supplies in. I was a Spc4 at the time and I was talking to a guy at the bar and I told him I could get stuff into that camp. My remarks were overheard by a full bird colonel that tapped me on the shoulder and asked me what I had said. The room was suddenly much smaller! I repeated my remarks as I gasped for air, and I told him my idea, which was to use high velocity drops. Not many people were using that technique at that time. I told him I would take a 500-pound capacity parachute and overload it to about 750 pounds. Pinpoint accuracy was a key on this technique. The colonel turned to his exec, a major, and said "Get this man an aircraft immediately." The colonel told me to get whatever I needed and get ready to go out and try this plan.

The Caribou was probably the ideal aircraft for this type of mission since it was vital that we be able to fly at somewhat slow speeds. This plane was twin-engine with some good features and some bad ones. On the bad side, it was a wet wing aircraft with self-filling gas tanks. The slow speed was a plus. We went in that night flying at about four hundred feet off the ground. The guys in the camp filled a can with gasoline and lit it and that's what we aimed on. I would kick the load out when the pilot gave me the signal. I was on a safety tie-down strap and the cargo was on rollers. When the pilot gave me the green light he pulled the plane up and I released the cargo out the tail. We dropped five chutes, three on the first pass and two on the second. All five chutes fell within friendly lines although two of the camp defenders -- Montagnard tribesmen -- were killed when a load hit them. They had been instructed to stay in their bunker but they wanted to see the show I guess.

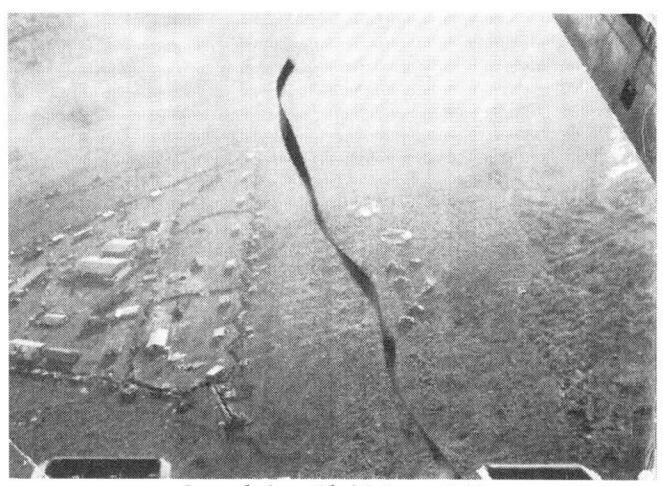

Supplying Plei Me -- 1965
Courtesy: Donald "Tip" O'Neill

We took twenty-one .51 caliber rounds in that plane that night; it sounded like somebody smacking the side of the plane with a chain. They knocked off about a foot of the inboard fuel line. We had taken off from the new asphalt strip at Pleiku for the mission but due to the damage to the Caribou we had to land at nearby Camp Holloway, which had a much shorter runway. There were four of us on board including the pilot, and when we landed, due to concerns about a crash on the short runway, and the fact that the pilot couldn't reverse props because of all the aviation gas pouring out of the wing, three of us jumped out of the tail of the plane at 35mph. We got bruises and scrapes but we were okay. I was awarded a Combat Air Medal with V for Valor. After the Plei Mei battle a major with Delta Force gave me a couple of rounds that the enemy had been firing at us. His name was Charley Beckworth and he became a legend in this unit.

I had free rein on these types of missions after that. I told them I could get arms and ammo, food and medical supplies in there, but not perishables. I flew in there the next few nights. After the battle I went in to the camp to retrieve my parachutes. The stench of death was terrible. There were loads of NVA soldiers that had been killed by bomb blasts or mortar fire, and in many cases the rats had eaten most of the meat off the dead. Not only did our Intelligence know that the NVA was in South Vietnam, we knew there were both Russian and Chinese advisors with them.

There were so many casualties in the Plei Mei camp during the siege that there was a need for additional medics in there. There was this young, black medic who wanted to meet with the chaplain before he went in to Plei Mei. He said he didn't think he was going to make it. The chaplain took him off to the side and prayed with him. The Vietnamese Marines flew the helicopter taking the medics into Plei Mei. Twenty minutes after they took off for Plei Mei they were back and the black medic was on board, dead. He had taken a round that hit his flak jacket on the lace on the sides and went straight through to his heart. Things like that got me to the point where I had seen enough; I just wanted to go home.

*Spc4 **Bob Janecek**, Crew Chief*

We sometimes flew Special Forces guys into areas following B-52 raids for them to assess the bomb damage. One time, as they were re-boarding the chopper for the return flight -- we were on the edge of a tree line, or what was left of the tree line -- I noticed the fins of a large bomb stuck in the ground nearby. I mentioned this to the guys and they said it was probably a delayed fuse meant to go off after the enemy re-entered the area. This was done because the VC liked to enter a bomb location to take any unexploded ordnance.

The 540 rotor head chopper would fly at least twenty miles an hour faster than the old Huey. When we first tried it out just the pilot and I were aboard. We caught up with a medevac helicopter, normally the fastest things in the sky, and the pilot decided to see what we had. He actually passed the medevac chopper from underneath and then flew a circle around them. All of this happened within sight of the Tan Son Nhut runway. When we landed we realized that we had quite a crowd of spectators watching us, curious as to what we were flying. The speed of this new chopper also helped us avoid a lot of ground fire since the enemy was used to the 85mph of the Hueys. At first glance this new helicopter looked like the old Huey but it was faster.

I was constantly trying to get the pilots to let me fly. I tried to convince them that if they were ever hurt they might need me to know something about getting us safely on the ground. They did let me take the controls when we were on long flights once in a while.

We did a lot of back loading wounded and dead soldiers. One time the VC detonated a mine under an armored personnel carrier which was part of a four or five vehicle convoy. The mine blew the APC upside down and one man, probably the driver, was trapped underneath. They had a wrecker in the convoy and it righted the APC. I helped get the guy out and I knew he was dead but I was surprised when I lifted the guy that all his bones were broken.

Spc5 **Mike Stockton**, *Army Security Agency, Saigon*

One side of Camp Davis faced directly at the Tan Son Nhut runway. We lived in barracks made of mahogany, which was hard as steel. We had a helicopter land on the runway once, and it had an arrow from a crossbow sticking out of the undercarriage. Talk about a culture clash.

AT2 **David Greene**, *Aviation Electronics Technician*

I can't really confirm that I was ever shot at but we did get intercepted by aircraft several times -- Chinese aircraft. We usually flew about twenty miles off the Chinese coast in international waters. One time they forced one of our planes to land in China. That's the kind of thing we always worried about. Our plane was not armed. Their planes would come out and fly on our wing and we had these big cameras that we could stick out and snap their picture. These cameras were big enough to be mistaken for cannon! I was always worried that they might get the wrong impression.

When President Kennedy was assassinated I was living ashore and the MPs came and got me and put me on an airplane. All I had on was my skivvies and a flight suit. They took us to a strip up in Honshu Island, up in northern Japan. This was in November. It was snowing there. They put us on that plane because they thought we might be going to war. A similar thing had happened a year before during the Cuban missile crisis.

I liked what I was doing so much that I extended my enlistment for another two tours. I was told one time prior to a flight that we would not be finding any radar sites on our mission. The CO promised us a case of San Miguel beer for each installation we uncovered. We found twenty! We never saw the beer but we did check out the R&R boat and got a nice tour of the Bataan Peninsula and Corregidor. I was recognized for my efforts in Patrol Squadron 4 when I returned to the states; my next duty station was as an instructor, and that made me feel good.

Shade is where you found it
Courtesy: David Greene

Spc5 **Mike Stockton**, *Army Security Agency, Saigon*

I witnessed some of the first B-52 strikes from the air; this was around Tay Ninh. We were flying at around 6,000 feet and all of a sudden we saw this eruption on the ground. I also had a chance one time to ride as a door gunner on a chopper. We flew to Can Tho, about ninety miles south of Saigon. We were flying about ten feet above the palm trees at 120 miles an hour. That was pretty cool. I fired at a few VC sampans going up the canals. We probably got shot at but we never knew.

LCpl **Doug Garrett**, *Comm Center*

Our air officer, Captain Henry, asked me if I wanted to fly in an F-4 Phantom jet. I jumped at the chance. That was a blast. Of course he tried to make me sick but I tend not to get air sick or motion sickness so I thoroughly enjoyed it. We were turning G's and my pressure suit was inflating like crazy. I would have liked to have landed on a carrier that day but we couldn't get authorization.

*CWO **Norris "Woody" Woodruff**, Pilot*

During one of our quieter moments we were given a mission to spray Agent Orange on the perimeter of our base, along the concertina wire. We had 55-gallon drums of Agent Orange on our chopper. The drums had a motor and a sprayer on top. This mission lasted three days. As we finished each day we were covered with Agent Orange residue. So was the inside of the chopper. We would fly to a nearby river and ease the chopper down just below the waterline to swab it out and clean ourselves as much as possible.

My friend "Woody" Woodruff died in February, 2012 of Agent Orange-related problems.

*Spc4 **Bob Janecek**, Crew Chief*

I did have one crash landing over there. The active runway and the taxi runway at Tan Son Nhut created a big oval. There was a shortcut from the taxiway to the active runway and four jets that needed to take the shortcut to get airborne quickly were on that shortcut. Meanwhile we were up about seventy-five feet on our takeoff procedure, traveling about sixty mph. When the jets turned on to the active runway their exhaust went under our chopper which blew out what they call the ground cushion. We came down like a rock. Our rotor clipped part of the tail boom in the back and bent the skids. Luckily this was mostly cosmetic damage.

CHAPTER SIX

ON LAND AND SEA

Spc4 **Frank H. Voytek**, *Quartermaster Supply*

When the coup started we were being trucked back from work in the back of a deuce and a half, with no weapons. I had a mechanic's grease gun and I held that like it was a machine gun. There I was, a crazy nineteen-year old kid, squeezing grease out of that machine gun wanna-be. We're driving through the streets of Saigon and the people were looking at me, and I was squeezing grease, and the sergeant threw me down and told me I was going to get everyone killed.

**A coup in Saigon. A very tense time.
Courtesy of Frank H. Voytek**

Around the time of Diem's assassination (1963) I saw several Buddhist monks burn themselves to death. They would sit in the middle of a Saigon street, and other Buddhists would gather around so you couldn't get to the guy who set himself on fire. The burning person would sit there cross-legged and pour gasoline on himself but he wouldn't yell or anything.

Finally when he was dead, he would just fall over. The joke going around then was "What uses a gallon of gas but doesn't go anywhere? A burning Buddha."

Saigon 1963
Courtesy Frank H. Voytek

Jokes aside, with Diem's assassination it was a very tense time. We were not allowed out into Saigon. We were in the middle of that but in a sense, we were not involved. It was like it was in a movie. The restaurants became off limits to us so we ate in the mess hall. The food was decent. No C rations.

LCpl Don Campbell, RTO

We had run a land line (wire) out to an outpost just outside a village bordering Route 1. Some of the wire ran down the inside of an abandoned railroad track. On troubleshooting the line the next morning (the line went dead the night before) we found the wire had been cut in too many places to count and removed. We abandoned the line.

Huts along the railroad tracks
Courtesy: Don Campbell

I was assigned to the furthest outpost on weekly rotation duty. I was informed on arrival that the week prior they had killed some VC sappers and buried them in the latrine dug on the hill. Fortunately, nothing of this nature occurred during my duty.

One night I was assigned to a night patrol beyond the outer perimeter through an area of rice paddies and small huts. We made no contact but it was spooky looking at my shadow reflected in the water of the rice paddy as I walked on the earth bank of the paddy. This was how it was during the first part of the patrol; later, the moon would rise and set which led to darker conditions where you thought every bush was moving. Our Fourth of July was watching the parachute flares at night.

One time after repairing a cut in the wire on a foot patrol, we continued walking to the outpost. We entered the outpost area through a break in the barbed wire, passing two marines in a foxhole. Fifteen minutes after returning to our area via chopper, we learned that a short 105 mm round had landed in that foxhole. Both marines were killed by concussion but their bodies were intact. This was during a fire-for-effect coordinate for night patrol beyond the outpost.

*LCpl **Larry Rock**, Embarkation Clerk/Driver*

I experienced twenty or twenty-five "alerts" during my stints on the defense platoon, all but one of them at night. One morning I was shaving -- using cold water in my helmet -- and the sirens went off.

I brushed the shaving cream from my face, grabbed my rifle, cartridge belt and helmet, and ran for my bunker. The other marine assigned to my bunker was not there, as usual. It was not yet seven o'clock and the sun wasn't up, but I could see a large group – perhaps a hundred or more – blue helmeted soldiers coming down the road. An officer walked beside them. They were a hundred yards away and I had no idea what was going on. No one came by to give me any information. As they approached I leaned my loaded M-14 on the bunker.

The landscaping consisted of sandbag bunkers and barbed wire.

The officer forced a smile as they passed by. I assumed them to be South Vietnamese. They were trailed by some of their vehicles. A hundred yards away the road made a dogleg left and they were out of my sight. Then a propeller driven Skyraider usually flown by the South Vietnamese flew by just a few hundred feet off the ground and began to machine gun the column. I got down that way a couple of days later and saw the burned out hulks of some of their vehicles. I don't know if any of these people were hit, but I assume some were. It was a strange war.

Spc4 **Frank H. Voytek***, Quartermaster Supply*

Soon after the coup started they moved us from the Army base to an old French hotel in downtown Saigon, close to our warehouse. But wherever they put us there were rats. Rats were all over the place in the barracks, down at the waterfront and everywhere. They were also at that old French hotel. The monsoon brought more of them and the sewers in Saigon overflowed. But we did our jobs.

*Spc5 **Mike Stockton**, Army Security Agency, Saigon*

As I walked to work at Camp Davis I would pass by rows of planes at Tan Son Nhut, and I'd see guys covered with this grey dust, loading Agent Orange on airplanes. I saw lots of coups and attempted coups; those were going on all the time. One time we had Vietnamese tanks facing Vietnamese Skyraider planes on the runway. Our commander didn't know what to do; we had trenches to go to for cover but he didn't react.

We were on our way to a remote location south of Nha Trang. There was my boss, Sgt. Brown, and the direction finder driving the jeep, each of whom carried .45's, and me with an M-14. This road was full of mud and holes and we're going about five mph when about a hundred black-clad guys stood up in front of us. They were carrying machine guns and had red scarves around their necks. That is as scared as I ever got over there. We rode by them at five mph and they just grinned at us.

*Spc5 **Donald "Tip" O'Neill**, 3-Qualified*

I went out on ambush when I was at Nha Trang. We walked through a series of rice paddies to catch the sampans coming down the river at night. There were two Americans with a squad of Montagnards. We set machine guns up. We could hear somebody walking down the river. The squad leader sent me out to check the walking noises. I low-crawled about thirty yards to the bank of the river. I could hear the guy walking but it was so dark I couldn't see him. I inched closer to the water and when I was within ten feet from the edge I could see that the "guy" was a huge rat.

Courtesy: Don O'Neill

Hospitalman 3rd Class **Scott Squires**

I had a chicken for a pet at Chu Lai. One day we were coming back to our tent area and the chicken was racing past us being chased by this big rat. We laughed for hours at that; the rat didn't catch the chicken.

Sgt. **Allen Thomas Jr.**, *Radio Relay Crew Chief*

A friend and I were at Korat for some reason, watching a movie when I noticed something around my feet. I looked to my left where my friend was sitting and I saw the head of a snake. I looked to my right and saw the rest of the snake; about thirteen feet of cobra. I told my friend not to move and the snake just kept moving away. Another time at Udorn we killed a Krait; these snakes were known as a step-and-a-half because that's how far you'd get if bitten. These snakes are small but very deadly. They killed this snake just outside the mess hall.

LCpl **Doug Garrett**, *Comm Center*

I came off duty one night and I was walking down Hill 55 to my cot. This was a well-worn path that I had taken many times. Something hit my boot. I had my flashlight with me and turned it on to see a snake slithering off and a yellowy, syrupy thing on my boot. I had been bitten by some sort of snake. We did have cobras around the compound. One of our guys, LCpl Warren -- an Indian from Arizona -- used to try to catch them. Somebody had told him that cobras were slower than rattlesnakes. It was his goal to catch a cobra with his bare hands. He didn't catch one while I was there. But somebody killed a 2 ½ foot pit viper under the boards at our shower. I killed several snakes on my tour, one of which was a cobra.

We were allowed to discharge our weapons against snakes and I put half a clip from an M-14 into this snake, to be sure.

Courtesy of Doug Garrett

Airman1st Class **Mike Tillman**, *Air Police*

I pulled guard duty one day at the bomb dump. A guy with a fork lift was picking up empty pallets and moving them around. As he picked up a pallet a cobra came up with it. This snake was about fifty feet away from me. It was standing up like they do and it was taller than me. I always carried a round in the chamber, which the lieutenant told me I shouldn't do, and I emptied a clip into the cobra. Remember I'm doing all this shooting at the bomb dump! The shooting scared the hell out of the fork lift guy who thought he was under attack. He jumped off his machine and ran. The sergeant called me and wanted to know what I am shooting at.

Hennessey, Tillman, Calsada, Espinoza – Phan Rang, 1966
Courtesy: Mike Tillman

I lived in a tent the whole year I was in Vietnam. Eventually we had wood frames for our tents. We had rats, snakes, rock apes, lizards, you name it. The worst I got hurt over there was from a scorpion. They had two main types of scorpions; they had a little brown one that was about the color of burlap sandbags, conveniently. There were also the bigger ones that you could hear clank when they walked. They were huge but you could kind of hear them coming. When you were out there on post your ears were real big anyway. I was dismantling a sandbagged bunker and one of the little scorpions got me. I was really sick. I had a high fever and spent two days in bed. When the fever broke I was fine.

*Spc4 **Jack Stroud**, Teletype Operator*

On the tour in Thailand we did a lot of recon river trips, and we worked with Air America (CIA). On the recons we experienced a lot of small arms fire. I carried an M14 and the first time I got shot at I pissed my pants. I was in charge of making sure the boats we took up the Mekong River had all the supplies they needed. We would follow the Thai patrols into Laos and wait for the Thai patrols to come back to debrief them. I wasn't supposed to be in Vietnam on this tour, but I was, reconning near Buon Ma Thuot. Strictly speaking we were only following the Thais; we didn't do anything! I ran into both South Vietnamese civilians and the guys in black pajamas on my treks into South Vietnam. Since this was a recon we tried not to get involved in any firefights or prisoner taking.

Courtesy: Jack Stroud

Our closest enemy was the Pathet Lao. From what I could see these people fought whoever they wanted, whenever they wanted, just to get out of it what they wanted. They were just trying to get ahead, and they were being led by a lunatic.

The major had a nine-hole putt-putt course built. That is how I spent my leisure time.

Allen Thomas Jr., Radio Relay Crew Chief

It was very hot there in Thailand so the uniform of the day was a bathing suit with a t shirt. The t shirt would have our name and rank stenciled on it. The three or four times we had some sort of visitor I put on a uniform. Some of the guys wore sarongs. Since we had just built the place everything was new. We had three houses to live in; two other sergeants shared one house with me. We had flush toilets into a septic tank system and we had a water tower which the sun kept warm for hot showers.

The danger was hitting a water buffalo on the Thai roads. Courtesy Allen Thomas Jr.

Highway 1 runs up and down Thailand. It was the only paved road in that area while I was there. We weren't afraid that something was going to happen to us; we were out in the middle of nowhere. We'd get these little Jitney busses and for a quarter you could ride all the way up to Vientiane, or wherever.

The biggest problems we had were running into a water buffalo in the middle of the road. We were never scared but as a young guy, I was just pretty much overwhelmed with the beauty, the culture. I'm looking at temples, and rice paddies and water buffalos; it was just overwhelming. All the colors; it was amazing to me that I was doing that. I was also amazed that I was doing this on my own without anybody being around. The army pretty much left us alone. I never carried a weapon, although I had one. I did carry a bowie knife. Right before I came home I bought a .38 from a civilian engineer who was going home.

For $.25 you could ride to Laos
Courtesy Allen Thomas Jr.

We got our pay every month. We had to block off the highway and a plane would land on the highway and give us our pay. In December of 1965 the plane had engine problems and landed in the trees. The pilot and the paymaster got out but our pay burned up! Up to that point we were being paid in military scrip but starting in 1966 we were paid in American money.

One day a young American guy rode up to our base on a bicycle. He was about twenty-three years old and in the Peace Corps. He was working down the road in one of the villages and he was happy to see us. He had been there seven or eight months and he had malaria for which the Air Force provided medication.

*Spc4 **William Wyrick**, Construction Engineer*

One of the enemy tricks was to plant mines at night after we had finished smoothing out our road during the day. They would put an unexploded 105mm shell under the mine, and place the mine on top. When the mine went off it would set off the much bigger 105 round.

*Spc4 **Gary Nunn**, Military Police*

We were on patrol once and some tracer rounds went over the jeep. I bailed out of the jeep in a hurry that time. I was on patrol another time with a QC (Vietnamese MP) and a mortar round came in and blew his leg off. In that case there was nowhere to run because you didn't know where the next round would land.

We were patrolling once in a VC graveyard. We had been told there was a lot of live VC in there. I didn't think I was going to get out of that deal, but then I realized that the people in there were ARVN, not VC. That was a helluva relief! Communication was poor sometimes. You never had the full picture.

While I was there the VC drove a load of plastique into the front of one of the downtown Saigon buildings and blew the front of the building off. A lot of people were killed or wounded in that explosion. They drove their vehicle right in the front door.

On 30Sep66, while on patrol, I went into a bar where a soldier shot and killed a Danish seaman. He then turned with a gun in his hand and looked at me. I thought he was going to kill me! In that brief moment I thought I was going to be killed by one of my own people! We jumped on him and wrestled him down. To this day when I go into a restaurant I cannot sit with my back to the door. I recently looked up this incident on maritime records and there is really nothing there. It was all covered up. Some of these seamen are at sea for quite a while and when they hit port they have a lot of pay coming. This guy may have gone into the bar with a Chicago bankroll (a hundred dollar bill wrapped around a hundred ones), and he may have tried to take a girl away from a black American soldier, who then shot him.

I received a Letter of Commendation from the general for the way we handled that shooting incident in the bar. There were four guys mentioned in the letter; three of the guys were Regular Army, and I was the draftee. My knowledge of Vietnamese really helped in that investigation, and was mentioned in the commendation.

LCpl *Doug Garrett*, *Comm Center*

Soon after my arrival in Vietnam, as a low man on the totem pool, I was assigned shit-burning detail. I poured my five-gallon can of gas into the barrels but since neither of us on this detail smoked, we didn't have a match. I ran back to the Comm Center where I knew one of the guys working was a smoker. Before I got back to the head (a four-seater) one of our new Second Lieutenants, who didn't heed the can of gas warning at the door to the head, had thrown his cigarette down one of the other holes. He was pretty badly burned and had to be evacuated but he also wanted to write me up. Our CO just laughed at him.

Airman 2nd Class **Pat Griffin**, *Medic*

A friend worked at a nearby Field Evacuation Hospital and I went to see him. As I arrived a chopper came in with some casualties aboard. A guy got off with his head completely covered in bloody bandages. Then they brought off a guy on a stretcher. The guy with the head wound insisted on helping carry the stretcher. I realized I was watching a true act of selfless heroism.

Airman1st Class **Mike Tillman**, *Air Police*

We had one period where we were awake for about three days. I think we were preparing for a visit from somebody. Anyway they gave us Benzedrine to keep us functioning. That kept us awake but I sat out there on guard at night and watched an entire circus train go by me elephants, tigers, lions, clowns, acrobats -- it was just as real as it could be. I got on the radio and asked them what the circus was doing out there. They came out and relieved me so I could get some sleep. Of course by this time I was so hopped up, how could I sleep?

*Striker **Rick Dolinar**, Fire Control Technician*

Refueling operations are not to be taken lightly. We were taking on fuel once from the *Sacramento*, a large oiler, and we rolled to within two feet of each other. It was actually our captain's fault, and it cost him his command. We had an Emergency Breakaway, where both ships should turn away from each other. Anyway, we came real close. I know I could have reached off the deck of the *Berkeley* and touched the *Sacramento*; it was that close!

My station during refueling was Midships Signalman. Refueling was going on fore and aft, but midships, you would transfer people back and forth between ships on a boson's chair, or medicine, mail, movies, or food would be coming aboard via the midshipman's high line. I was the signal guy with the flashlights, like the guy at the airport with the wands, moving planes around. The high line was a very large steel cable. There was a flinching device on it that would adjust as the ships came closer or moved further apart. Well the clutch on the flinching device froze, the ships moved apart, and the cable snapped. If I hadn't hit the deck I probably would have been cut in half. The cable hit our ASROC locker so hard it dented it, so badly that it required service before it could be used again. It was a very touchy, scary situation. There were a lot of people on the deck when it snapped, but luckily no one was hurt. We were taught that if you ever heard a snap you should hit the deck, and we all did.

Courtesy: Rick Dolinar

At one point on our first tour, our ship was relieved of duty and sent to Australia to participate in the Coral Sea Celebration, recognition of one of the main WW II battles in the Pacific that helped safeguard the lifeline to Australia. As part of this event, we had to cross the equator to get there and I was initiated into the Shellback fraternity. That was a lot of fun. We got whacked in the butt with fire hoses, forced to eat baked beans with coffee grounds, and kiss the royal baby's belly, which belonged to a big fat old gunner's mate. On this trip our captain really wanted to travel about a hundred miles out of our way to let him qualify as a Golden Shellback, someone who crosses the equator at the International Dateline, but that didn't happen.

*Airman 2nd Class **Pat Griffin**, Medic*

At Bien Hoa, we were picking up a GI to take to Saigon for evacuation home. We had to drive through this big walled compound, and we saw a big stack of aluminum caskets, and the ground was sloped toward a central sewer. They were doing autopsies behind these canvas walls. We went through two sets of double doors and found ourselves in a room full of multiple amputees. (*pauses here*) Okay, so our kid had no arms or legs and his head was shaved; apparently he had some head injuries as well. So we took him back to Saigon like that. He was medicated; he just laid there and moaned. The whole ward was full of people like that. It changed me and my whole view of the war, the whole deal.

There were eighty-three guard dogs at Cam Ranh Bay. I occasionally went with a friend to feed them and play with them. I always knew how many days I had left on my tour, and it occurred to me as night was falling and I returned to my cot, that the dogs never got to go home; they were there for the duration.

CHAPTER SEVEN

GUYS AND DOLLS - ASIA CHAPTER

"When a man enters military service, where he can be ordered to do things that endanger his life; this is an act of bravery. Anything he does afterward, as a serviceman is in the line of duty." -- George Orwell

During the Vietnam years about twenty-five percent of the 8.6 million who served were drafted. The 1964 draft of 112,000 was more than doubled in 1965, to 231,000.[xxvii] The 1966 draft exceeded 383,000.

*Sgt. **Allen Thomas Jr**., Radio Relay Crew Chief*

The young guys I had there were amazing. Usually you have to keep on guys but all I had to do was tell them what we needed and it was done. I had four guys working directly for me. Several times they tried to move me but my replacement was not able to work with the technicians at the radio relay site. My would-be replacements were trained as leaders and supervisors but not technically and the guys wouldn't work with them.

My guys: Koestner, McKee, Sloss, and the Thais: "Butch" (cook) and Liek, the generator man. Courtesy Allen Thomas Jr

*Spc5 **Donald "Tip" O'Neill**, 3-Qualified*

The Special Forces were like a football team. There were no racial problems. I worked with some great people and I stayed in the Air National Guard for three more wars and thirty-three years all told.

Jayne Mansfield goes to War, Danang, 1966
Courtesy Doug Garrett

LCpl ***Doug Garrett***, *Comm Center*

We had a good bunch of guys but we had a Staff Sergeant, a big, fat guy with glasses who somehow found a snake in his pillow. He also had a grenade (a dummy) thrown into his hooch. This SSgt was a replacement for the Comm Chief that we all loved. He wanted to hold inspections. He wanted to put us on the top of the hill on the skyline to do close order drill. They finally rotated him away from Hill 55.

*LCpl **Don Campbell**, RTO*

I was single when I was in Vietnam, and had no commitments. I really respect the married men and officers for their sacrifices. I sometimes wish I had stayed with my unit for the duration, instead of getting the early discharge to go to college. At times this makes me not want to acknowledge that I was in Vietnam. The unusual thing about that war was that we were the first to go in and went in as a complete unit, but we came home individually, as our tours were up. Replacements coming over were just assigned to a unit when they arrived. I believe this helped complicate and extend that war and helped divide a generation.

*Spc4 **Louis Kutac**, Heavy Equipment Operator*

When I was working in Saigon at the heliport I went to see the Ann Margaret Show. There were only a hundred of us there due to rumors of VC activity and I got to dance with her. I think she spoke with every guy personally. I also sneaked over to the Bob Hope Show; this was in December, 1965. I had some kind of duty but I drove over near the show; I didn't see him up close. There were thousands of guys for that show. An Australian group came up to see us at Long Binh. They put on a real nice show.

The 49th were the best guys there ever were. I really had a good experience with those guys. As the replacements came in over the months, I just didn't get that close to the new guys, for whatever reason. There is much to be said for going over as a unit.

Bob Hope visited four or five sites in Thailand in 1965. In Saigon he entertained 20,000, an eight-fold increase over 1964. He begged the audience not to applaud too much because he didn't want to be "held over." He told his Cam Ranh Bay audience that their sandy camp was an R&R center for camels. At Bien Hoa he cautioned the soldiers to be alert; "they found a manger scene with four wise men!" At An Khe he reminded the troops that "last year you were all advisors. Now that you've seen where it's gotten us, maybe you'll keep your traps shut!" At Danang he said it was "a pleasure to be at such a Top Secret installation as Danang. This place is so hush- hush the bugler doesn't blow reveille. He creeps from tent to tent and whispers "The general's up, how about you?'"

The Hope Show lost an engine flying into Chu Lai and he applauded the sailors on the USS Ticonderoga for donating 11,000 pints of blood for the troops in-country. They visited Nha Trang, Clark AFB in the Philippines, and ended at Guam, where Bob noted that twenty B-52's just took off on the Hanoi Milk Run, nineteen to bomb Hanoi and one to cool the beer."

Hospitalman 3rd Class **Scott Squires**

I spent some time catching passes from Roger Staubach while I was at Chu Lai. Staubach was a Navy officer and future Dallas Cowboy quarterback who ran the offloading of ships at the Sand Ran. The river ran into the ocean at that point and they had cut out a ramp for the LST's to unload. I played football in high school and I thought I could play but he threw the hardest footballs I ever caught. He wanted to keep his arm in shape for after his Navy tour.

Spc4 **Gary Nunn***, Military Police*

Late in 1966 a major tried to bring some girls into a Saigon mansion for some entertainment. I would not let him enter the building and he was upset with me. I called the duty officer, a captain, who arrived and proceeded to chew the major out.

Spc4 **Frank H. Voytek***, Quartermaster Supply*

Despite the limitations I was very proud of our work getting supplies from the Navy and out to the Army. The guys I worked with were wonderful. They showed me the ropes. I still communicate with one of them. When I was ready to come home I was the old guy showing new guys how to do it. Just before I left in April of 1964, we moved into our new, modernized supply office, which I had helped build. I spent my last week helping to set up the new facility and then I was gone.

New Supply Facilities – Saigon 1964
Courtesy: Frank H. Voytek

*Airman 2nd Class **Pat Griffin**, Medic*

I took great pride in the gratitude of the doctors and nurses with whom I worked and mainly from the wounded themselves, who were sincerely appreciative of our help. One time I volunteered to help a pathologist do his work, a grisly job. I didn't know anything about what he was doing so I just handed him things and helped where I could. When he finished he told me he appreciated someone helping out with such a difficult task.

*Hospitalman 3rd Class **Scott Squires***

I was a corpsman with the Marines but nobody ever called me "Doc" until they saw I could do the job. Once I did the work under less than favorable conditions they started calling me "Doc," and they're still calling me "Doc." I saw a number of corpsmen who were grievously wounded but never recognized with medals because they did what was expected.

When I first arrived at Chu Lai there was a veteran corpsman there that had seen action in Korea. He was with Charley Med in Korea and the Chinese overran their unit. This guy sprawled on a stretcher atop a dead guy and pretended to be dead himself. The Chinese bayoneted him repeatedly but he stayed still and survived. He left the service after Korea and they called him back for Vietnam. He was the unhappiest person I had ever seen! Another corpsman had once been kicked out of the navy for stealing an X-ray machine and they called him back because they were so short of corpsmen. With all that went on nothing ever seemed to change. I never really felt that we were winning over there.

CHAPTER EIGHT

THE END OF THE EARLY YEARS

In December of 1966 Bob Hope visited several sites in Thailand, including Korat, Udorn and Takhli, before getting to Vietnam. When he reached Vietnam he visited Ti An, where only half of the Big Red One could be spared to see the show, and had Christmas Dinner at Cu Chi with the 25th Infantry Division. Hope's writers gave him no jokes about the Viet Cong tunnels underneath them, indicating that perhaps this central issue still was not fully appreciated. As Hope told the 25th I/D: "The country is behind you 50%." Protests at home were noted if the tunnels were not. As Hope joked at Pleiku, "The Defense Department gave me my choice of combat zones, Vietnam or Berkeley."

Hope also visited the carrier Bennington and when he returned to Vietnam he hit An Khe, where he commented on their "new mud," Saigon "there's a lot of brass here. They have more guys in the hospital with tennis elbow than with shrapnel." He also went to Cam Ranh Bay and Qui Nhon, where he came in "on the 9:00 monsoon." When he hit Danang it was pouring again, as it was in 1965, and then it was home, with stops at Clark AFB and Guam on the way.

The curtain that came down on Bob Hope's last Christmas Show of 1966 also marked the end of the Early Years. As Winston Churchill once observed, referring to World War II, "it was not the beginning of the end, but it was the end of the beginning," But was that the case at this point in Vietnam?

* *

By the end of 1966 most Americans knew we were in a war, although war had not been declared. The closest our Congress came to a declaration of war was the Gulf of Tonkin Resolution, which gave President Johnson a free hand. Political obfuscation aside, it is doubtful that the military in Vietnam during the Early Years would have had more spring in their step behind a Declaration than they demonstrated after the Resolution. That would change. But war it was; the draft had been tripled over the past few years,[xxviii] public opinion and the press had changed sides, and even some in the administration began to doubt what was going on in Southeast Asia. Our first war to "stop the spread of communism," Korea, was termed a "conflict," or a "police action." (Here's some free advice: Don't ever tell a veteran of Korea that he served during a police action or conflict!) Although we never declared Korea a war there was at least United Nations support for the effort. Vietnam received neither. Apart from the United States five nations provided troops and/or medical personnel for Vietnam, including the Republic of Korea, Thailand, Australia, New Zealand and the Philippines, and over 5,000 of these people died.[xxix] *How many countries have to be involved to earn the designation of World War?*

By the end of 1966 there were 385,000 American troops in-country, but the buildup was far from finished. In 1965 1,369 Americans died, and 5,300 were wounded. In 1966 the death toll was 5,009 and 30,093 were wounded. Any idealism about the war also died in the Early Years.

The buildup was not just about men. The logistic infrastructure that was missing when the Marines came ashore at Danang in March, 1965 was well underway by the end of 1966. Ports, airfields, hospitals, communication towers, and improved roads were sprouting up seemingly overnight. Vietnam was being force-fed into the 20th century. Five jet air bases were added to Tan Son Nhut, Bien Hoa and Danang, six new deep-water ports were constructed to reduce reliance on Saigon, four supply and maintenance depots, and twenty-six permanent base camps were erected, and seventy-five tactical airfields able to accommodate the transport planes sprang up. Twenty-six hospitals with over 8,000 beds and a two-story, air-conditioned office for Westmoreland and a staff of 4,000 were also built.[xxx] *Everything would be connected with a new, direct-dial telephone network called the Southeast Asia Automatic Telephone System with 14,000 circuits. The 3,000 miles of roads needed for our lines of communication was the largest engineer project ever undertaken by our military in a foreign country.*[xxxi]

The repair parts shortage that plagued the early days began to disappear by mid-1966. Thirteen Japanese-owned warehouse facilities with dirt floors were acquired by 1966.[xxxii] *Civilian contractors emerged; the Vinnel Corporation provided trucking services and stevedore support, beach and port clearance and vessel maintenance beginning in the spring of 1966. Han Jin Company of Korea provided trucks and stevedores in the Qui Nhon area.*[xxxiii] *Another civilian contractor, RMK, built the airfield at Cam Ranh Bay, with Army engineer help.*[xxxiv] *The first use of the mobile De Long piers,*[xxxv] *(90' X 3,000', which were towed across the ocean and through the Suez Canal) also occurred at Cam Ranh Bay. With this success, eight more De Long piers were ordered.*

The Vietnamese railway system, a one-line track which ran along the coast from Dong Ha to the DMZ, began restoration in June, 1966. Although the condition of the rolling stock was poor, the road was well-engineered, with 413 bridges and 27 tunnels.[xxxvi] *Down in the Delta, Dong Tam was begun as a IV Corps staging area. The camp grew to 600 acres, a 1,670 foot runway, and a home for the U.S. 9th Infantry Division and many other assorted units. Dong Tam was named by General Westmoreland. It means United Hearts and Minds.*

Much had been accomplished in the nearly two years since the insertion of Marines at Danang (March, 1965), and much of it under fire. We still had advisors working with the South Vietnamese military but the ARVN were no longer the main show. The war had become Americanized. Defense Secretary McNamara and others who anticipated Vietnam serving as a lab for testing our military's new weapons found mixed results;[xxxvii] our combat troops had early problems with the M-16 rifle, which were eventually overcome although the communist version, the AK-47, was always considered the better weapon. Helicopters, perhaps out of necessity, had proved their worth. Vietnam's harsh climate required new jungle clothing and boots.

Initially, supply support units and logistic supervisory personnel were inadequate for the numbers of combat troops they supported and were also deficient in training.[xxxviii] Support troops used the Early Years to update supply, communications and other systems. Base and unit commanders had the option of picking what level of comfort they wanted for their base camps. Due to the climate, air conditioning and refrigeration units were requested far in excess of unit Tables of Equipment and with more equipment came the need for additional maintenance personnel. As the bases were completed, more of the engineer's efforts began to be directed toward improving the Vietnamese infrastructure.[xxxix]

At one time, General Westmoreland estimated that the enemy received 70% of his supplies by sea. Operation Market Time, which covered 1,200 miles of the South Vietnamese coast and extended forty miles out to sea which closed down enemy lines of supply by sea! This major success went largely unsung. Conversely, attempts to shut down supplies and personnel moving down the Ho Chi Minh Trail were not successful.

Since we were forbidden from committing troops to Laos[xl] the burden of cutting this supply line was given to the Air Force. We had learned -- or should have learned in the Korean War -- that air power by itself cannot sever a supply line. In 1966 alone the U.S. flew 13,000 air raids against North Vietnamese targets (roads, rail lines and vehicles) but Westmoreland saw "no indication" of weakened resolve and McNamara would conclude (1967) that air bombardment alone would not impact the Ho Chi Minh Trail.

The Ho Chi Minh Trail hugged the Vietnam border with Laos and Cambodia. It was a superhighway with 12,500 miles of road 22-feet wide with redundant lanes and over 3,000 miles of pipeline to carry fuel. It was well hidden by jungle canopy. Over twenty thousand tons of supplies and thousands of NVA troops moved down the trail each month; by the end of 1965 the communists were building up at twice the rate of our effort. Over 100,000 North Vietnamese support personnel worked on this artery, which gave our enemy the advantage of interior lines of communication. Without this supply line General Giap could not have won. Thus, the war was compromised at the Geneva Conference in 1962 when U.S. Ambassador Averill Harriman agreed to keep the U.S. out of eastern

Laos while ceding NVA freedom of movement in western Laos.[xli] Those who argue that the war was lost in Washington were partially right, but it was also lost in Saigon, where the instability of the government was always a problem.[xlii]

The biggest killer of Americans and Vietnamese alike also made its debut in this early period. One of the many concepts being tested was not supplied by an arms manufacturer but by several chemical companies, including MONSANTO Corporation and Dow Chemical. They were some of the makers of herbicides and defoliants known as Agent Orange. This product was discovered by a plant biologist in 1943 and various mixtures of it were tested in Florida in 1945. It was later used at a utility company in New Jersey and at many military bases in the United States.

As early as 1962 spraying began in rural South Vietnam, designed to destroy foliage which could conceal enemy troops and supply lines and to deny agricultural crops to the enemy. The spraying lasted nine years during which over nineteen million gallons were dropped on 6.5 million acres – over 30,000 square miles or about 12 - 18% of the country. The aerial spraying was done by C123 "Provider" twin-engine aircraft and helicopters. Eleven million gallons were sprayed from trucks, APC boats and backpack sprayers. The short term results of the spraying ignited a migration to the cities; the long-term results are still being tallied.

PART TWO: WAGGING THE TAIL

MIDDLE YEARS (1967 – 1969)

As the Middle Years (1967 – 1969) began, according to military analyst Hanson Baldwin, President Lyndon Johnson continued to be distrustful of the military.[xliii] Public opinion had turned against our involvement in Vietnam; over half of the American public disapproved of Johnson's policies and 56% of those polled believed the war was a stalemate.[xliv] Historian Stanley Karnow notes that Johnson had also lost faith in McNamara and began to consider dumping him.[xlv]

On the military front General Westmoreland was getting most of what he wanted, in terms of men and equipment, but so was the enemy. North Vietnamese infiltration rose from 35,000 in 1965 to 150,000 by late 1967 and maintained over 100,000 every year after 1966.[xlvi] Despite our success in interdicting enemy supply movement in the Delta we were unable to stop or even slow enemy troops and supplies on the Ho Chi Minh Trail. The antiquated Japanese and French rifles once used by the Viet Cong were replaced by Russian and Chinese-made AK-47's, probably the finest assault rifle on the Vietnam battlefield during the war. There were also no "secure" rear areas. Some bases were poorly chosen and subject to pilferage, sabotage and attacks.[xlvii] The roads were insecure and could not be traveled at night.[xlviii] Some would maintain that the use of helicopters was an admission that we didn't control the roads.

On the support side by 1967 hooches had replaced tents, and then, in many cases, barracks replaced hooches. Although each unit had, to some extent, the opportunity to determine the level of comfort for their base camp, ice plants, walk-in refrigerators, ball fields, pools, clubs and even miniature golf courses were still the exception rather than the rule. Our attempt to be comfortable in Vietnam was at odds with a North Vietnamese slogan seen on the Ho Chi Minh Trail: "When marching leave no tracks, when eating make no smoke and when resting build no house."[xlix]

It became a different war with a different enemy and different weapons as the Middle Years unfolded. Despite the frustrations of "ticket-punching" commanders, micro-management of the war from Washington, D.C., and the safe sanctuaries given the enemy in Laos and Cambodia, the American combat troops and their support personnel soldiered on. Vietnam lacked the full participation of the American public seen in the Second World War; the Vietnam War even lacked the indifference the public showed to the Korean War. As the cost and casualty lists rose each week, as trumpeted by the nightly news broadcasts, the public grew more hostile to the military. Enemy body counts became the measure of success; our own body counts the price of an uncertain victory.

CHAPTER NINE

1967: OUR NUMBERS SWELL

Nearly all troops coming in to Vietnam after 1966 came individually – not as part of a unit – and most arrived by plane. A higher percentage of them were also draftees, including some drafted into the Marine Corps. Career soldiers were beginning their second or third tours.

*Sgt. **Jack Stroud**, Teletype Operator, HQ IFFV*

After my tour in Thailand I was assigned to Signal Company Support with the 569th in Arizona, where we were on call 24/7 to fix communications problems anywhere in the world. We spent a fair amount of time getting ready to respond to some emergency but then they would tell us to stand down. After my time in Arizona I went to the 177th at Fort Benning as their Comm. Chief. They were in the process of converting C-47's into gunships. My job was to move the radio equipment into a bay in the back of the Chinook's to give the radios a little more protection armor-wise. From there I flew into Tan Son Nhut in June of 1966. I went by truck to Nha Trang, where I spent my second tour. My first child was born just after I arrived.

After the first couple of months of circuit chasing VHF sites I got involved in profiling. This involved being dropped off in certain spots to determine the viability of using it as a communications site. This was always as a prelude to an upcoming operation. I worked with Captain Thomas and a couple of other men. We tried to pick areas of high elevation where we also determined we would be able to get vehicles in there. When we finished our field work we had to make our way to the pick-up point. When we returned the captain would write up the After Action Report and

I would do the profiling on the map to see if our "shots" (line of sight) would work. They had just started a 24-hour monitoring of the circuits so everyone had to take a turn working nights. We actually set up some sites that came in handy during the upcoming Tet offensive. The work we did was for LZ Bird.

*Spc4 **Ron Kappeler**, RTO, 198th Infantry Brigade, Americal Division, USA*

In October of 1967 I sailed over on the troopship *USS Gordon*. While at sea a guy jumped overboard. A few life rafts were thrown and we turned around, which takes a few miles for a big ship to do. When we returned there was no sign of him. Most of us rushed to the side of the ship to look for the guy. This created the possibility of the ship listing too much so they ordered everyone to their compartments where they checked ID's. An hour later they let us back on deck. We circled for a while looking for that guy, and it was an eerie sight looking at the expanse of water and the empty life preserver. We stayed there for four hours. They alerted all ships in the area but this person was never found. We passed ships in the night and I could read the blinking lights. We would ask them their destination and they would answer CONUS (Continental US), and they would ask our destination and we would answer CONFIDENTIAL. We did get to go ashore at Subic Bay for a few beers on the base.

Aboard the *USS Gordon*, October 1967
Courtesy: Ron Kappeler

We reached Danang, and were transferred to an LST. Before the transfer took place we noticed a lot of men with carbines looking over the side of the ship for sappers or air bubbles signifying someone was in the water near the side of the ship. Once on the LST we sailed down the coast that night and went ashore around midnight at Chu Lai. My unit, the 198th HQ unit, ended up just west of Chu Lai at Landing Zone Bayonet

One of the jobs they gave me at LZ Bayonet was every morning I would take a deuce and a half truck and drive south on Hwy 1. I was in the truck by myself. In front of me was an APC (armored personnel carrier) or a tank with a squad of infantry and two minesweepers (men walking with the metal detector on their back) sweeping the road in front of the tank. I would follow them for a mile or so then I would make a left and head toward the beach, about a mile away. This would be not too far from the My Lai area. I had heard that if you drove 40 mph and you detonated a mine it might miss the cab. So I tried my darndest to go 40 mph along this rutted road that made turns left and right, but I was never able to do it. I did this job every day for over a month

The purpose of my trip was to pick up about twenty-three villagers who were the work force for our camp. I had no security with me other than my rifle. I picked these people up and drove back along the beach road to Highway 1 and then we went north to LZ Bayonet and just pulled into a field along the highway and we worked there filling sandbags all day. I was responsible for these people and their food (couple cases of C rats) and a five gallon water which I buried to keep it cool.

When I worked with the infantry I would get dropped on a hilltop somewhere to set up the radio equipment to be the basis for their communications. We were sometimes dropped by Chinook helicopters. Sometimes we had a jeep that had three different types of radio capabilities; radio, radio teletype and voice communication, Morse code etc. We were trained on Morse code but we didn't use it much. The Special Forces guys communicated a lot with code and they were so fast I couldn't keep up with it. I also pulled a lot of perimeter guard duty and shit burning details.

*Spc4 **William Wyrick**, Construction Engineer, A Co., 46th Engr. Bn., USA*

In 1967 I went back to Camp Bearcat. Troops had already been living there over a year, but they sent me there with a wheeled entrenching machine to dig a ditch two feet wide by six feet deep to serve as a septic system for their mess hall. After this task was finished I went back to check on it and it was working very well for them. It was probably one of the first systems like that.

*Hospitalman 3rd Class **Scott Squires**, 2nd LAM Bn., 1st Marine Air Wing*

At Chu Lai we continued doing MedCaps almost every day, delivering babies and sewing up the Vietnamese. I also rode a lot of weekly convoys up to Danang. We had some days where we were going all day long and some days where there wasn't much to do, but if you were a lower-ranked person they soon found tasks for you.

We did a lot with the Vietnamese under the heading of pacification. We helped them a lot with medical problems. There was an island, I think the name was Ky Kao, right near the Sand Ran at Chu Lai. They used to run a load of Marines out there in mike boats to visit the girls there. Part of my job was to check out the girls at the cat house.

*A/M 2nd Class **Tom Emmons**, Loadmaster, 374th Tac. Air Sqdrn*

I asked my air force recruiter if I could get in. He asked if I could walk, talk and breathe, and when I said yes, he told me I was in. The day I was sworn into the Air Force my draft number came up. It would not be the only close call I would have in the military.

After six weeks training as a loadmaster in Texas and duty in Columbus, Ohio I flew into Okinawa in January of 1967. We would be flying over to Vietnam for two week stretches, and then back to Okinawa for a bit. This meant we were not included against the total military in Vietnam.

The closest thing we had to home in Vietnam was Cam Ranh Bay. During our two-week stints in-country, we'd usually take off empty from Cam

Ranh Bay. We landed at all airfields from Khe Sanh to the Delta. We went to fields that were nothing but a dirt strip. Our mission in Vietnam was to haul anything that the army needed to be moved from one place to another, whether it be dead bodies, soldiers, ammo, beer -- I remember one time we had I don't know how many pallets of beer. They were stacked 8' x 8', 6' tall; all beer.

The C130 model A was a four engine turbo-jet that could land on an aircraft carrier. It was a real workhorse. The Army used a 2-engine version. We carried 32,000 pounds of fuel and burned 4,000/hour, so we had about eight hours of fuel aboard. We were lucky to get four hours of flight time a day. We had a crew of five; pilot, co-pilot, navigator, flight engineer and me. I was the loadmaster and low man on the totem pole. I was the first guy to jump if we went down.

When we landed the plane the rest of the crew just sat there. They'd watch me bust my ass, but when we took off they'd do their thing; fly the airplane and land it. The more landings the harder I worked. And it was a hustle. Once you hit the ground you got the plane chocked. That was my job. Then I'd load it making sure everything was tied down. Vehicles were the biggest pain in the ass. Loading a deuce and a half was a pain because you had to really chain it down. It was 8G's forward, and 4G's to the rear, so a 10,000 pound truck was 80,000 going forward. So it took all kinds of chains. It took about half an hour to secure it. I was never on the ground for less than half an hour loading vehicles. If I was lucky they'd roll pallets in; all pallets meant you were gone in fifteen minutes.

You were never assigned to the same plane. You'd get up in the morning and they'd say "this is your plane today." These are the problems the plane had. It might be red x'd and you couldn't fly it that day. At the end of the day we'd come back and you'd be met by the chief maintenance man. That was his baby. He would want to talk to the flight engineer. What's going on? What do we need to fix? So then his work started. And there was pride there. Real pride.

Airman 3rd Class **Frank Towns**, *Jet Mechanic, 436th Org. Maint., Dover, Del. USAF*

Both sides of my family had a military background. My father was a Marine wounded on Guam in WW II, in August of 1944, and he was on 100% disability. I received my draft notice in June of 1966 and when I went to Indianapolis to report they told me I wasn't required to serve since

I was the only son of a 100% disabled veteran. I said it was they who didn't understand. I went back and talked to my parents and my uncles -- my uncle Bill was one of the survivors of the USS Indianapolis – and they advised me to go into the Air Force or the Navy. The Army recruiter was somewhat unpleasant when I returned since he wasn't going to get me. I enlisted in the Air Force in September. I did basic training at Lackland AFB. They told us in training that for every man in a combat role in Vietnam there were thirteen people in support!

My plane had a tail number of 40613. We also helped out each other on the other planes. The crew on the C-141 included pilot, co-pilot, flight engineer, navigator, cargo master, mechanic, radioman, and a few others. The cargo master was the most important guy; he had to balance the aircraft -- he used a plumb bob -- and he was required to have a Top Secret security clearance. Mine was Top Secret also. Only about 300 of the 6,000 military at Dover held a Top Secret clearance. The paperwork on any type of security clearance ends up at Langley (CIA). Apparently my great-grandfather, who I never met, was a German officer under Hitler. During the investigation for my clearance, by the FBI, I was asked if I had any communist ties. After six hours of their seemingly pointless questions I grabbed one of the G-men by the tie and made a fist. The other agent laughed and said "Well, I guess we've found the point where you're going to break," and I told them I found the point where this agent was going to lose his teeth. But I got my Top Secret Clearance.

We never knew where we were going until we took off and the pilot unsealed his orders. Our usual trip consisted of flying cargo from Dover, DE, usually with a first re-fueling stop at Elmendorf AFB after about 3300 miles, since we lacked the capability to refuel in mid-air, and then sometimes a second stop at Clark AFB in the Philippines. We usually flew into Cam Ranh Bay, then on to Tan Son Nhut. Then we flew to Bangkok. A one-way trip took about 22 hours. We usually spent a couple of days on the ground before returning, sometimes longer if major maintenance was required. Our last stop was always Cam Ranh Bay where we sometimes back loaded medevac patients, but always caskets coming back to Dover. We never came back empty. I was the jet mechanic on the flight. There may have been about thirty planes doing these flights out of Dover and thirty or more out of Charleston. Those were the two largest cargo bases. We carried about 280 caskets on a trip, twelve to a pallet. On the trips over we often carried beer (144 cases to a pallet); never premium beer, usually Pabst, Weidman's, Carlings or Ballantine ale; all donated by breweries.

We carried ammo, weapons, peaches and pound cake. Some peaches and pound cake would be snatched during the unloading process and maybe sold on the black market. Since there might have been eight or ten guys unloading the plane, usually with two or three forklifts, it was hard to keep an eye on everything. Other planes flying out of Dover were high-altitude reconnaissance planes that did filming of various areas of Laos and Cambodia. This activity also required a high-level security clearance since we weren't supposed to be in those areas.

BMC *Don McMurray, WFMB-17, Dong Tam, USN*

I enlisted in August, 1960. We arrived by plane for my first Vietnam tour in February of 1967. There was supposed to be a truck there for us but of course there wasn't. We spent the night sleeping on the tarmac at the airbase. I woke up with a face full of mosquito bites. Welcome to Vietnam! I went to Cam Ranh Bay for a month, building sewage trenches, and then flew to Yokohama, Japan to pick up our repair vessel which we towed to Dong Tam.

Dong Tam – 1967
Courtesy: Don McMurray

Our responsibilities at Dong Tam were basically to repair, replenish and service the river craft. So if the engine broke down, as the boson mate I was the one that lowered the hook down, grabbed the engine and pulled it up. I would swing the bad engine over and drop it into the engineering bay of our repair vessel, pick up a new one, swing it over and drop it into the boat. The average work day was ten to twelve hours. We worked on ASPB's, Monitors, and LCM's so basically I was a coxswain of all three; I had to know how to drive them.

By May 1967 five Navy support ships arrived to contribute repair and logistic support.

Captain **Chuck Glazerman**, *RF/PF Forces Advisor*

I came through the ROTC program at a military school so I entered the Army as a lieutenant. After a tour in Korea I was assigned to Recruiting duty. This bored me so I volunteered for Vietnam. Before I went over I had to go to the Defense Language School to learn some Vietnamese. I was a combat arms officer with the Armored Cavalry but when we arrived there was little need for armored guys so they converted us to advisor roles. I flew into Tan Son Nhut around May of 1967 and after a brief orientation I was choppered to Long An, southwest of Saigon, in III Corps.

I was an advisor to the Regional/Popular Forces, a battalion size group in Long An Province. We actually had responsibility for more than Long An Province; we flew into several neighboring provinces from time to time. I usually had a radioman and an interpreter right beside me. I called in air strikes and artillery and medevac's. The Ruff Puffs took good care of me because if I would get hurt they wouldn't get the help they needed.

We would go to the field after breakfast, and return at the end of the day. With additional planning and perimeter duties I worked at least 12/7. An American Brigade had a fire base near Long An and we sometimes coordinated action with them.

The town of Long An had old French villas which we used. I shared a hooch with four or five other guys. We didn't have any problems with rodents or bugs since we had sort of an in-city location.

*2ndLt **Eric Dauphinee**, Pilot, HMH-463, Danang, USMC*

I was born in a rural part of Maine and graduated from high school at 17 in 1964. I enlisted in the Marine Corps with my cousin Will Basque. My goal was to be an MP and stay in the Marines or return to Maine and become a state trooper. The Marine Corps made me a better offer. After Parris Island, South Carolina I went to Supply School. Then I went to Pensacola, Florida for flight training. I completed training and got a commission as a 2ndLt in December 1966. I transferred to El Toro, California where I was assigned to HMH-463 in Santa Ana. This kid from the backwoods of Maine was now flying the free world's largest helicopter, the CH-53A.

The CH-53A Sea Stallion is a Sikorsky-built heavy-lift helicopter that carried a combat crew of five, pilot, co-pilot, crew chief and two door gunners. We carried an internal cargo on pallets rolled in or out the rear ramp or we could be rigged to carry patients on litters or we had seats for 38. At 72 feet in length and almost two stories tall at the tail, it was one very large helicopter. Our cruise airspeed was 170 knots or about 200 miles per hour. There is a hook at the centre of mass used for attaching external loads such as downed aircraft, 155 mm guns or cargo nets full of ammo. The crew chief, lying on his belly, looked through a hole in the cargo deck to guide pilots into position over these loads. The only armor plating was in pilot seats and the two jet engines. Fuel cells were self-sealing against small arms fire. I have landed with so many bullet and shrapnel holes in it that you could recognize the guy standing on the other side, yet it flew home. Thank you, Sikorsky!

On May 1, 1967, I left San Diego on the LPH Tripoli for Pearl Harbor where we picked up "secret" orders for our true destination, Marble Mountain, Danang, RVN. We launched off the ship with this brand new helicopter pre-dawn on May 23 and I got my first look at my new home. Upon landing at Marble Mountain my pilot and I were sent to Operations for a mission briefing. We flew the rest of the day into the night. When we got back we stumbled to our quarters in the dark. Someone had placed my stuff in the 6-man hooch so I unpacked what I needed and hit the rack

Courtesy: Tom Petersen

My duties changed as time went on. We flew often for the first month or so. After that, there was a concern that our aircraft was so valuable it needed to be held in reserve or used sparingly until we could gain more experience. Therefore, missions were assigned to pilots on their second tour and the new guys flew second seat on test flights or trash missions. This lasted until the brass actually started to use our abilities to benefit the cause. After that, we got many "exciting" missions and the seats were occupied by almost anyone nearby when a mission came down.

We did external load missions to lift ammo and artillery into fire bases throughout our area of operations, I Corps in the northern portion of South Vietnam. We did a little work in northern II Corps and some in points west. There was the occasional lift of aircraft downed by accident or enemy fire. Each of our aircraft had a silhouette painted by the door of these aircraft picked up and returned to base. There were Huey's, Ch-34's, CH-46's, O-1 Birddogs and an occasional jet. We brought beans, bullets and mail to the men operating in the field. Our Sikorsky hauled some unusual loads. We hauled lumber; we hauled a water buffalo. Those loads tend to shift around in flight and can be a hazard. Who would have prioritized a water buffalo over ammo and mail?

We were all assigned additional duties in operations, administration, supply, intelligence or maintenance. Some maintenance required a test flight which we did out over the South China Sea. Checks of the flight line for foreign objects were made. There was the occasional screw up by an individual that required investigation and maybe judicial action. Some personnel were sent to Japan or the Philippines for schools or specialized training in accident investigation, survival, Forward Air Control or whatever served the Corps. I was sent for survival training and to Manila as the R&R Officer attached to the embassy.

Helicopters recovered over 10,000 downed aircraft during the war.[1]

*Hosp. 1/C **Alexander Phillips**, USS Cleveland, LPD-7, USN*

I entered the Navy May 14, 1963, in New York City. Prior to departing for our WESTPAC (read Vietnam) tour I attended VD Contact Interviewing; finding all the contacts was important in the containment of sexually transmitted diseases. The date set for moving onto the *Cleveland* -- a beautiful new ship -- was April 5, 1967. The work was easy at first since Sick Bay consisted of one First Aid Box with a bottle of Bayer aspirin and a package of J&J band-aids. Everything else was sitting in a warehouse somewhere. When the medical gear arrived it was smeared in Cosmoline which required lots of Acetone to make the equipment ready for sterile surgery.

The *Cleveland* had a 16-bed ward, a laboratory, a Sick Call area, a Medical Officer's Exam Room, a Dental Room -- though we had no dentist, nor the prospect of ever having a dentist -- an Operating Room and a Central Sterile Supply. We had three storerooms; supplies were divided so that in case of a catastrophe in one location we would still have supplies available.

We donned our whites and massed on the flight deck on April 31. The Chief of Naval Operations and other flag officers joined us for the commissioning ceremony. Our pennant was hoisted to the after truck of the mast, the watch was officially set, and we became a ship of the line, official homeport at San Diego. Before we even left for the west coast we had our first suicide attempt.

We were underway on June 28 for San Diego via the Panama Canal. Our passage through the Canal was very tight and in some areas we could have shaken hands with the monkeys in the trees. We also observed Army paratroopers making an early morning jump nearby. We had a short liberty there before getting underway on July 4, which necessitated a cookout on the flight deck.

On July 6 we christened the OR when one of our Firemen developed a felon on his right thumb that required I&D (incision and drainage).We also had our first brig physical two days later; a seaman was placed on bread and water for three days and my job was to make sure he was alive each day. He was!

By July 11 we were nearing the California coast. We were applying the final coats of paint for our entry into port when we heard the Man Overboard call. One of the electricians assigned to boat painting detail had missed a step on the Jacob's ladder. He was already being hauled back aboard when I arrived. We took him to Sick Bay for a shot of rum; I told him that this was a cheap way to get a drink!

We began additional training on July 28; I again went to Firefighting School and I also was sent to Landing Craft and Surf Salvage training. We took our utility boat to where the surf breaks, stayed there and threw a line to a beached craft. Then our engines were reversed to pull the beached craft off the beach and refloat her. On August 11 we took on AMTRAC's and 300 Marines for training off the coast of Camp Pendleton. I was amazed that those big tank-looking things would float. When they exited the well deck they would momentarily disappear under the blue waters of the Pacific, then bounce back and bob like corks.

We departed on October 18, 1967, along with the *USS Iwo Jima* (a helicopter carrier), one cargo and personnel carrier, the *USS Cavalier*, the *USS Tulare* (LKA-112) and the *USS Comstock*, for a nine-month deployment. We stopped briefly in Hawaii, where I heard Don Ho sing, and had liberty on Okinawa. Somehow we gave our Fruit-of-the-Looms to some bar girls, and then after some more time at sea someone said "There it is," as Vietnam came on the horizon.

We anchored in Danang Harbor on November 13 and began to backload equipment and Marines. Five days later one of the Marines, some of whom were already battle hardened, was diagnosed with malaria. This jarhead became our first medevac as he was sent to the helicopter carrier for treatment. The following day we diagnosed our first Combat Fatigue case and helo'd him to the hospital ship USS *Repose* (AH-16). We had a visit from the TV cast of Rat Patrol the next day as part of their USO tour.

In mid-November a Marine battalion landing team (1/3) from the Cua Viet/Perfume River areas boarded the *Cleveland*. This involved 900 troops and their equipment and we acted as their staging area; they were destined for the LPH. We did Medical Civic Action Programs

(MedCaps), Rescue Operations and PsyOps. My day was tending to the sick and wounded and assisting in surgery.

FCTG **Rick Dolinar**, *Fire Control Technician, USS Cleveland LPD-7*

On my second tour, I was on the *USS Cleveland*, LPD-7. LPD stands for Landing Platform Dock. We left San Diego in November of 1967, and this was the first cruise for the *Cleveland*. All of us on that first cruise became what is known as "plank owners."

I was still doing my Fire Control Technician job this tour, on the *USS Cleveland*, but now we were primarily off the South Vietnamese coast. The LPD was primarily designed for the marines; it was amphibious but not a man-of-war type of ship. Although it was a newer ship it had older technology in terms of guns; it carried Mark 56 and 63 guns, which were smaller than the 5" 54's on the *Berkeley*. But the fire technology system was essentially the same and that was still my domain.

About half the LPD is hollow, and we had a tailgate on the stern, much like a station wagon, and if you put the tailgate down the water would rush in and fill the well deck. The seawater would be let in or pumped out to accommodate embark or debark of the landing craft.

The flight deck of the USS Cleveland (LPD-7)
Courtesy: Rick Dolinar

On the *Cleveland*, I worked eight hours a day but, as an E-4 and E-5, I didn't have to stand any watches. So the work day was a little less intense for me.

Cook 3rd Class **Vic Griguoli**, *USS Cleveland LPD-7, USN*

After high school I was working in a butcher shop. By August I was in the Navy. Probably because of the butcher shop experience the Navy made a cook out of me.

On the *Cleveland* we fed about 750 sailors and a marine battalion (about 1,000) each day. As soon as breakfast was completed you had to start fixing lunch. The captain inspected the galley and he told us if we kept it clean he wouldn't bother us. I was in charge of the menu for each day. Our food was requested from Palo Alto, California. The guys still talk about my lasagna. As cooks, we worked 24 on/24 off, or 48 on/48 off.

Courtesy: Vic Griguoli

Lt. Col. **George B. Gray**, *Commanding Officer, 46th Engineer Bn., USA*

I assumed command of the 46th Engineer Battalion in May, 1967, the fourth CO for the battalion since their arrival in Vietnam in September, 1965. We were based at Long Binh, a base that the 46th built upon their arrival. Our strength was usually 750 men but we were at 1200 by the time I took over.

Lt. Col. George Gray
Courtesy: Gary Sigafoo

The highest priority field assignments during my tenure in II Corps were the Bien Hoa bypass and Bearcat Road projects. These routes would improve the quick reaction forces of the 9th Infantry Division in their defense of Long Bing, which was the home of II Field Force, the largest ammunition and POL supply areas in Vietnam, and the Bien Hoa Air Base.

46th Engineer Battalion – Long Binh
Courtesy: Harley Brinkley

The Bien Hoa Bypass Road had made no progress in two months, partly because they had begun it in a deep and lengthy section of quicksand, rice paddies and rubber plantations. We began a night shift on this project which was frequently attacked by snipers. They had stripped junk yards of artillery shells, jeep bodies and everything else to try to provide a stable sub grade for the road and the pressure from II Field Force was intense and embarrassing. We started a new approach in May 1967. Using 25-ton Euclid dump trucks and every other truck we could find, we hauled very large rocks from the Bien Hoa quarry and dumped them in the quicksand. By the end of the first day we had 300 yards of stable grade! In November, 1967, the nine mile stretch of paved road was opened with great ceremony! Our success with the Bien Hoa Bypass Road led to our employment on the Bearcat Road. This completed road provided the 9th Infantry Division quick access to Long Binh area.

*Sgt. **Allen Thomas Jr.**, Section Chief, 124th Signal Bn.,*

After Thailand I spent the next year in Germany at a place called Goeppingen. We were way too busy since most of the battalion had been cleaned out to support Vietnam; all we had there was five sergeants trying to do all the work. There was no down time. That is where I was when my orders to Vietnam arrived. I flew into Tan Son Nhut in May of 1967 and was choppered to Pleiku. After just a few days I was attached to the 173rd Airborne Brigade at Dak To, in the Central Highlands.

My small unit maintained seven radio sites at Dak To and in the neighboring countryside. This was a "line of sight" concept and the satellite sites were always on high ground, usually in a small clearing big enough to support several howitzers which were in turn supporting the infantry. My job was to maintain these vital communications and to take care of my people. Our antennas were usually crank-up types, about 75 to 90', but here that was not high enough to get above the trees, so we built towers. But at the fire support bases, small clearings at the top of a hill somewhere, we just had small antennas that were air-lifted out to them. A hole was dug in the ground and the antennas plopped in there. As long as colonels and generals could talk to each other nobody bothered us.

We were just three or four guys there at Dak To working in support of the 173rd Airborne Brigade, parts of the 4th Infantry Division, the MP's; we were their communications link to the outside world. We just had to stay on the air. So we were important and they treated us royally. They made sure we were safe and had enough to eat. The biggest threat to our safety was our commanding general! General Stone insisted that all the NCO's should be leaders; regardless of your daytime job, you should be out leading patrols at night. I must have led about fifty of these patrols.

Our living conditions were not very good. We lived in tents in a hole in the ground. We had a tent and three trucks. The engineers built us a shower and a laundry and a mess hall. We had a refrigerator; we had a

Courtesy: Allen Thomas, Jr.

coffee pot. We had cold Cokes! Perhaps because of our elevation (we were too high up for snakes – too cold) and the fact that we had cleared much of the underbrush, we probably avoided some problems, but we had lots of bugs and rats and lizards. They called them FU lizards; that's what it sounded like they were saying. Our bunkers had been there so long they had grown moss, which brought the mosquitoes, then the lizards would come to eat the mosquitoes, then the rats would come.

*Technician **Dick Trimbur**, Communications, 7th Fleet, USN*

After my tour in Turkey I arrived at Danang by plane in October of 1967. The monsoon had just started and it was a real joy to walk into that.

The duties included message traffic interception from enemy planes (Migs) and North Vietnamese land batteries. We worked twelve-hour shifts on the *Coral Sea* carrier and four to eight-hour shifts at Danang or up to a couple of days when we were in the field.

Petty Officer 3rd Class **Vince Malaterra**, *Engineer Aide, MCB-3, Seabees, USN*

After high school, I worked as a rodman for a survey company while I contemplated college. The draft was rapidly approaching and I was advised to join the Navy, since they did a lot of construction-type work, which would keep me out of Vietnam? Of course I fell for it! But due to my experience I was able to go in as an E-4.

I arrived in October of 1967. During my first tour we built bridges and roads between Danang and the DMZ. I was also a gunner on the 81mm mortar. Whatever we did and wherever we went, that mortar went with us. That was the first thing we set up when we got to a work site. With a full charge the range on that mortar was about a mile. It was a close support weapon. We fired quite a bit of HE (high explosive) out of that, but at night it was mostly illumination.

Living conditions sucked. At Danang we started out in hooches, maybe for two weeks. Then we lived in tents until we got rocketed one night. After that I just slept in whatever I could find. We had lots of rats and lots of snakes; little pit vipers, small but deadly. We were sitting around somewhere and we had a bunch of body bags near us, waiting to be transported to Saigon. Suddenly, we noticed movement in two of the bags. Rats had gotten in there at some point.

CHAPTER TEN

ALLIES: MIXED REVIEWS

1967

Khuong Beeler performed housekeeping duties for men of the Army's 46th Engineer Battalion, first at Vung Tau and then at their new home in Long Binh. When the 46th left Vung Tau they asked her to come with them. She told them she didn't know anybody in Long Binh. They told her to bring her friends with her so she brought her sister. She cleaned hooches, shined boots, and did general housekeeping chores. "Housekeeping is hard work!" she remembers. Some things never change.

When I began this project I did not anticipate talking to any Vietnamese people so when I met her at a reunion of the 46th Engineer Battalion (she married an American and moved again – to the United States, where she has lived since the 1970's) I had no questions prepared. She was called "Babysan" in Vietnam and still is. I asked her if she was happy when the Americans first arrived in Vietnam. "Yes," she replied. I breathed a sigh of relief. "Why?" I asked her. "Because the VC execute my father," she replied.

Courtesy: Harley Brinkley

*Spc4 **William Wyrick**, Construction Engineer*

There wasn't much socializing with the Vietnamese people in 1965, but that started to change by 1966. Rules had been relaxed. You could go into the village at Long Binh/Bien Hoa and when you did you didn't take any weapons. In 1967 you couldn't take a weapon into the village.

*Sgt. **Jack Stroud**, Teletype Operator*

I never took my eyes off the Vietnamese; I was just afraid of them. You couldn't trust them.

*Petty Officer 3rd Class **Vince Malaterra**, Seabees*

On my first tour, we recognized that Dogpatch, near the airfield at Danang, was not a pleasant place.

*Airman 2nd Class **Tom Emmons**, Loadmaster*

We had a Vietnamese hooch girl at Cam Ranh Bay with a festering sore on her arm. Our flight surgeon gave her some medicine. There were no hooch girls in Thailand. I found the Thais more attractive and they also liked us. The Aussies also liked us; I got a kick out of their bush hats and iced coffee.

*BMC **Don McMurray**, Boat Engine Repair*

VC posing as workers paced off distances at Dong Tam for their mortar ranges. And when I'm in the head I see their women. Why do we have

Vietnamese on the base when we don't know if they are VC or good guys? They were being used to book kick their economy, I guess.

Hospitalman 3rd Class **Scott Squires**

The Marines gave me a lot of flak for working on the Vietnamese. The enemy. At that time we didn't see many VC in this area; we were fighting the NVA. I had no problems treating a wounded enemy soldier; I figured there was no reason why they should suffer any more than anyone else. I had no problems with us shooting to kill them because they were soldiers, but once they were hurt I figured it was my duty to treat them.

Captain **Chuck Glazerman**, *RF/PF Forces Advisor*

The Regional/Popular Forces guys were somewhat derisively referred to as the Ruff-Puffs. They weren't like the regular ARVN army. As a comparison maybe they were somewhat like our National Guard. They lived in the town they defended so they actually had an investment in its' survival. They were always under-equipped; in my early time with them they were using the old M-1 and perhaps an occasional Thompson submachine gun. If better weapons were supplied to the ARVN they didn't necessarily filter down to the Regional/Popular guys. At the end of the day, literally, when the Americans were back in their bases and the Viet Cong were roaming the street, it was the Ruff Puffs who were right there to intervene. Were they good soldiers? Hell no, but they had a lot of experience fighting the French and toward the end of my tour they started getting the M-16. When you got right down to it it was the Ruff Puffs who had to defend their families and their village and they did. During the night when the VC came to cut the head off a teacher or savage the mayor it was the Ruff Puffs who would respond.

For the most part, the Ruff Puffs were brave, brave enough to put on a pack and go out there and do it. They were also pretty savvy; they knew that come noon it was lunch time and they would stop and go find a chicken to steal or a mouse to throw in a stew pot. The VC seemed to do the same. And the war resumed at 2:00. These guys had been fighting this war for a long, long time; long before I got there. And the contributions that people like myself made, if we went out with twenty and came back with twenty, well, that was a success.

A Ruff Puff standing next to me while we were getting air support during a fight was awed by the firepower the planes were throwing out. He was smiling from ear to ear one minute and knocked unconscious the next from an empty shell casing falling from a plane.

2ndLt **Eric Dauphinee**, *Pilot*

The Vietnamese people have a sauce they like to pour over their rice. They call this *nuoc maum* sauce. Any American that ever sees how this sauce is made will never eat it. Fish is placed in a hole in the ground and a wooden press screws down on it squeezing all this wonderful juice out. Now if you are the first one to ever use this press, perhaps it would simply pick up some of the earthy flavor. However after long-term use the fish is poured in on top of whatever might remain from the last batch and all the critters that have come to the banquet. Cockroaches, flies, rats and things yet to be named are all now part of this delicious sauce. ARVN troops wouldn't go anywhere without this stuff and had to get re-supplied frequently. I'm pretty sure I hauled more of this savory sauce to them than bullets. To accommodate our ARVN friends we had to devise a way to get it to them without crashing the helicopter due to the stench. We found some drums that could be sealed and this is how their sauce was packaged and sent to the field.

So, enter our aviation community to deliver this sustenance to our friends who like to leave grenades in our helicopters. We plan our flight to allow us to get some altitude because it's hot in Vietnam and temperatures cool at about 3 degrees per thousand feet. Being aviators trained in pressure differences we know any sealed item cannot be opened even at say 10,000 feet. A soda can would become a missile and spread the contents all over the cockpit. What we don't know is the point at which this sealed can of sauce will self-relief. I found out: It is somewhere just below 10,000 feet. That helicopter still had an odor when I walked by it the day before I rotated back to the States.

Lt. Col. **George B. Gray**, CO 46th Engineer Battalion

Our Bravo Company Carpenter Shop, begun in May, 1967, employed 500 Vietnamese workers by October and was producing four million board feet/month of pre-fabricated erection kits for bunkers and latrines. The Carpenter Shop became a byword throughout Vietnam as the source for building kits with instructions for every kind of wooden buildings and bunkers commonly used in Vietnam. Delta Company erected and operated a Concrete Block Shop; using one soldier and Vietnamese workers and they turned out about 1,000 concrete blocks per day.

**Prefab Work in the Carpenter Shop – Long Binh 1966
Courtesy: Harley Brinkley**

When the contractor RMK/BRJ phased out the 46th took over a completely equipped rock quarry at Bien Hoa AFB, with two 75-ton rock crushers and a fleet of 25-ton Euclid dump trucks. Lacking experienced soldiers in quarry operation, the Vietnamese at the quarry were hired and soldiers of the 46th were trained.

*Sgt. **Allen Thomas Jr.**, Section Chief*

We had Vietnamese working in the laundry and jobs like that. We had a papasan who we used as an interpreter; he had fought the Japanese during WW II. He spoke English well although he was not educated. He liked to come over and we would give him C rations. He had five kids. Papasan was on his third family; his first two families had been wiped out by all the fighting going on there in Vietnam. The ARVN unit nearby were solid troops; in my view probably the best in Vietnam. They "owned" Kontum. Their colonel was another guy who had fought against the Japanese. His unit fought, they didn't run! We could listen to him on the radio sitting there on the ARVN patio.

We occasionally took food, clothes and other things from our CARE packages from home to the orphanage in Kontum where our papasan interpreter came in very handy.

*Hosp. First Class **Alexander Phillips***

We came into contact with the Vietnamese in the villages we visited. Vietnam had an old world charm; the only thing missing from the old hotels that were built during the French colonial period was Claude Raines making small talk with Bogey. Vietnam was beautiful women and children; women in the overdress with some floral appliqué, or hand-sewn dragon motif. Yellow fever, a very intense appreciation of the Asian females, was always an issue.

*Spc4 **Ron Kappeler**, RTO*

After driving these villagers to work for a few days, and being responsible for their food and water, I became friendly with them. I picked up their language a little bit. One day a group of these people were resting at lunch time and reading a book. There were about ten of them looking over the shoulder of the guy that was reading. The book was written in Vietnamese. Since I had been around these people I thought I could pronounce these words. I asked if I could look at the book and I sat down amongst them and, as though I were the teacher, they looked over my shoulder as I read the words in Vietnamese, and it was so cute because most of these people were my age or younger, and every time I made a mistake they would correct me. But I held their interest long enough to read a few pages.

The Vietnamese men were small but highly competitive. In their minds they were strong. They always used to play games with me. They would throw sandbags at me, like a half-filled sandbag. They would throw it in the air and catch it on their forearm and they would look at me and say you do that. No matter what it was I had to equal them.

The Vietnamese would fill up cans from our garbage each night. They would tell us they were going to feed their pig but we were never sure.

*Communications Technician **Dick Trimbur***

We also had ARVN assigned to our unit. They were happy for the food and cigs. Everything we took for granted was a luxury to them. We depended on each other. No women cleaned our hooches due to the classified stuff. Some thought to be disloyal were executed at various camps.

The first troops from Thailand arrived in September of 1967. South Koreans had been in Vietnam since January 8, 1965 – months before the Marines arrived at Danang. Filipino non-combatants came in October, 1966.[li]

CHAPTER ELEVEN

A MOMENT OF JESUS

*Sgt. **Jack Stroud**, Teletype Operator*

My job was to get Colonel Coe down to Cam Ranh Bay for his biweekly briefing. We had to go through the rubber plantation and on this particular trip I had noticed some differences in the road; it looked like somebody had spilled water or something. On the return trip I drove over one of those spots and the explosion threw both of us about thirty feet. It banged up my back a bit and he got a few cuts and bruises. I refused to take a Purple Heart because I didn't get it under fire.

*Airman 2nd Class **Tom Emmons**, Loadmaster*

We were shot at lots of times. We took lots of fire. You could see it. Sometimes you had to fly through a valley coming in and that was always a sticky wicket. The worst time was a night mission where we flew to a star base that ran out of ammo. It was a volunteer thing; that's how I got my DFC. We went in hot, dark and hot to almost a black runway. Guys on the ground provided suppression fire, we popped the doors open, our engines were screaming, we unloaded, cranked up and left. We were only on the ground five minutes, but it was a long five minutes.

*Captain **Chuck Glazerman**, RF/PF Forces Advisor*

The key road down to Saigon came right through us and there were a couple of strategic bridges on that route and we had to deploy several times in the middle of the night when the VC were threatening those positions. We were often exposed to small arms fire during ambushes. I had my Vietnamese counterpart killed during one of these fights. We had rockets, mortars and small arms fire on many occasions.

I was pinned down more than once by enemy fire where I got myself as close to the ground as I could possibly be, and I'd see stalks of rice above my head quivering due to the rounds whizzing by. That brings you a moment of Jesus!

*Sgt. **Allen Thomas Jr**., Section Chief*

Our bunker was blown up the second day I was there. We got mortared, we got rocketed, and we got shot at up and down the road. I hit another land mine while driving from Dak To to Kontum; this was the same stretch of road where I had hit a land mine on my first Southeast Asia tour. In fact, this mine was only three hundred yards away from where I hit the first one. Although lightning had struck a second time, no one was injured.

At Dak To, we were close enough to the Ho Chi Minh Trail and the NVA infiltration route that we could hear and feel the concussion from B-52 raids over there in Laos. We also had battleships firing support missions. That is amazing. You could actually see those huge rounds going over.

*Spc4 **William Wyrick**, Construction Engineer*

I was at Camp Bearcat in 1967 and we were mortared and took a lot of sniper fire.

*Airman 3rd Class **Frank Towns**, Jet Mechanic*

We picked up mortar fire fairly often during our down time at Cam Ranh Bay, usually coming from the north or the west. The Marines guarded the perimeter to the south, and they were pretty aggressive in their patrolling and keeping the enemy off balance.

On orders from our State Department prior to February, 1967, American artillery could only shoot at targets after our troops were fired upon.[lii]

During the 77-day battle for Khe Sanh, American planes, including B52's, dropped 100,000 tons of bombs, which made the meaningless patch of ground around Khe Sanh the most heavily bombed target in the history of warfare.[liii]

Spc4 **Ron Kappeler**, *RTO*

There were occasions when people would try to come in through the wire at night. And we would fire back; an exchange of fire. Sometimes we were exposed to sniper fire. We underwent mortar fire one time while we were at LZ Baldy and in a number of other places. A lot of times you could see the mortar fin sticking out of the ground. A lieutenant was pulling on one of fins one time and we suggested he get away from there.

Hosp. First Class **Alexander Phillips**

We were doing another PsyOps on December 22 along the Quang Tri coastline when we were sniped at from shore. I stayed low and counted my morphine in the event the SOB gets lucky and hits someone. It must have been a disgruntled employee of the South Vietnamese government taking his unhappiness out on us. Just as the sniping quieted down I heard a loud "boom" out to sea. I didn't see anything out there that looked like a destroyer. Then I heard a freight train go overhead and explode inland with only a "thud." This went on for five or ten minutes, then it stopped. We learned later that the battleship *New Jersey* was doing the shelling but we never saw her. We certainly heard her!

The sniping resumed in the afternoon, interrupting our box lunches. We returned fire from our .50 caliber machine guns. Despite all the shooting I decided to take a peek at what was going on. I saw mortar rounds walking towards us. Someone yelled "Mortars," and we started evasive maneuvers. The mortar fire stopped and we returned to the *Cleveland* to report. Two of our gunwale mounted speakers had small caliber bullet holes. I don't know if this was excellent shooting on Charlie's part or just pure serendipity hits; I prefer the latter explanation. Anyway it was over, and it came to a draw.

Hospitalman 3rd Class **Scott Squires**

There were frequent mortar and rocket attacks at our base at Chu Lai, random small arms fire on the convoys, automatic weapons fire while we rode the choppers, and worries about mines on the road with the convoys. If they disabled a truck on the road the whole convoy was at risk so they gave the truck thirty seconds or so to get things working. If not, they just pushed it out of the way and went on.

BMC **Don McMurray**, *Boat Engine Repair*

We'd work all day repairing boats and engines and about 0100 or 0200 we'd start getting incoming. The rounds would be falling every four hundred yards or so, walking straight toward us, then they'd hit the barge next to us; the next round would be us. But it stopped.

2ndLt **Eric Dauphinee**, *Pilot*

We would find lots of bullet and shrapnel holes in our helicopter on post-flight inspection, some of which were a surprise to us. As a helicopter pilot, we seemed to get into situations regularly where the other side would get off a few rounds in our direction. Some days it seemed we couldn't find a place where Charlie didn't have some extra ammo to expend in our direction. One day I was Major John Cooper's co-pilot. We flew a couple of simple missions with usual ground fire incidents and then got tagged with taking some news media from Dong Ha to Con Tien. Dong Ha was a large base close to the DMZ and just inland a bit. Con Tien was more inland and nearer to the DMZ. It was a big listening post and arty site that took a lot of incoming from the north. They had been taking some extra pounding and the media wanted to capture some of that footage and talk with the troops about how they felt getting pounded by all these explosives.

On our approach to Con Tien, they waved us off early as they heard the rounds on the way. We did a 180 and orbited well south for a while. It soon became apparent we were not going to get an opportunity to land there on this fuel load. We returned to Dong Ha. As we approached the base, Charlie got a lucky round into the ammo dump and all hell broke loose. I believe that place exploded for at least THREE days. Anyway, we were now going to have to find fuel elsewhere. Phu Bai was our alternate and we got in there without incident.

Our mission with the media was cancelled. That left the media well south of Dong Ha, a base they had left to find trouble and a place where trouble had arrived. They weren't getting any footage of some terrific stuff to send home. We, on the other hand, were now given a mission to deliver some much needed supplies to a small outpost in the mountains to the south and west of Phu Bai. Contact with the outpost was promising with their radio operator speaking in normal tone and volume. He reported no enemy fire for months, something nice to hear. We made our approach and knew the landing area was far too small to accommodate our helicopter. We'd have to hover over the edge and offload to the helipad out the back of the helicopter. It's sort of like backing your car to a needlepoint and holding it there while weight is transferred around in the back – except with your car you don't deal with winds and altitude changes. It really is a skill and challenge that all helicopter pilots like to do with precision. Anyway, on our second trip in, we are neatly in place offloading when the whole area starts taking automatic weapons fire. The little firebase tuned up their 105 and silenced the guns, but John looked at me and said, "This is the last day you and I fly together, Magnet Ass." And it was.

CHAPTER TWELVE

WORK IN IT, PLAY IN IT

All Americans serving in Vietnam dealt with an inhospitable climate, dangerous wildlife and an often treacherous host country. The combat troops were also impacted by micro-management of the war from Washington, D.C., "ticket-punching" commanders and the enemy sanctuaries in Laos and Cambodia. Those issues also affected the support troops, but their primary day-to-day issues were the difficult soil (laterite), lack of indigenous rock in places like Cam Ranh Bay, spare parts, challenging weather and the sometimes overpowering demands of satisfying all the Free World forces.

*Airman 2nd Class **Tom Emmons**, Loadmaster*

We fly high and if we had to land in bad weather we relied on our navigator. The engineer would say, "Does anybody see the ground yet?" We're coming down. The navigator would say "You're doing good, you're doing good." He's not even looking out the window; he's looking on his radar "You're getting closer. You're getting closer." Boom. You found it! The pilot says "Holy shit. I'm not doing this again!" But we did.

I was always wet, but not from the rain. It was sweat. I would carry two gallons of drinking water each day because I would really sweat. The guys on my plane would laugh at me; they'd say "We've seen people who sweat before but you gotta' take the cake." It was so hot that clear liquid would just run out of my nostrils. I was drenched from my nose to my ankles.

*Airman 3rd Class **Frank Towns**, Jet Mechanic*

Flying all the way from Delaware we didn't let the monsoon deter us but it was like a thousand bullets hitting the aircraft. We only tried to go through that on an emergency basis, like if they needed ammunition or something. When we took off you could look down and see massive mud slides; what a helluva way to live.

*2ndLt **Eric Dauphinee**, Pilot*

Weather in combat is not a helicopter pilot's friend. We like to be able to climb up a few thousand feet to get out of ground fire range. When the ceiling gets down to only a couple hundred feet we have a couple of things not going our way. Traffic is now crammed together within this limited space. Bad weather usually brings a decrease in visibility. We want to keep our speed up to decrease exposure to ground fire. There is no trained air traffic controller with radar and navaids bringing all these together. It's usually some E-3 or E-4 who is hunkered down behind some berm or rice paddy getting his butt shot off while trying to coordinate extraction or what help his commander is demanding. He's probably just finished high school last spring and now here he is. The Air Force had an asset on Monkey Mountain that was a big help more than once.

*Hospitalman First Class **Alexander Phillips***

The Danang Harbor is easy to enter since the port is open to the sea, but this also allows the Northeast Monsoon seas to enter the harbor. The anchorages assigned to naval ships are exposed and on November 13, when we entered the harbor to relieve the *USS Duluth (LPD-6)* we found 6-8 foot seas. We were off-loading some material and also taking on Assault Craft Division 13. While this was going on our Fire and Rescue Team was dispatched to aid the *USS Beauregard*, a merchant vessel, in combating a fire in her superstructure. Nothing scares me more than a fire aboard ship! There is no alarm to pull and run, as there is no place to run!

*BMC **Don McMurray**, Boat Engine Repair*

If we an engine needed to be pulled during the monsoon, we were out there. We got used to the monsoon and the heat. One minute you're soaking wet and then you're dry, and then you're soaking wet again. One Saturday we were all off and it was raining like heck, and we figured "we can work in it we can play in it." We went out and got kegs of beer and started playing ball in it. That was a memorable moment.

*Sgt. **Jack Stroud**, Teletype Operator*

When the weather was a problem we always had previously begun files we could go back to from other areas. We did more than one or two locations at a time so we had options.

One frustration was the time I pulled guard duty down at the PX. We were having a big pilferage problem; people were raiding the CONEX containers. We didn't have a problem with rats in our barracks because they were all down at the PX. The colonel needed me as his driver and that is the last time they put me on guard duty.

*Spc4 **Ron Kappeler**, RTO*

The heat and the humidity were the most frustrating things, because you could do nothing about them. And the mosquitos. The elements were one of the most frustrating things.

After you are used to temperatures of 100 the change during the monsoon felt very cold. There were times when you had no choice but to sleep in water 3" or 4" deep. There was always rain. It was difficult to bear; difficult to live. We would take the little white pill every night. And another pill, salmon colored, we took once a week.

*Communications Technician **Dick Trimbur***

The monsoon didn't affect us. One was hitting when I first arrived at Danang. It created miserable conditions but didn't affect how I did the job. I spent most of my early time either in the hooch or on the *Coral Sea*.

*Captain **Chuck Glazerman**, RF/PF Forces Advisor*

Well, I used to be two inches taller but all that walking with boots full of water and mud during the monsoon took its' toll. A good friend who was in an armor unit rescued his men but his vehicle got stuck in the mud. He won medals but was horribly wounded in the process. Insurgencies are not meant to be fought with armor. The monsoon in our area did not hurt too much the ability of aircraft to support us but it did make things very sloppy on the ground.

*Sgt. **Jack Stroud**, Teletype Operator*

Out in the field it was always frustrating trying to find the designated pickup spot for our retrieval after the job was done.

*Sgt. **Allen Thomas Jr.**, Section Chief*

It seemed like the monsoon started and it was real heavy for a couple of months, then it would slow down for a while, then it would pick up again, but it never stopped. That's how it seemed. I still have problems with rashes from that dampness. The equipment in our mobile vans stayed dry; these were located at the sites around Dak To. Conditions were worse for guys at the satellite sites than for the main location at Dak To. We used sand, pallets, or whatever we could get to move ourselves up off the ground. We were able to use the facilities of the 173rd and other units to help alleviate our suffering.

*Petty Officer 3rd Class **Vince Malaterra**, Seabees*

The government can be so wasteful. Sometimes the machinery and tools that were parachuted to us would be damaged and we would just blow it up so the VC couldn't use it.

*1stLt **Eric Dauphinee**, Pilot*

A major frustration was finding enemy troops in the open and being unable to get artillery, naval guns, attack aircraft or permission to fire upon them ourselves. There often didn't seem to be enough time or assets to accomplish what needed to be done let alone some of the things you'd like to get done. Some of those routine missions turned into emergency missions and still didn't fester to the top to get done. Sometimes a medevac went from emergency to routine. You knew some loved ones back home were about to get the worst news they had feared.

*Sgt. **Allen Thomas Jr.**, Section Chief*

The 173rd Airborne Brigade lost a lot of people at the battle for Hill 875. I heard most of that battle over the radio network, and I helped load many body bags onto planes and choppers.

I felt we never got the support we needed. As a result I did a lot of trading with other units. For example we traded much of the stockpile of C rations we had to a nearby unit for hot chow.

*1stLt **Eric Dauphinee**, Pilot*

I hated dealing with the media. They were demanding and always tried to get us to do more for longer than the assigned mission. They often interviewed troops and edited it to show a question asked while the answer given was to another question. They asked stupid questions of young men not equipped with life's experiences to give a sane answer. Some of the answers given exceeded my wildest hope but I'm sure none of those ever made it back to the States.

CHAPTER THIRTEEN

HEARING THE LIGHTS

One of the major criticisms of our handling of the Vietnam War was the decision to NOT call up the reserves.[liv] By increasing our troop strength via the draft, we gave the North Vietnamese time to stay apace of our buildup. Some (mostly middle and upper class men) managed to avoid military service by staying in college. By 1967, nearly one third of eligible whites were drafted; the figure for African Americans was nearly two thirds. Most of the veterans I interviewed that served during the early and middle 1960's either volunteered or considered the military an economic opportunity if not a duty.

Airman 2nd Class **Tom Emmons**, *Loadmaster*

Our navigator did more than his share of drinking and one day it nearly cost him. We had an early start. By 0700 we were ready to taxi and the navigator was nowhere to be seen. It was hot as hell in the cockpit even at that early hour and we had the cockpit hatch cover open. We decided to go without him. As we started to taxi we heard a pounding noise on the side of the aircraft loud enough to be heard over the roar of four engines. It was the navigator! He had fallen asleep on the wing next to the engine and didn't wake up until the engines came to life.

Hospitalman 3rd Class **Scott Squires**

There was a corpsman who won a medal charging a hill during the Korean War with a machine gun under his arm. They did a documentary about this guy. He was a legend. I met this man in Hawaii. He wore a Marine Corps uniform despite being in the Navy. He was a died-in-the-wool jarhead. He was a Navy Chief but you'd never believe it to hear him talk. Like him, in my twenty years in the Navy I spent more time with the Marine Corps than I did at sea! I always felt good if I treated someone who could then lead a better life because I helped them.

We had a First Sergeant at Chu Lai that had actually been in the cavalry in the Marine Corps before WW II. At that time he had over thirty-five years in the Corps. I think he needed congressional permission to stay in that long because after thirty years they make you get out. I was planning on extending my tour there in Vietnam but he is the one that persuaded me to leave. He explained that if I extended they would transfer me to another unit. He said it was bad enough how much combat I was seeing now but if I stayed in I would be in it every day until I was killed. I thought about it overnight and knew he was right. The First Sergeant did me a big favor.

*BMC **Don McMurray**, Boat Engine Repair*

There was a bar at the base at Dong Tam and I was the bartender. We always knew when the army was going out. They would come in and buy cases of beer. We normally sold a case for $3, but we sold it to them for $5 to $6 and they were paying it. We knew guys from the boats that carried them up the river; they were charging them another $5 a case to carry it. So much for the secrecy surrounding the move.

*Captain **Chuck Glazerman**, RF/PF Forces Advisor*

I got to talking with a stewardess on the Northwest flight into Ton Son Nhut and we corresponded during my tour. When she had a flight coming in somewhere near me I found a way to get over to see her and have a cold coke in the plane.

I was up near the Plain of Reeds one time and a mortar attack began on the base. I jumped into a bunker and an officer I knew from training was there and recognized me. While the mortar attack unfolded he and I were talking about the old days!

*Petty Officer 3rd Class **Vince Malaterra**, Seabees*

We saw the Bob Hope show in December of 1967 at Danang, at the foot of Hill 327. We were quite a ways from the stage but we made up for it by partying with his Australian dancers until the wee hours.

1stLt **Eric Dauphinee**, *Pilot*

When I was in high school in Maine I dated one of the cheerleaders from a rival high school. We grew apart as most adolescents do and each went on to marry. Her husband was in Vietnam at the same time I was. He worked at a special facility on the top of a mountain north of our base and overlooking Danang from the east. There was one road up the mountain and at the bottom drivers were told not to stop for any reason. Wild monkeys in very large groups would attack, seemingly unprovoked, any lone individual. It was better to put a broken vehicle in neutral and let it coast down the mountain rather than stay on this road. Anyway, I visited Joe a couple of times before he rotated home. One day he told me what they did at that facility. I could tell it was a radar site and had always figured it helped control traffic in and out of Danang, one of the world's busiest airports and the busiest airspace anywhere. They had a section that could put aircraft to a spot on the map. We could give them ten-digit coordinates and they would ask if we wanted to pop out over the spot or at some distance and direction from it. We'd come down through the clouds and pop out exactly as described and clear of air traffic. They weren't always available for us to use as they were a small unit with only a few dedicated folks to do the work. But they were a godsend on more than one occasion. When we first started using them I was telling my pilot the story about Joe and that I used to date his wife before she met him. The pilot was more than a little concerned about how well I had treated this lady and whether or not Joe knew any of the details. There were no untoward events to relate and we had never "gone all the way" so I assumed Joe knew all he needed to know. After all, she married him a couple of boyfriends after she dumped me. Besides, Joe wasn't the kind of guy who would intentionally auger in an aircraft full of people to get one guy. But my pilot was still concerned.

When asked what my proudest moment was in country, I often think of delivering the bread to weary troops, getting that first Air Medal, missing-man formations flying overhead and all those kinds of things. I suppose it always gets around to October 10, 1967. When I got to the squadron that morning, I was called in to see the "Old Man." The orders were in and I was now a First Lieutenant. The butter bar was gone. I was still the youngest but I was no longer the most junior officer in the Marine Corps. I was given the day off to go visit my cousin Will at Red Beach supply center on the north side of Danang. Before I could go I got a phone call from the Red Cross. Some lucky guy got to tell me my normal, healthy daughter had arrived and the mother and baby were doing well. That doesn't seem like much today as communications with combat troops is available through cell phones and email. In those times it was just short of a miracle. I got promoted and became a father all within minutes. Guess which one was the proudest moment for me?

*Lt. Col. **George B. Gray**, CO 46th Engineer Battalion*

John Paul Vann was appointed Province Pacification Officer for Bau Trac Province, formerly part of Long An Province. II Field Force encouraged John Paul Vann to enlist the support of engineer battalions to build schools and other facilities. Vann enlisted the 46th for two Task Forces; Rach Kien, then occupied by the 3/39th Infantry Battalion, was selected for the first location. This location had once been a VC R&R location until they were driven out by the 3/39th.

To construct a base camp at Rach Kien we filled a rice paddy and built a chain link fence around an area 80 X 200 feet that was within the town itself. Although General Westmoreland had outlawed sleeping bunkers I believed that the 46th hand-picked volunteers, 58 fine young men, would be able to stay awake on guard duty and avoid the problems encountered by previous army and marine units. The Brigade and Group commanders left the decision to me and I initially decided against sleeping bunkers.

On December 10, 1967, a surprise mortar attack by a 5,000 man NVA force on Task Force Builder and the 3/39th killed Spc4 Donald Guittar and wounded eleven of his comrades of the 46th Engineers. No U.S. intelligence was aware of the presence of this NVA unit. The enemy threat to our endeavors had risen with the introduction of NVA heavy mortars.

We sent a convoy with bunkers and other building materials to Rach Kien from Long Binh in the morning. In one day sandbagged bunkers were erected for our Task Force Builder men. Sleeping bunkers were offered to the 3/39th but were refused and a fearsome price was paid for this refusal one night in January, 1968, when about 200 men of the 3/39th were killed.

The 46th men in Rach Kien were living in crowded, hot, poorly ventilated, rat and bug infested smelly bunkers, subjected to mortar attack, road ambushes and job site sniper fire, but what made the work of building schools and other village facilities so special for the men of Task Force Builder was the importance to the rural villages. The Vietnamese had a deep and passionate desire to educate their children. Any schools that had existed in the area had been destroyed many years earlier, mostly during the fighting of WW II. Thus the US-built schools were met with incredible enthusiasm. Our men of TFB told stories of local housewives confronting VC cadre's intent on destroying American-built schools. Armed with only brooms and at great risk to themselves, these village matrons saved the schools on numerous occasions. On other occasions villagers risked all to warn Americans of impending ambushes and attacks.

Facilities such as our Carpenter Shop and the Concrete Block Shop received widespread attention and were frequently visited by dignitaries such as US Ambassadors to Nepal and Vietnam, General Creighton Abrams, Lt. General Bruce Palmer, the II Corps Commander, and General Harold Johnson, Chief of Staff of the Army. We understood why the VIP's came to visit our facilities but many did not listen. As we had done in Korea US soldiers and native workers routinely worked together productively, forming teams without bureaucrats or corruption, providing desperately needed facilities to rebuild villages and win the "hearts and minds" of the Vietnamese people.

The reputation of the 46th was unusually good because of the men. Handed some unusual and difficult challenges, the young men of the 46th -- boys in their late teens and early twenties -- rose to meet and conquer these challenges. Young leaders always came forward as needed and the young men responded to them with vigor. They were America's best.

Sgt. Allen Thomas Jr., Section Chief

The actor Robert Stack showed up one day. He said "I can't sing, and I can't dance. I don't know what I'm doing here but I felt I should do something, so here I am." He spent the whole day with us. I'm not a celebrity fan but I appreciate the fact that he was there.

My people were highly educated. I had a high school diploma; I had seven guys working for me and three of them had Masters Degrees and the other four had BA's; young people that just got out of college and joined the service. The guys were technically on top of the work. They could read maps, they could shoot azimuths, and tune radios; learning all this only took a little while. It was important for me after we had them trained on the technical part of the job, to stay on top of their health, both mental and physical. By that time the equipment had become containerized; you didn't have to replace tubes, you just put in a new module. My job was to keep them sane! Out there, if you received an insect bite or a cut it could become a big problem very fast. Guys had to keep taking their malaria pills. A big problem I had was making sure everyone stayed clean.

The experienced sergeants, guys who had one or tour tours in Vietnam already, were amazing. We'd be playing cards, and a guy would just jump up, say "wait a minute," and run to his equipment. He could **hear** that his lights were going to go out.

One sergeant was blown off a ramp by a mortar shell. He wasn't hit by shrapnel but he scraped his face on the ground. He was a dark-skinned guy and he had this white where his face was peeled. After seeing the medic he went right back to his site because he wanted to see to his boys. NCO's that took care of their people brought people home. I understood that from having talked to my uncles from other wars. I had a theme: make me look good. Don't stand around doing nothing. Do something. And I'll take care of you. If you make a mistake I'll take care of you. And I did. I was awarded the Army Commendation Medal for my service on this tour in Vietnam. I never knew about it until I left there and arrived in Germany for my next tour of duty.

Airman 3rd Class **Frank Towns**, *Jet Mechanic*

The things that needed maintenance the most on the C-141 were seals and engines. The dusty conditions in Vietnam probably accounted for that. We always assisted the specialists on the big jobs. Changing the fuel bladders was a tough job; I don't know how those guys could breathe in there. Part of our job after each landing was to grease the struts on the plane. They give you gloves to deal with the graphite grease but you couldn't spread grease as well with gloves as I wanted to, so I used my hands. So I was in the wheel well at Dover, with this grease, stripped to a

T-shirt due to the 95 degree heat. I hear a voice yell "What the fuck are you doing in there, airman?" "None of your fucking business," I responded. Then I hear a stern voice telling me to step out there. I looked down and saw three pairs of patent leather shoes. I get out of the wheel well and see three generals, a one, two and three star. I'm hatless and covered with grease. I salute. One of the generals was "Hap" Arnold, the AF Chief. I figured my second stripe, which I had just received, was now history. They laughed and told me to go back to work. They made a lot of surprise visits to the Dover flight line. They had a lot of fun with me that day.

On any given day, there might be about 300 hearses lined up to pick up a body for transportation to another location. There was a transient barracks there at Dover for the escort, who would arrive a day early to accompany the deceased to his hometown. One time I was going somewhere off base and I was pulled over. In fact all the cars on the highway got pulled over. The FBI, MP's and the CIA were swarming all over the place. They were investigating a guy that was transporting drugs from Thailand via military aircraft, in caskets. A second guy had been transporting cigarettes. We had to prove who we were. They made a movie out of the guy shipping the drugs. He said he was making a million dollars a day.

Cook 3rd Class **Vic Griguoli**

On Sundays aboard the *Cleveland* we had brunch, and the guys were allowed to sleep a bit longer. One Sunday we had a Second Class Yeoman who demanded more food than we gave him. The Mess Cook told him to eat what he had then come back; we had a lot more guys coming through the line. But the guy kept pointing to his two stripes and demanding more eggs. I made a suggestion as to what he could do with his two stripes. He told me he'd get even with me and he did! I got my orders for the LST and that was a rough tour of duty.

Spc4 **Ron Kappeler**, *RTO*

Four of us were on perimeter guard one night and it was really hot, so I volunteered to go back to the base camp for two six packs of beer. Two guys were supposed to be watching at all times while the other two rested. Each one us had a can of relatively cold beer when the officer of the guard, a captain, walks up. We saw him and we challenged him: "Who goes there?" and "Advance to be recognized," and the password and all that. Meanwhile we hid the open beers and put the other eight beers in a grenade box. When he got there the captain asked us if we have everything we're supposed to have, flares, claymore mines, etc., do you have hand grenades? Yes sir. Where are they? "In that box over there, sir." "Let me see them." I said, "Sir, I just counted them about ten minutes ago and there are fourteen in there." If he would have opened up that grenade box, the four of us would still be in Leavenworth.

Marijuana was prevalent over there. Some guys would amuse themselves by shooting at the feet of Vietnamese civilians. I had some infantry guys shooting at the feet of my work party one time. I did my best to persuade them to stop.

I was always amazed by the number of accidents among the servicemen. We did some stupid things. I remember unscrewing a hand grenade and removing the charge. I would pull the pin and throw the charge minus the casing which constituted the shrapnel.

Communications Technician **Dick Trimbur**

We had an aviation guy on the flight deck of the Coral Sea who pushed an F-16 off the deck into the Tonkin Gulf. Turns out he was under the influence; they used to melt aspirin into Listerine and drink it. They'd get aspirins from the px and dissolve it into Listerine and get goofy that way. He was dishonorably discharged in a hurry.

Hospitalman First Class **Alexander Phillips**

One hilarious night we were bunking with Navy SEALS in Danang and watching a striptease by one of the sailors who ended up wearing only a red ribbon in his pubes. Of course this was alcohol fueled but nevertheless funny.

Late in the evening on Christmas Eve the *Iwo Jima* came alongside and we serenaded her with carols from an ensemble assembled on the open flight deck. It was a nice gesture; they in turn played Christmas music on their flight deck announcing system. Then it was business as usual. I didn't see anyone who was homesick in Sick Bay. Perhaps the combat pay was a strong motivator and when you are at sea for extended periods of time that money stacks up real fast! Most folks just take what they need and let the money accumulate until liberty ports are announced.

U.S. troop levels reached 463,000 by Christmas.

CHAPTER FOURTEEN

"WE'RE NOT GOING TO MAKE IT!"

*Spc4 **Gary Nunn**, Military Police, 716th MP Battalion, Tan Son Nhut AB, USA*

In my last few months I had won the Soldier of the Month award in my 900-man battalion. This was probably the reason the lieutenant picked me to be his duty driver. We went to several altercations between various Vietnamese factions and it was more interesting than sitting on a post watching a specific area. It was also more dangerous.

In my final days over there I was filling out my short-timers calendar and I started to carry more ammunition. I picked up a bandolier from the Air Force that allowed me to carry six additional clips instead of the one the Army issued me. I also carried a .45 with three clips.

*Sgt. **Jack Stroud**, Teletype Operator*

The last profile we did was in the Pleiku area. There was some intelligence about expected action by the enemy in this area and Captain Thomas and I went in there to do some recon. We worked on that job a long time and chased down some bad VHF sites that we couldn't use, and we had to borrow a tent for our work. When we looked for a tent we saw that the general had brought in a house trailer for himself. We'd always go down and bang on his door and get coffee in the morning. We finally found a suitable site. Trees usually weren't so tall that our antennas wouldn't work so most of our profiling was successful.

*Airman 2nd Class **Tom Emmons**, Loadmaster*

The time I was the most scared was when we lost the two engines. We were dropping flares over Laos, illuminating the Ho Chi Minh Trail. We cut out the two outboard engines to conserve fuel and when we restarted the outboard right it flamed out. The other engine on that wing also went out. This was very close to China, maybe fifteen miles away. And I really thought we were going to have to parachute into the jungle. I think the entire crew was petrified. The pilot says "We're not going to make it so start throwing stuff out. So anything that wasn't tied down I threw out the door. And he said "I still don't think we are going to make it so the load master is the first one to jump." I was in the back, and I pushed the talk button and said "Bullshit! I'm not going first. You guys can jump and I'll fly the damn plane!"

I remember another night in Laos, where we weren't supposed to be. We were dropping flares again. These flares weighed 64 pounds so after a night of throwing them out of the plane you were really whipped. They were shooting something at us that would explode. I don't know what it was but it would come up so high then it would explode behind us. We almost bought the farm; we're flying along dropping these one million candlelight flares in a line so that the F4s could see and come in do their bombing runs, but the guys on the ground were getting better. I'd be sitting there dropping flares, and boom boom, and I'd hit the mike and say "Turn right, **now**!" The guys on the ground figured it out; if you're dropping in a straight line they just have to lead you.

We'd be flying along over that beautiful green jungle canopy and you'd suddenly hit a brown stretch of totally defoliated ground – Agent Orange!

*Spc4 **William Wyrick**, Construction Engineer*

After I made Spc5 (1967) I was taking a guy out in a ten-ton tractor with a tanker hooked onto the back to teach him to drive. He was watching me closely. I stopped at a stop sign. I was planning to make a right turn but I changed my mind. This truck is long and hard to maneuver so I put it into reverse to help make the left-hand turn. As I backed up there was a jeep behind me. I hit the jeep and boy did I feel small, out there trying to teach a new guy and I have an accident.

*Airman 3rd Class **Frank Towns**, Jet Mechanic*

The biggest mechanical problem we had with the aircraft was a time we took off from Dover and then turned around and went right back. We had hit a flock of geese, which shut down three engines.

*BMC **Don McMurray**, Boat Engine Repair*

On the river I'm working a crane doing some loading on our Mike boat and the army was nearby offloading ammo and I see the army guys throwing the shells to each other. Just as I notice this, one goes off. Guys were killed. Mortar rounds have a large bursting radius, even when they're used improperly!

*2ndLt **Eric Dauphinee**, Pilot*

A jet went down, and they wanted it retrieved from the jungle RIGHT AWAY. There was a huge, Wing-level briefing with zone prep and troop insertion to secure the area followed by rigging specialists and an experienced hook-up man for the most dangerous part of the job. An F-8 jet was picked to make the first run. The plan was for the jet to bomb in close proximity to the downed aircraft, but not too close! The F8 put its' bomb right on top of the downed jet. So much for all the planning. We just went home.

Sgt. **Allen Thomas Jr.**, Section Chief

I led about fifty of the night patrols initiated by our commanding general. On one patrol a GI tried to throw a grenade; we all heard it hit a nearby tree and fall to the ground nearby without exploding. We were all afraid to move. On another patrol I was sitting there in the dark with rain flowing down and through my poncho when we heard VC approaching. They weren't even trying to be quiet figuring we wouldn't be out in that kind of weather; they were talking noisily as they moved along. With all this going on I realized I was crouching on an ant hill. It was miserable but they moved by us without an incident.

Communications Technician **Dick Trimbur**

We had four or five different supervising stations on the radio intercepts and you would get their attention when you thought you had something hot. And he would make a determination. There were more dummy communications than live ones. When we intercepted stuff it was usually a radio transmission in Morse code. Of course it was encrypted; we taped it and the intelligence people were responsible for breaking the encryptions. With so many dummy communications it was tough to discern. My boss disagreed with me on one and told me to ignore it. I thought it was hot and I went over his head. I got a commendation and he lost a stripe.

One time we intercepted a communication that discussed a proposed new North Vietnamese tunnel system. This communication was between the VC and the NVA. We got some fighters in there and bombed that out before they could get it underway and we got a Captains Commendation for that. Another time we intercepted stuff on enemy ground-to-air defenses around Haiphong. We diverted some fighters to take that out which prevented a possible catastrophe.

Hospitalman First Class **Alexander Phillips**

We conducted two Psyops missions in December, 1967, both preceded by a leaflet drop. Assault Craft 11 didn't have a corpsman so I volunteered. This mission was on December 10, and we pulled out of the well deck for a routine trip up the Cua Viet River, a fairly narrow body of water. Our job was to cruise up and down the river as far inland as Dong Ha blaring messages in Vietnamese. We broadcast for 4.5 hours without incident on the first Psyop. I thought the mission successful since we returned without Incident, but the military planners probably thought otherwise. We know that our broadcasts reached the civilians. People already alerted by the pamphlets stopped working to listen and children ran along the banks of the river with us. The VC's hostile reaction confirmed that they considered us a threat.

We brought a casualty aboard on December 17, a man with a fractured leg. We splinted the leg and airlifted him off the following day to the hospital ship. This event pointed out that the LPD's, because of their design with no direct access to Sick Bay, cannot be designated as casualty receiving ships. We had to lower this young man into Sick Bay with a winch. We learned this limitation of the LPD's after building seven of them. The planners also probably never considered our medical personnel limitations.

We executed a medevac of one of our injured sailors on the aft end of a PBR in the middle of a tossing sea. It was difficult to see as I wear glasses, and the sea was whipped up by the helo's rotors and the rough seas. However with the cooperation of the PBR's CO and the expertise of the helo crew, we pulled it off.

Bob Hope began his 1967 tour with stops in Thailand (Ubon and Udorn) and then he reassured Marines at Danang (not raining!) not to worry about riots back in the States. "You'll be sent to Survivor School before you go back." The tour then visited Takhli, in Thailand, that Bob Hope called the "Megalopolis of the boondocks." Hope made his first visit to the 9th Infantry Division "Old Reliables" at Camp Bearcat and showed off Raquel Welch at Plei Ku. "Why not? We've tried everything else." When Bob spoke to the Americal Division at Chu Lai he called it "the Malibu Beach for losers." At Lai Khe Big Red One troops took two hundred pounds of dynamite and some claymores out of the nearby village just prior to his arrival.

The tour stopped at Phu Cat then did their first nighttime show at Phan Rang. Bob and his troupe then made their first arrested landing on the USS Ranger – Hope cracked that he hadn't been hooked that like since vaudeville! He then landed on the USS Coral Sea, which he called "our 51st state" due to its' size. Then it was back to land, or at least what Cam Ranh Bay called land. Hope told the 27,000 GI's that Cam Ranh Bay was the "Sahara of the Far East." He also referred to it as a "million dollar cat box." Cam Ranh Bay was the home of the 1st Logistical Command, where half "of everything that arrives is on the black market within twenty-four hours."

Hope picked up sniper fire at Cu Chi where he entertained the 25th Infantry Division. The sniper fire delayed his departure thirty minutes, but Bob always liked being held over. He then traveled to Korat, Thailand, which he called the "Peyton Place of Thailand," and then played to his largest audience up to that time – 28,000 – 30,000 – at Saigon, on Christmas Day, including General Westmoreland and Vice President Ky of South Vietnam. They did their last show on Guam.

CHAPTER FIFTEEN

CALMS BEFORE STORMS: 1968 ARRIVALS

During late 1967, with the buildup completed, Secretary McNamara initiated efforts against inventory excesses similar to those found after WW II and other conflicts. [lv] Army supply experts were sent to Vietnam on temporary duty to assist in-country personnel with supply management problems.[lvi]

Clark Clifford replaced Robert McNamara as Secretary of Defense on March 1, 1968. Creighton Abrams replaced William Westmoreland on July 3, 1968. Richard Nixon defeated the Democrats in November of 1968.

CTG **Rick Dolinar**, Fire Control Technician

We carried a battalion of marines and their heavy equipment, such as tanks, for insertion on land as needed. We provided support for the war in-country, in terms of helicopter landings and also putting troops

USS Cleveland LPD-7

ashore in the small boats that were part of our LPD. During the course of this tour, we had over 1,000 helicopter missions from the *Cleveland* and hundreds of landing boats went ashore. Sometimes the landing boats returned to the ship with damaged equipment like trucks, and we had repair facilities aboard to deal with that. The boats also returned sometimes with wounded Marines, and we had medical facilities aboard as well. If the injuries were severe, we choppered them to a larger facility.

Cook 3rd Class **Vic Griguoli**

My run-in with the sailor who demanded more food while I was on the *Cleveland* got me orders to the *Meeker*. I only had about two weeks leave between tours. In all I spent over two and a half years in and out of the rivers.

Pfc **John Lawrence**, *Crew Chief, 101st Aviation, Udorn Air Force Base, Thailand, USA*

After high school I had a good job at GM in Norwood, a suburb of Cincinnati. I had a new car, I had two girlfriends, and then I was drafted at age 20. I was mechanically inclined -- I had worked on cars and hot rods and things like that -- and I also had a few rides in planes while working carnivals, so after testing I was sent to bird dog school. I did well there and they sent me to school to work on the Huey.

I flew into Udorn AFB, Thailand, in January of 1968, just before the time Tet occurred in Vietnam. Udorn is very close to the Laotian border. I was assigned to the 101st Aviation.

Courtesy: John Lawrence

I was a crew chief on a Huey helicopter. I had four guys working for me. We flew out of Udorn airbase over Laos and Cambodia, places we weren't supposed to be. I did thirteen medevac's. We also delivered supplies and soldiers. I worked seven days a week! I was either flying or on call 24/7. I often slept in the Huey. We didn't have a door gunner on our Huey; the guns were electric, wired to the pilot's helmet.

The 101st Aviation had two choppers, two turbo-prop planes and one bird dog. One of the choppers was a lemon. Eventually they took both of them away and gave us two new '68 models. In September of 1968 they brought two more helicopters with full crews over to help us because we just couldn't keep up.

*Sgt First Class **Jim Kuipers**, 46th Engr. Bn., USA*

I joined the Army out of high school. After basic training I went to Germany where I was in a Transportation battalion. Then I was a wheeled-vehicle mechanics course instructor at Fort Leonard Wood, MO. At that point I got orders for Vietnam, which was kind of common back in 1967 and 1968. I had just made Sergeant First Class (E-7) and anybody that got promoted back then was on their way to Vietnam. In the Army's way of doing things my MOS (military occupational specialty) was abruptly changed from wheel vehicle mechanic to tracked vehicle mechanic. I was sent to Vietnamese language school at Fort Bliss, TX prior to going overseas.

I arrived by plane at Bien Hoa on 3 February, 1968 and was sent to the 90th Repo Depot. My arrival was delayed several days due to the eruption of the Tet offensive. I was assigned to A Company, 46th Engineer Battalion; wheeled vehicles. This would have made sense but the Sergeant Major who interviewed me told me the battalion commander would want to talk to me. I no sooner sat my bags down at A Company when the phone rang telling me to report back to battalion HQ.

I went to see Colonel George Gray and he started asking me questions about engineer equipment, and I told him I knew nothing about it. He pointed out that I had advanced awfully fast to E-7 (six years) and I agreed, and I asked him if he had technical manuals for the Corps of Engineers. He said "Of course we do; you're about a cocky son-of-a-bitch." I told him I didn't get to be an E-7 because I was quiet. Anyway he sent me to Charlie Company where I was completely out of my MOS. Naturally their wheeled-vehicles were not a problem since I trained on those, but the dozers and graders and tractors and pans; I had no clue about them. They had manuals and I started reading them and they had some good men and I set about learning about engineer equipment in a short span.

When I first got to C Company they were running two crews. The equipment was being worked 24 hours a day by two crews, and that was a downfall in my opinion. Maintenance was being ignored with that schedule. I got the battalion commander to agree to at least one maintenance day a week where we could shut everything down and pull some maintenance on it. He finally agreed to it, much to his displeasure since his job was making progress on the roads, but we began to shut down on Sunday for maintenance.

After several months at C Company the unit moved to Camp Bearcat, where I was acting First Sergeant since an E-8 had left. We had our own area at Camp Bearcat (Camp Castle); we provided our own security and we continued our mission of repairing roads and bridges on the way to Vung Tau, one of our major sea ports along the South Vietnamese coast. We spent a lot of time repairing roads and bridges that had been blown up by the VC. When we were at Bearcat sometimes the Company Commander and I would go out to recon the road. We'd have an infantry escort with us or sometimes we would be in a chopper if it was too late in the day to get there by wheel. The CO and I also went back to Long Binh for numerous meetings while we were out at Bearcat. We returned to Long Binh after a few months when a new First Sergeant came in. I went back to my Motor Pool where I was happy.

*1stLt. **David Cass**, Plt Ldr D Co., 46th Engr. Bn, USA*

I flew out of San Francisco in late April of 1968 – Steve McQueen was filming *Bullitt* while I was in the airport. In Vietnam I had a lot on my plate and I loved it! I was the platoon leader of 45 men of the 2nd platoon, the Class "A" Piaster Conversion Agent, PX Inventory Team, MPC Conversion Day Collection Officer, Customs Control Officer, Alt. Classified Documents Custodian, Alt. Security Control Officer, Voting Officer, Member Unit Fund Council, Unit Historian, Trial Counsel (prosecuted 3 cases while in country), Lost Weapons investigating officer, construction supervisor of three bridges (two outside Long Hung, one in Long Binh), and construction of one eleven-chair dental clinic in Long Binh. I also supervised a gravel pit outside Saigon, the removal and replacement of one steel bridge in Saigon, repair of a floating dock in Saigon, installation and maintenance of security lighting on several bridges from Saigon to Bien Hoa, installation of power poles and wiring of 650 family units in Cholon, O. D. (officer of the day), night time officer in charge of security at Battalion, Long Bien Post and task force, highway repair, gravel convoy duty, and pile driving in the Saigon River.

My first task each day was to coordinate with SFC Carter on personnel, materials, tools, motor vehicles, including sick-call list. Then I would visit all projects and make up a punch list of items needed. I prepared design and materials lists as well as estimated cost of upcoming projects and reviewed the fly-over report of bridge lighting and visited all bridges to check status of generators, light fixtures, fuel supply and personnel status. I investigated charges for up-coming trials I would prosecute and wrote up Article 15's as required. I wrote letters to families of injured personnel, checked that the block shop and culvert shop had enough materials. I coordinated with the Vietnamese foremen to resolve any problems with the 200 Vietnamese we employed. I worked with the 720th M.P. Battalion for security on bridge sites. I handled recommendations for promotions or awards of enlisted personnel. When the work crews returned to the Company area about 1755 hours I inspected weapons and uniforms before posting night guards. Another responsibility was to check that all flat tires have been fixed and fuel tanks are topped off in case we were called out during the night. My evening work was to review platoon and squad leader reports of the day's progress and meet with the Commanding Officer and fellow platoon leaders to discuss tomorrow's projects. I usually visited the bridges after dark to check on lighting. Around 2200 I would write letters home if I didn't have Officer of the Guard.

*Lt. Col. **Bud Might**, Pilot, Spcl Ops/Psy Ops, Saigon, USAF*

I had flown 35 bombing missions with the 8th Air Force over Germany in WW II and was involved in the Berlin airlift of 1949. I was in Iceland during Korea but after jungle survival training in the Philippines, I flew into Tan Son Nhut in 1968.

After my orders for Vietnam came in I went to Louisiana for training on how to drop leaflets and do "ground talking;" a new trick for an old dog perhaps. In Vietnam our job involved dropping leaflets and using a loudspeaker to talk to people on the ground.

Ex-VC Commander Meets Psy War Pilots

BINH THUY (USAF) — U.S. Air Force psychological warfare pilots and crewmen based at Binh Thuy Air Base recently met a former Viet Cong company commander, who had rallied under the Chieu Hoi program.

The ex-VC Nguyen Dong Tang, former company commander with the 269th Viet Cong Battalion operating in Kien Hoa province, was treated to a close-up view of U.S. Air Force psywar activities during a visit with the "C" Flight, 5th Special Operations Squadron at Binh Thuy.

Tang was escorted on a tour of the "C" Flight facilities by Captain Stanley F. G. Jones, a 5th SOS C-47 pilot.

Briefings

The visit included briefings on C-47 Skytrain and U-10 aircraft used by the unit to drop leaflets and broadcast appeals to enemy forces, urging them to rally to the side of the government, promising rehabilitation, amnesty, vocational training, job opportunities and reunion with families.

The unit is the only such Air Force psychological operations organization in the IV Corps Tactical Zone, and was directly responsible for Tang's decision to rally to the Republic of Vietnam, officials said.

"My company came down from Tay Ninh to support Viet Cong harassment in Kien Hoa province," said Tang during his visit.

"We were primarily an anti-aircraft unit, armed with 57mm and 100mm anti-aircraft guns," explained Tang. "Kien Hoa province was the closest I had been to my family in a long time."

He is a native of Vinh Binh Province and his wife and family were there at the time of his repatriation.

"It was a very hard decision to make," he said. "I had been a Viet Cong for about 20 years and I feared for my family's safety. I had heard the broadcasts from the airplanes and read the leaflets which were dropped, but I still was not sure what would happen to my family." Tang continued.

Brother

After much deliberation, Tang contacted a brother — not a VC — and told him of his plans. Following their meeting, they went to the nearest Chieu Hoi Center, where Tang surrendered.

"I guess I came over to the Republic's side because I realized the Viet Cong can never win. And, of course, I wanted to see my family again," stated Tang.

Useful Citizen

Now living with his family, Tang goes to school. Later, he will return to a Chieu Hoi camp where he will teach newly arrived Hoi Chanh how to become useful citizens again.

"I thought that Americans would be mad at me for being a Viet Cong," he said, "but now I know they are friendly and I like them very much. I am very happy I became a Hoi Chanh. It is much better this way."

"Tang's visit marked the first time we met a Hoi Chanh in person," said Lieutenant Colonel Gerald W. Might, "C" Flight commander. "We seldom have the privilege of seeing the results of our work."

All these efforts were done in IV Corps, around Saigon and the Delta. There were six planes assigned to these tasks; two C-47's, including mine, and four smaller planes. The C-47 had a crew of about five, including the pilot, co-pilot, navigator, flight engineer, and a loadmaster, or interpreter, or somebody.

We would meet with representatives from the Army and get our directions for the week. The composition of our crew depended on the mission. If we were going to be talking to the ground with the loudspeaker we would have an interpreter who spoke English and Vietnamese. If we were dropping leaflets we would have a crew member, maybe a loadmaster, who handled the drop. We also did flare dropping missions and we would need someone to handle the machinery to eject the 64-pound flares.

**PsyOps flight crews; Saigon 1968
Courtesy: Shirley Bachus**

*1st Lieutenant **Edie Meeks**, Army Nurse Corps, 3rd Field Hospital, Saigon, USA*

I had been practicing nursing for about eighteen months prior to joining the Army. The reason I enlisted is because my brother was a Marine and my younger brother was of draft age. I come from Minnesota, and at the time there was a lot of anti-war rumbling, mainly from the coasts. I had no feeling one way or the other about the war but I did know that if something happened to my brothers I wanted somebody to be there who wanted to be there. I had a lot of mixed emotions during training at Fort Sam Houston, in Texas. For one thing they teach you how to do tracheotomies. This would be in case of a major disaster where all the doctors were busy. Then we had these colonels come in to tell us about the "kill power" of our new weapons. I found it bizarre. I wasn't there to kill people; I was there to help and cure.

After Fort Sam Houston I went to Fort Ord in California for three months. I had volunteered with a guarantee that I would go to Vietnam. At that time all of the women who went did volunteer. I had been dating a guy at Fort Ord who asked the chief nurse in Vietnam if I could stay in Saigon because that is where he was stationed. I flew into Tan Son Nhut the only woman among about two hundred guys and they served us three breakfasts during that flight. I questioned the stewardess about this and she told me they always did that. We were flying east and kept hitting the sunrise. I thought: This is nuts! On arrival I went to 3rd Field Hospital ICU in Saigon for six months. We were supposed to be the medical showcase; we wore white uniforms, white nylons, and white shoes. And yet we got the same patients that the people out in the field got.

When I arrived the chief nurse asked me where I wanted to work. I had done emergency room nursing and intensive care nursing before and I opted for ICU, not knowing what it was going to be like. It turned out to be nothing like the United States. It took me years to figure out what the difference was. In the U.S., when somebody comes to the ER for drunk driving or a sports-related accident or whatever, everything made sense! Over in Vietnam you would have a perfectly formed young man come in and he was blown to pieces. It didn't make sense.

*Sgt. **Floyd Jones**, Med. Admin. Spec. USAF*

I landed at the 100th Medical Air Evacuation Squadron at Tan Son Nhut in August of 1968. On arrival I was treated like a long lost relative by my co-workers. No one in my unit was below the rank of E-4 or Sergeant. Most of my co-workers were E-7's or above.

Our primary role was simple: Move our wounded troops from primary in-country treatment facilities to the best American military hospitals around the globe that best fit their treatment needs. The most popular destinations were Brooks Army Hospital in Texas for burns, and Walter Reed Army Hospital in Washington, D.C. for surgery. If no military hospital had the facilities or staff to treat wounded heroes they were then sent to civilian institutions. This was rare as nearly all injuries and diagnoses were treatable through the military system.

Each and every night the field hospital at Tan Son Nhut would communicate the specific needs, diagnoses and number of patients scheduled to be moved. We would pass this along to Clark AFB, Philippines. They would configure the C-141 aircraft to fit the needs of our patients. In the morning, "am-busses" arrived and patients were placed in a pre-planned section of the aircraft. Many carried IV bags or had other special needs. They had to be firmly in place to ensure nothing moved or came loose on the flight. The aircraft held four medics and one nurse. The transfer process took 3-4 hours of manual lifting, twisting and bending to ensure stabilized positioning.

*Airman 1st Class **Bruce Quinlan**, Instrument Repairman, 315th Consolidated Aircraft Maintenance Squadron, USAF*

I was a 1967 high school grad. When my draft number started to get close I wanted to get into something I liked. I was always interested in airplanes and cars -- I had a car since I was fourteen -- and I wanted the Air Force. I wanted to learn something. I hoped to get into electronics. I enlisted in November of 1967 and went active in January of 1968. After basic training at Lackland I went to school and became an instrument repairman.

I flew into Cam Ranh Bay in August, 1968. It was very hot and I was very scared because I had no combat training and only fired the M16 one time in basic training. When I saw all the veteran Army and Marine grunts with their weapons and backpacks, I thought I was out of my element.

**Airman 1st Class Bruce Quinlan, Phan Rang AFB – 1969
Courtesy: Bruce Quinlan**

When I reported in at Phan Rang AFB the first thing I did was go on sandbag detail. The irony of all our technological weaponry and gadgets being protected by sandbags was not lost on me. After filling sand bags for a while they asked if any of us could drive a truck. With all my experience on cars and motors, I raised my hand. They handed me a wheelbarrow! New war – old joke.

We had F100's at our base and I helped build the Quonset-type revetments for them. I did that for a couple of weeks and then I finally went to my outfit. The 315th was on the remote (east) side of the Phan Rang base, about nine miles from the Phan Rang Harbor on the South China Sea. We were surrounded by high hills. Our planes, about thirty, were housed in the revetments we built and we had about eight repair shops. I was assigned to the ComNav (Communications/Navigation) Instrument Shop where I worked exclusively on C123's.

We all worked twelve-hour shifts. I worked nights, 4:00 am to 4:00 pm. We were responsible for evaluating and fixing all the navigation, engine, hydraulic and electrical equipment in the C123. We also did the routine preventative maintenance; every sixty operational hours or so we'd pull the planes in for this. We'd actually go through the operating systems for the whole plane before they were given the green light. A lot of my stuff was in-shop repair, evaluating the computers and control boxes and things like that. There were eight of us on nights and about twelve on day shift in the Instrument shop. There were more guys on the radio and other shops.

C-123 cockpit
Courtesy: Bruce Quinlan

In all we had eight maintenance buildings. Engines, sheet metal, hydraulics; there were a lot of different functions going on. If we ever had a problem getting a spare part we would cannibalize a damaged or shot-up plane. Parts were not a problem for us. We had about thirty C123's and probably four or five of them were out of service on a given day.

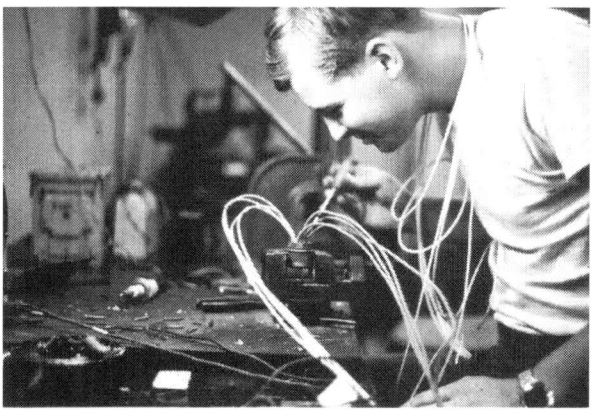

**Soldering a C-123 Wiring Harness - 1969
Courtesy: Bruce Quinlan**

Due to the electronic equipment we were the only air-conditioned maintenance shop. We had to have a hermetically-controlled environment. We also had radios which put us in direct contact with Base Security. We were also the Disaster Control Center so we had all the M16's, flak vests, etc., for the unit. Any time there was an alert we had assigned posts that we were to man. My post was in a crow's nest in the dock area, about fifty yards from the perimeter.

Spc4 **John Martin**, *Radar Tech., 1st Logs Com, USA*

I enlisted in the Army and selected a job that I hoped would serve me after I got out. I was hoping for something like television repair but was steered to a Weapons Support Radar Repair School. Once there I learned that the radar in question was used to locate enemy mortar firing locations so I knew where I was headed. I arrived by air at Bien Hoa in September of 1968 and flew from there to Qui Nhon where I ended up trying to guard some Vietnamese workers with an empty M-14.

AN/MPQ-4 RADAR
Courtesy: John Martin

We supported two different radar sets, the old MPQ-10 left over from the Korean War and the MPQ-4. They are mobile units but very large. The MPQ-4, for example, is a dual-beam radar set. When an enemy mortar round is fired and enters the track of the first beam a dot is plotted on the computer screen attached to the unit. When the mortar round breaks the second beam another dot is plotted. The operator's analog computer has vertical and horizontal crosshairs and he will crank those crosshairs until they go over the plotted dot on the screen and the computer will then read out the coordinates to identify the source of that mortar round. This information would be passed on to an artillery battery for a fire mission. A good operator could have return fire on the target within 90 seconds! Over time Charlie learned to change positions after a few rounds.

Each unit had a repairman but when he couldn't fix it we were called. We did most of our work out in the field, traveling all over II Corps either in our vehicle or by chopper.

*Pfc **Tom Petersen**, Radio Repairman Tower Team, 459th Signal Bn, 21st Signal Corps, USA*

I was not doing so well in junior college. The Army recruiter appeared at our school and I decided to enlist. I took their tests and basically qualified for everything the Army had. I opted for the microwave radio repair program. This was the longest school the Army had at that time, lasting about nine months. The school was in Fort Monmouth, New Jersey.

I flew into Cam Ranh Bay in July of 1968 with orders to report to the 518th Signal Company. Within a few hours of my arrival I was on a short hop over the mountain to Nha Trang.

Most of the guys in our company were what was called radio repairmen. They were assigned to a specific signal site and they did rotating shifts keeping the radio sets tuned, replacing parts, and stuff like that. They also monitored the signal to ensure that it was clear. Each radio set had forty-seven voice channels. Channel #1 was always ours so we could call each other to monitor the signal strength. At least once a shift these guys would call around the network just to talk to each other and get a sense of how clear the signal was. Channel #1 was also kept open for what was called the command call; this would involve some important general needing to send a message or something from the Pentagon. Sites had three to five radio sets. So if a site had three radios, they could handle up to 3X47 messages. This is primitive to what they could have today, of course, but some towns in the U.S. still use that microwave technology.

It is my understanding that the U.S. Army handled the long distance communication for all of South Vietnam from I Corps down to IV Corps in the Delta. Some of the radio relay towers were on air bases or naval installations and some were on a mountaintop somewhere. This was a line-of-sight system with a tower every thirty kilometers or so from the next one. The maximum distance was around 45 kilometers.

In my first year I was part of the Tower Team, which involved the erection and maintenance of the radio relay towers and antennas. When establishing a new radio relay site we looked for high ground. We also had to lease this ground from the South Vietnamese government. It was our job to go into this new site and make it habitable and defendable.

We were given our assignments each day by our Operations Officer. Of course some of these jobs lasted three or four weeks. The radio relay from one point to another was known as a "shot". An average day would be like the time they wanted to connect a shot from the Phan Rang Air Base to Nha Trang, Cam Ranh Bay and Da Lat. The latter three were already connected and Phan Rang was kind of outside the loop. We spent three weeks at Phan Rang, spread across two separate trips, trying to get this shot to work but never did. But we were able to hit the "repeater" site which was Pr' Line Mountain. The land they leased for this repeater station was on a mountain owned by a Frenchman who used it for a tea plantation. By getting this shot to Pr' Line Mountain we were able to include Phan Rang. It was a funny, kind of triangular link, but it worked.

**The Pr' Line Mountain "Repeater" Site
Courtesy: Tom Petersen**

We traveled a lot so most of our living was done at other sites. We used whatever accommodations were available at each site for our bed that night. It was really hit or miss. For example, Lang Bin Mountain was a pretty big signal site with tropo gear (tropospheric scatter, or big billboard antennas -- long range), the barracks was half dug in with sandbagged walls. But at LZ Betty where we did a job for the artillery guys, they just lived in holes in the ground. When we stayed at the air bases you felt like you were living in the states. Those guys had nice mattresses. We ended up scrounging some of the mattresses from air bases for our permanent living quarters at Nha Trang, but of course we were not there that much.

*Engineman **Jim Fritz**, Mobile Riverine Force, USN*

I arrived by plane in Saigon on May, 1968. We took a Korean ship to Dong Tam, in the Delta. We were ambushed the following morning. On the riverboats, everyone had to know everyone else's job. I was an engineman, gunner (.30 cal., .50 cal., and 20mm), radioman, and coxswain. We worked about 12/7 checking sampan traffic on the river and canals, looking for weapons and things. Every fifth round in the 20mm cannon was armor piercing but those rounds were slightly too big for the gun. We had to take every fifth round out of the belt.

*Chief **Sidney Brown**, Hull Technician, USS Luzerne County (LST-902), USN*

I joined the Navy in 1954 so I was an E-7 (Chief) by Vietnam. In September, 1968, I received orders to join the *Luzerne County* in Saigon. I flew to Tan Son Nhut and was greeted by MP's telling us to exchange all U.S. currency for MPC (military payment certificates) down to the denomination of a nickel or face five years in jail!

We were billeted in a U.S. run hotel in the Cholon section of Saigon, near the racetrack. The smell from the racetrack each morning drove us out of the area! We ended up there for six weeks since the *Luzerne County*, our ship-to-be, broke down on the way over. This LST was of WW II vintage and had to be re-commissioned to rejoin the fleet. They realized they would need a lot of veteran sailors who had some experience with the old vessels and the rumor was that they had emptied the brigs for old salts that had been imprisoned for one thing or another.

Meanwhile I and some of my future *Luzerne County* shipmates were being issued jungle fatigues, web belts, an M-14 and a .45, and things that are normally worn by an infantryman. "But I'm a sailor," I protested, showing them my blue dungarees. "Nope, this is what you're supposed to have," they responded, checking their clipboards.

Finally we were bussed over to the pier and met the crew that had brought the *Luzerne County* from the west coast. They certainly looked the part of brig rats, what with long hair, shirt sleeves cut off, and menacing scowls. We exchanged conveyances; they took our bus and we boarded the ship.

USS Luzerne County LST-902
Courtesy: Sid Brown

I had eight guys working for me. They were electricians, ship fitters, pipefitters, metal smiths, etc. Our job was to keep that rusty old WW II ship running. We picked most of our cargo up at Vung Tau and hauled it up into the Delta. We hauled some of the first steel matting used to build landing strips in the Delta. The first time we lowered the ramp in the Delta the elephant grass on the bank of the river was eight or nine feet tall. Over time I was qualified as an officer of the deck and I stood watch just like the officers. Somebody is always on the bridge. Unloading cargo we'd work around the clock until that stuff is off there.

Aboard the USS Luzerne County
Courtesy: Sid Brown

A common cargo was bags of cement. They'd put twenty-four bags to a pallet and each bag weighed eighty pounds. They'd stack cement four pallets high. But the worst stuff we would haul was ammunition. At times we would have the tank deck stacked to the overhead (ceiling) with ammunition; 105mm shells, rockets, cordite. We stored lube oil in 55-gallon drums on the main deck because it would be slower to go off than gasoline. We laid 2x12 lumbers across the top to chain them down. If a round came in we got a lot of splinters but not shrapnel or a big explosion.

*Spc4 **Noah Dillion**, Aircraft Mechanic, 221st Recon Aircraft Company, USA*

Many of Noah Dillion's stories may be found in his book: Surviving VietNam: Tales of a Narcoleptic Hangar Rat

I turned eighteen in January of my senior year. Late bloomers were skipped over by the Draft Board because we were already eighteen when we graduated. I started to work at General Electric as a drafting trainee. I avoided the draft on my nineteenth birthday but the notice came on my twentieth in January, 1968. I went into downtown Covington, KY and enlisted on the new "Green Army Contract" for aviation mechanics school.

I completed school third in my class, was promoted to PFC and sent to school for Single Engine Observation Aircraft Crewman, receiving my wings in June, 1968 along with a promotion to Spc-4. I applied for OCS Engineering at Fort Belvoir, Virginia and went through the first eight weeks before the Narcolepsy whacked me.

Narcolepsy is a sleeping disorder which affects over 250,000 Americans and for which there is no known cure. Simply put it is an uncontrollable desire to sleep. I can fall asleep very quickly – I have had many forty-five second naps at traffic lights – but I've had one major and three minor traffic accidents due to sleep attacks. Obviously a combat zone is not the ideal place for a narcoleptic, but the Army didn't screen for Narcolepsy so I had to deal with it. It is a neurological disorder, not a mental illness, and recent medications can improve the quality of life for victims. I have had this sleeping monster with me all my life.

I received orders for Vietnam and arrived on a Braniff 727, flying via Hawaii and Okinawa on Nov. 6, 1968. I was assigned to the 221st Recon Airplane Co. (0-1) by the 90th Replacement Battalion.

My first meal at Soc Trang was very good. I was surprised at the availability of cold Kool-Aid (the mess hall NCOIC told me he made it from large packs of Jell-O mix watered down) and cold, real milk. These delicacies were part of the deal struck between the Army and the Air Force for the latter's landing privileges at the airfield. I never saw powdered eggs and I never ate a box of rations while at Soc Trang. But sleep was a bigger issue to me than food. My sleep was always an adventure but my first night at Long Binh was the scariest night of my tour. A disgruntled soldier popped a tear gas grenade in an NCO's hooch to register his discontent about how things were being handled.

Courtesy: Noah Dillion

The heavy use of aircraft increased the need for maintenance despite the fact that overhaul time was raised from 2,140 hours to 3,300.[lvii] Direct air shipment of parts from Corpus Christi, Texas was begun.[lviii] The authorized parts list grew from 8,000 in 1965 to 46,000 by late 1968.[lix]

*SSgt **Bill Roy**, Environmental/Occupational Medicine, 14th Combat Support Group, USAF*

I worked at both Pleiku and Nha Trang during 1968 and 1969. My job was environmental and occupational medicine. I would inspect work sites to ensure compliance with health and safety regulations. I was doing most of the things that OSHA does now. For example, I found welders not wearing proper safety attire or people sawing through asbestos during hooch construction and I would see that things were fixed; among the things that came under my wing was giving the new arrivals a VD bracelet and conducting a lecture on the types of diseases they could contract.

*Pfc **Garry Ramsey**, Supply Clerk, 524th Quartermaster, USA*

I was drafted at age 19. I arrived at Tan Son Nhut by commercial airliner on December 13, 1968. After orientation we flew a C130 to Cam Ranh Bay.

Courtesy: Garry Ramsey

I spent several months with the 524th Quartermaster when I first got to Vietnam. That was part of the 1st Logistics Command. I worked at the tank (fuel) farm. We would bring fuel in from ships with a big hose and transfer it to tankers at our fuel farm. I would climb up on the truck and monitor the pressure gauges. I also did some guard duty on the perimeter. We had over twenty fuel bladders there holding about a million gallons.

*Petty Officer 3rd Class **Vince Malaterra**, Engineer Aide, MCB-3, Seabees, USN*

On the first tour we were just like a construction crew. We'd get to the site in the morning in these cattle cars and sometimes we pulled guard duty or we had guys from the First Marine Division with us. We'd work to dusk and they'd come and get us out of there. Many nights you'd end up with guard duty somewhere so you'd end up with a 20-hour day. The VC would come at night and blow up whatever we built and then we'd come back the next day and rebuild it. We'd also patch the roads; the mortar rounds would leave a big hole in roads. We had to keep the civilian population moving through there too.

CHAPTER SIXTEEN

THE ASIAN MELTING POT

Nearly forty nations provided some sort of help to the effort in South Vietnam, but only five countries sent troops – Australia, Thailand, New Zealand, South Korea and the Philippines. Australian jungle specialists arrived first (1962) but the Koreans sent the biggest contingent – two Army divisions and a Marine brigade. These allied forces reached a peak of 69,000 in 1969, and over 5,000 of these allied soldiers died in Vietnam.[lx]

Vietnamization was announced on April 16, 1968. Westmoreland (now back in Washington as Army Chief of Staff) quickly claimed credit for the policy, most American generals and the top ARVN soldier said it "should have been done years ago," and many more U.S. servicemen were to die.

*Captain **Chuck Glazerman**, RF/PF Forces Advisor*

If you are assigned to the Vietnamese you are expected to eat with them. I ate two meals a day and I tried to eat meals where I knew where it came from. I could handle their tea and a few other dishes but I often used the guise of a "delicate" stomach to avoid some of the things they ate. I was not about to eat rat. We also had some C rations. The American brigade located near us had a PX and we could sometimes go there to get things. As far as mess halls go it seems like the bigger the city the better the food. Province food was better than food in the district, and the big city was better than the provinces and so on. I'd go up to Long Binh and it was like two different worlds from what I was used to. There did not seem to be a shortage of beer or liquor over there.

*Sgt. **Floyd Jones**, Med. Admin. Specialist*

The momma sans would do their laundry in and around the men's showers even when we were showering. It was more embarrassing to me than them. For a fee of $50 per month we employed a momma san who kept our barracks clean and washed and ironed our uniforms. She was very honest and treated each of us like family.

Courtesy: Floyd Jones

*1stLt. **David Cass**, Platoon Leader*

We used house girls for laundry and we bought lumber and electrical supplies from the Vietnamese. We rented sampans to be used as a pile driving platform and we hired a Korean barge with a crane to help remove a collapsed bridge. I coordinated with Vietnamese foremen to resolve any problems with the two hundred Vietnamese we employed.

*Sgt First Class **Jim Kuipers**, 46th Engr. Bn.,*

They had Vietnamese people working in our compound, some in the carpenter shop and I had two or three at the Motor Pool. They stayed out by the bunker when I first got there and I didn't even know I had them. When I first arrived the Motor Pool was like a junk yard. You couldn't even put a vehicle in the shop there was so much junk in there. And I only had three bays. When I learned that I had three or four Vietnamese mechanics assigned to work in the Motor Pool I brought these guys into my small office and took their ID cards away. I told them to come see me at the end of the work day and they would get them back. This is how I got them to work for me. Hell, they were being paid, they should work!

*Spc4 **Noah Dillion**, Aircraft Mechanic*

At Vinh Long we lived in a stateside four squad two story wooden barracks. We had stateside wall lockers and metal bunk beds just like the ones in basic. We built our own bunker between the two wooden buildings using 55 gallon drums and PSP. We paid 1600 Piasters to a mamasan to do our boots and laundry at both airfields.

My only other contact with Vietnamese was when I watched one of them pace off the airfields. I reported this to the First Sergeant. He told me nobody would be that stupid to do something like that in the middle of the day. That night three mortar rounds came in. Next morning the First Sergeant and two navy Seals approached me. They had the Vietnamese civilian blindfolded and handcuffed and I gave them a thumbs-up; he was the guy! I omitted the part about having reported this to the First Sergeant the day before; it would have put him in hot water. Two weeks later fifteen mortar rounds came in; the three rounds had been an accuracy check.

Airman 1st Class **Bruce Quinlan**, *Instrument Repairman*

I went to Phan Rang City maybe six times when I was over there. We also had an area outside the base that we called "the strip" that was frequented by a lot of guys. And we had mamasans in our barracks that cleaned up and did our laundry and things. I thought they were primitive, somewhat aloof; they didn't seem to want much contact with you. They seemed to make an attempt to avoid you. They often tried to take you for a ride in the market place. A bunch of them came on the base every day to work there. Most of them did not work in our area and we were actually told to avoid contact with them.

One of the barbers from our base px was killed one night setting up a mortar. This guy had cut my hair more than once. There were also stories of the Vietnamese civilians "walking off" certain areas to help them pinpoint our facilities. On one attack the rounds landed within ten feet of our buildings.

There was a group of young Vietnamese punks called cowboys. They would harass and take advantage of GI's who were in the towns and villages off base. I remember one time on my way through the countryside on a motorized rickshaw-type vehicle that held about six people. I was hanging on the back with my right hand and my left arm just hanging free when a group of these cowboys on their 50cc Hondas and wearing their black cowboy style hats came flying up to us and in the matter of seconds one of them took the Seiko watch I had on my left wrist right off. Another guy was taking pictures of these dudes and they snatched the camera right out of his hand and took off in different directions; gone in 60 seconds. We were told about these juveniles but it was the only time I saw them.

*Chief **Sidney Brown**, Hull Technician*

During December of 1968 we hauled several loads of cement to build revetments for helicopters. At the same time the US Aid International Development, which was an arm of the CIA, was trying to help the Vietnamese farmers grow more rice. The soil was so devoid of nutrients that we hauled bags of lime down to the delta and we'd drop a third at one place, a third at another place, and a third somewhere else. We unloaded this lime and at night we'd have lights on our surroundings with M-60's to protect us from sappers. We stacked all this lime on the bank and I don't know what happened to the guards that night but when we got up in the morning the only lime left was the row facing us. The five rows behind it had been pilfered during the night. So a few of us went into this little town to drink some of the local Tiger 33 beer and we were going to order some pork and fried rice. On my way through the kitchen I found out this pork was dog. They were cutting up these dogs. And then it started raining; it was the monsoon season. And we're watching these guys across the road building a cement wall. And I observed that I had never seen such white cement before. What it was, they had stolen our lime and they were mixing it with sand thinking they had cement, and we sat there for about two hours just watching the rain collapse their wall.

*Engineman **Jim Fritz**, Mobile Riverine Force, USN*

We saw the Vietnamese every day moving their sampans down the river. We learned to watch for signs of nervousness as we inspected their sampans for weapons, or we took note of the absence of birds in an area or a bunch of sampans hurrying in the opposite direction we were going, which could be signs of an ambush.

*Pfc **John Lawrence**, Crew Chief*

We had a small group of marines with some Cambodian and Laotian troops near our area. It was like they put a rag in the mouths of my pilot and co-pilot; they were not supposed to talk about where we'd been or what we'd done. There was a Captain Ferguson that I ran into, and he had been held in a POW camp in Laos. We bombed the camp and he was able to escape in the confusion.

*Spc4 **Ron Kappeler**, RTO*

I was up at LZ Baldy, near Danang. Three of us were up north of Danang in a ¾ ton truck; it was really hot and we stopped in to a Korean base camp. As naïve as we were we walked into the beer hall. We were oblivious to how much we stood out until we saw them staring at us. We bought a couple of six packs and left.

*1st Lieutenant **Edie Meeks**, Army Nurse Corps*

We had Vietnamese working in the hospitals with us and you didn't know if they were VC or not. They would come and do their job during the day but you didn't know what they did at night. You never trusted anybody.

I found that I had to really work to be kind to the enemy patients we had. I had to will myself to remember that I was a nurse no matter what. The reality was I had a limited amount of time and to whom do I allocate that precious time? My boys! I really had to work to give good care to the enemy. I had to choose if I was a nurse for everyone or if I would pick and choose. I realized that I could not pick and choose. But I did have to work at it!

*Spc4 **John Martin**, Radar Tech*

Within my first hour at Qui Nhon, I was told to guard some Vietnamese who came on base to work. I was given an M-14 with no magazine. I was told that if they gave me "any trouble, just point it at them."

I supported a Korean radar MPQ-4 and on one of my visits I left my 35mm camera in the truck. It was stolen. I reported this to the Koreans. On my next visit I was handed the camera. The camp commander had called a formation of his troops and asked the guilty person to step forward, which he did. He was sent to the stockade. I admired the Koreans. Unlike our soldiers they didn't have to ask permission to fire their weapons.

Korean Radar Operators – Phu Cat
Courtesy: John Martin

CHAPTER SEVENTEEN

LOVE FROM NEW JERSEY AND DRAGONS NAMED PUFF

In addition to the 10:1 ratio of support troops to combat troops in Vietnam, the kill ratio of enemy to U.S. was also 10:1, if not higher. But as Ho Chi Minh once said to the French, "you can kill ten of my men to each one of yours, but in the end, we will win."

*Sgt. **Floyd Jones**, Med. Admin. Specialist*

Our barracks had previously been hit by a rocket during the Tet offensive of February 1968. No one was injured but we all felt the chance of another rocket hitting the exact location was remote so none of us was concerned. During my stay in Vietnam we had four actual rocket alerts.

*1st Lieutenant **Edie Meeks**, Army Nurse Corps*

They built our beds a little higher so that you could get under them during a rocket attack. The first time rockets came in I got under my bed and three other girls joined me. You just didn't want to be alone.

I arrived for work one morning and they told us we would be receiving ten to fifteen guys that had been standing on a corner waiting for a bus when somebody threw a bomb at them. You weren't safe anywhere. They had always told us, if you're walking down the street, don't kick a can.

*Communications Technician **Dick Trimbur***

Danang was occasionally mortared but the rounds never hit near us. We often took small arms fire during helicopter insertion or extraction. We'd yell at the door gunner to shoot back. "Do you gd job; don't let them hit us". Sometimes we caught sniper fire in the landing zones. We occasionally fired back to defend ourselves. I carried an M-16 and a .45.

*Lt. Col. **Bud Might**, Pilot*

We took a lot of small arms fire and we got mortared three or four times a week at the base. No ack ack, like over Germany. They hit a gas tank once. I made two emergency landings.

*Airman 1ˢᵗ Class **Bruce Quinlan**, Instrument Repairman*

I was in the mess hall for midnight chow and the sirens went off. We all ran out of the mess hall and jumped into the nearby bunker. This was more of a trench than a covered bunker. Just after we reached the trench mortar rounds blew up the mess hall. We just missed real injury by a few seconds.

We had radio contact with everything going on around the base. One night the *USS New Jersey* was in Phan Rang Harbor, about nine miles east of us. We could hear them fire their 16 inchers and we ran outside; a few seconds later we could hear the rounds go over our heads and land on the hills west of the base. The shells traveled about eleven miles as I recall. It was pretty awesome and to have radio contact with the *New Jersey* made it that much more incredible.

*SSgt **Bill Roy**, Environmental/Occupational Medicine*

We picked up frequent mortar fire from VC in caves in the mountainous area around Nha Trang. There was talk of bringing in the battleship *Missouri* to shell the caves. I guess the assumption was that the trajectory of naval gunfire would be more effective than bombs or artillery. I argued that the risk of short rounds was too great. They decided to bring in Korean troops who got the job done the old-fashioned way: Boots on the ground. When finished they showed us all the neat stuff they dragged out of the caves.

*Petty Officer 3rd Class **Vince Malaterra**, Seabees*

We had so many mortar and rocket attacks, after a while you didn't have to wait for the siren. You could just smell the arrival of the rounds. When the nearby villages were completely dark and you didn't even hear the dogs barking, you knew it was coming.

*Sgt First Class **Jim Kuipers**, A Company, 46th Engr. Bn.*

One time the Company Commander and I were coming down the road at dusk and just before we turned off to Camp Bearcat there was a jeep that was hit by a mortar or RPG or something a hundred yards in front of us. The jeep was blown to smithereens. As we passed the jeep bullets came whizzing over us. You couldn't see them but you could hear them. When we approached the village there was a fire fight going on. Finally the infantry got it cleaned out and we were able to go on into camp.

In the middle of the night a mortar round came in and landed beside the bunker I was in. I ran outside and popped some hand-held flares so we could see if anything was coming in on us. Then I called battalion and told them I wanted some fire support in front of the 46th Engineer bunkers. They asked me if I was sure and I just keyed the button on the phone and they could hear the firing. They agreed that we needed some help. So they sent Puff the Magic Dragon and artillery put some illumination over the area. Puff did his thing and the firing stopped.

*Pfc **John Lawrence**, Crew Chief*

The enemy located around us in Thailand we called the VC. Udorn AFB was hit one time by a plane. We think it was an M-15, a new plane. Somebody had a new toy. The plane knocked out our tower and killed some guards. They were probably trying to hit the ammo dump.

We were flying along one time in the mountainous part of Laos and I happened to be looking at the ground and I saw this puff of smoke come out of the trees. I told the pilot to bank right. If I hadn't done that we would have been hit.

Udorn Air Base, Thailand
Courtesy: John Lawrence

The Air Force should have warned us not to fly in that area because they knew where the hot areas were. We were often shot at but never shot down. And I thank God for that because some of my buddies did get shot down. We had our share of bullet holes in the chopper.

"We covered Laos, Thailand and Cambodia"
Courtesy: John Lawrence

*Spc4 **Noah Dillion**, Aircraft Mechanic*

On one of my guard details I called the officer of the day to ask about a large clump of elephant grass I had seen between two rows of concertina on the perimeter. He told me there was no elephant grass on the perimeter. Then one of our gunships came by and fired mini-guns into the mysterious grass. When they went out to reset the claymores and trip flares they found a dead VC mortar crew in the elephant grass.

*Engineman **Jim Fritz**, Mobile Riverine Force, USN*

We arrived by boat in the Delta on May 26, 1968 and we were ambushed the following morning out on the river. We had four men severely wounded, requiring helicopter evacuation for medical treatment.

On November 1, 1968, we were tied up at Station 1 with the LST *USS Westchester County* (LST-1167), a supply ship and floating barracks. At 0300 two VC sappers evaded the patrol screen, maneuvered between the pontoons and the ship and placed satchel charges under the LST. We were tied up along the pontoons and sleeping at the time. Seventeen sailors were killed, the largest in-country loss of life at one time for the Navy during the Vietnam War. Eight soldiers also died in that attack.

In December of 1968 our ASPB was on patrol as part of Operation Giant Slingshot with a PBR (patrol boat river); we came under heavy automatic weapons and rocket fire and our boat was knocked dead in the water. Our boat had suffered a direct rocket hit in the engine compartment, knocking out our electrical power to the .50 caliber machine gun and the

ASPB Patrol
Courtesy: Jim Fritz

20mm cannon. We had to push off the bank of the river with bow hooks, while under fire, in order to get out into the current to float downstream until help arrived. After delivering a suppressing fire against the enemy I jumped into the river to lead our boat out into the current. Eventually our big guns began operating and we were then towed back for repairs. I was awarded the Bronze Star for this action.

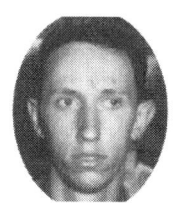

Pfc ***Garry Ramsey****, Supply Clerk*

We took rocket fire at the compound at Cam Ranh Bay. One of the rockets split a telegraph pole between two of our barracks.

One of our convoy drivers was shot in the head. It was always a stressful trip. We were coming back from Da Lat one time and on the mountain side of the road, there were six or seven black-pajamas clad guys wearing straw hats. I assume they were VC. Choppers came and cut them down.

Hospitalman First Class **Alexander Phillips**

Occasionally we would see vapor trails and sometimes those trails would end up in fireballs. I thought to myself how well electronic counter-measures work on the B-52's. You never heard them or saw them but the SAM's created a lot of attention for the B-52's. I regret that I never had a camera when these events occurred but they were a sight to behold against a bright blue sky.

1stLt. **David Cass***, Platoon Leader*

I had rocket close calls twice. A dud landed a few feet from me on a bridge one night. I was sniped at while on bridge projects, at the gravel pit and housing project. There was a fire-fight in the motor pool in Saigon while trapping thieves.

It was Sunday morning 22 September, 1968. Hershel Gossett was one of five men sent to evaluate a bridge outside Ben Hoa in respect to installing security lighting. Up till this time we had been lighting bridges in Saigon and highways north to Long Bien with American gasoline powered 5KW and 10KW generators at 60 HZ. We installed 1,000W sealed spots in a pattern designed to overlap, providing thorough illumination for bridge protection forces to spot sappers, especially those floating charges in the river towards the bridge abutments.

Our mission that Sunday was to evaluate, measure, and tag existing power lines on a high tension line supported by steel power poles that ran parallel and over the granite combination railroad and highway Song Dong Nai Bridge that spanned a river outside Ben Hoa. We were to evaluate the local 50 HZ (cycle) Vietnamese power available on the existing power poles. We had been on sight for an hour or so. Hershel and two other electricians had been taking turns climbing every pole in the area. They were short of breath and we were late for our next job so I went up to help Hershel on the last pole. The clay buildings across from us were higher than us with false fronts above the roof, some with clay tile decorations. The poles we were climbing were made out of angle iron and they had steel spikes closely spaced, pointing down so the kids wouldn't climb them. We would just lean out to get by them. I was holding Hershel's legs so he could lean out with an electrical multi-meter to measure and tag these lines when we were hit by a hand thrown concussion grenade (very few fragments). The blast knocked Hershel and myself off the pole. He hit on his forehead and did not survive. Local Vietnamese guards on the bridge were trading shots with someone on a rooftop above us. I was medevac'd to the 24th Evac. Hospital in Long Binh, paralyzed from the neck down. Hershel was a good soldier, a nice guy and a great worker. He was smart and could handle plumbing, electrical and carpentry equally well.

CHAPTER EIGHTEEN

REPLACEMENT PARTS AND RAINDROPS; THE FRUSTRATIONS CONTINUE

We can complain because rose bushes have thorns, or rejoice because thorn bushes have roses. -- Abraham Lincoln

Sgt First Class **Jim Kuipers**, *46th Engr. Bn.,*

My main frustration was a lack of replacement parts. That Red Ball supply system, or whatever they called it, did not work well. When you ordered a part you were supposed to receive it within a couple of days. That often didn't happen. My view was that when you ordered something they were supposed to check in-country for availability before that request went back to the states. I could usually go out and scrounge the part before it came from the states, which tells me that it was already in-country and they didn't know it. Their monitoring of the supply system really wasn't great. One possibility is that parts arrived in Saigon and got ripped off before anyone could get to it to distribute it where it was needed. I know that happened.

Many units didn't have all that they needed to properly support us. For example: Engineer units have lots of equipment that require hydraulic lines. Our support unit didn't have the lines or the machine that did the replacing of the damaged line. What I did was I went to the Air Force Base at Bien Hoa and said to the young man there: "Son, I'm in the Army. I need hydraulic lines. What do you need?" He told me he needed boots and fatigues. I told him I'd be right back. I returned with a box of boots and fatigues. He asked me what I needed. I showed him my hydraulic hoses. He asked me what kind of pressure I had on those hoses. "Do they exceed 10,000 psi?" I said "Hell no!" He told me that everything he had would withstand 10,000 psi since they were used on jet aircraft. So I got all my hydraulic lines that way. This was one of the reasons I was successful running the Motor Pool; I went out of my way to get what I needed.

*Pfc **John Lawrence**, Crew Chief*

The units in Vietnam had top priority for repair parts. Stationed in Thailand, an Army unit on an Air Force Base, we got the step-child treatment most of the time. I had to fly down to Saigon to get the stuff we needed.

*Spc4 **John Martin**, Radar Tech*

Highways 1 and 9 were paved and they became very slick when the rain hit the oily surfaces. I nearly rolled the jeep over on a turn. The monsoon did not affect the radar sets but the MPQ-10 was particularly vulnerable to humidity.

*1stLt. **David Cass**, Platoon Leader*

I got wet late in the day and stayed wet thru the night. We had a lot of road accidents when the laterite-built roads got wet and slippery and we did continuous wash-out road repairs.

*PFC **Tom Petersen**, Radio Repairman/Tower Team*

We were part of a multi-vehicle convoy on our way to repair typhoon damage at the Vong Ro Mountain site in November, 1968. Vung Ro was the repeater site between Tuy Hoa and Ninh Hoa.

The monsoon had taken out a bridge on Highway 1 leaving nothing but an I-beam going across. Four or five of our tanks were sitting on the other shore, led by a major, and our lieutenant volunteered me to walk across this I-beam to communicate with the tankers. So I balanced myself across the I-beam for 100 feet, and the major watched my every move.

Vung Ro Tower
Courtesy: Tom Petersen

When I made it across the major told me to go back and tell the lieutenant to bring our convoy down into the ravine and across the river and up the other side and they would cover us. He said when they crossed the ravine they would chew it up and no one else would be able to cross. I got back across to the lieutenant and told him "You get your vehicles down into that ravine and up the other side and you do it now!" And that is what we did.

*Airman 1st Class **Bruce Quinlan**, Instrument Repairman*

Just walking in the monsoon was tough. These were raindrops like you've never seen, almost like liquid hail. During the monsoon I had a job to do out on the flight line. I was carrying a fuel capacitor tester and wearing a parka, since it was actually rather cold during the monsoon. I worked the night shift. I couldn't see a thing. It was raining so hard I couldn't see the roadway or the white lines on the side of the road. I ended up walking off the roadway into a water-filled culvert. I was immediately up to my chest in water and my parka parachuted around me like a tent. I was in total darkness with my parka billowing around my head. I think it was the funniest thing that happened to me over there. Looking back I don't remember if that fuel tester ever worked again or not.

*Chief **Sidney Brown**, Hull Technician*

We would have mud above our shoes when we went ashore during the monsoon. But it was worse on board. Our drains would clog from the cement dust that had been activated from the rains.

*Airman 2nd Class **Tom Emmons**, Loadmaster*

One morning we landed at a field and loaded up. We flew that load to another field and unloaded it, and picked up a load from there for the field we had just come from. We unloaded at the first field and they told us to load more stuff for the second field. When we arrived there and unloaded they told us to load the stuff we had just brought them earlier this morning and return it to the first field. "We just brought this stuff from there," I barked. "You don't get it, son" they explained. "It's all about tonnage. We just need to move a lot of tonnage."

*Lt. Col. **Bud Might**, Pilot*

We would have a gunship in the air over Saigon at night. They would get a call for a disturbance somewhere and just after they left we would be mortared and they weren't there to spot the source of the fire. That disturbance was probably a diversion. About the time you'd get another gunship in the air the mortars would stop.

*1st Lieutenant **Edie Meeks**, Army Nurse Corps*

This general had been walking around the ICU handing out Purple Hearts. This one fellow had a trach and he had his eyes covered; we weren't sure if he was going to be blind or not. He was missing both legs and an arm. We were trying to stabilize him so we could ship him out to Japan. The general pinned the medal on his gown and I don't know if the guy even knew what was going on and you think to yourself: Is that an even trade? It was just so overwhelmingly bizarre.

The Army Nurse Corps motto was to preserve the fighting strength but I really wanted to preserve them so they could go home. The patients were all my brothers ages and I could see what a waste this all was. I loved my brothers so much I wouldn't want to see them wasted this way. Maybe it would be all right if there was a focus, a purpose, and we were actually doing it. I just got angrier and angrier that they were just trying to throw these guys away.

It was difficult not being able to write to the parents to tell them how brave their boy was and how hard he fought to stay alive.

*Cook 3rd Class **Vic Griguoli***

Among other things guys in the brown water got sprayed with Agent Orange all the time. Of course they told us they were spraying for mosquitos.

CHAPTER NINETEEN

TET

1968

Tet was the bloodiest single week of fighting in the war; 543 Americans were killed and 2,500 wounded. The VC lost 33,000 killed. Both the Chinese advisors to the NVA and General Giap himself were against the Tet Offensive, thinking it premature, but they were overruled.

*How to assess Tet? It was an undisputed military defeat for the enemy to the extent that it marked the end of the Viet Cong, for all practical purposes. It was also an overwhelming strategic defeat in that the main objective of the plan – the mass defection of South Vietnamese to the North Vietnamese cause – did not occur. That Tet helped pave the way for ultimate victory for North Vietnam traced to **their** "hidden army" – the American protestors.*

*Captain **Chuck Glazerman**, RF/PF Forces Advisor*

During Tet (February 1, 1968) they rocketed the city and we counted 214 VC dead in the wire in front of our camp.

*Sgt. **Allen Thomas Jr.**, Section Chief*

When Tet started we were in the village a few blocks outside our wire. When the shooting started we ran back to the base under fire, but when we arrived they had locked down the gate. We had to climb the wire which cut us up pretty good. When we got inside we ran to our bunkers.

There was a *Chieu Hoi* Center building across the street from our perimeter wire where they processed enemy soldiers that surrendered. These "surrendered" guys were shooting at us from the roof of the building. We returned fire for a while and then leveled the building with fire from two of our supporting tanks.

The 173rd had fought a battle against Hill 875 earlier in the year, before Tet, and the VC pulled out. The 173rd was then pulled off the hill. Later, for Tet, the NVA went onto Hill 875 again and entrenched themselves in well-placed bunkers. One of our companies lost ninety-some people in five minutes. One of the stupid things that happened is our guys were calling in for artillery support and the artillery had to call and ask for permission to fire. Guys are dying and they can't go to their aid. Finally some of the artillery guys just started firing. All of us on the hill at Dak To were listening to the Hill 875 battle on the radio. Finally they brought in a Marine Fighter Wing to Dak To for increased support. This battle went on for days.

Communications Technician **Dick Trimbur**

During Tet we had a lot more radio traffic to analyze; a lot more classification. We had to be more cautious on the job. They were hitting everywhere. We were quite busy. If you could pick up some classification that was in the works, naturally that was helpful.

Petty Officer 3rd Class **Vince Malaterra**, *Seabees*

There were times during Tet when you got no sleep at all; you were working 24 hours a day. All hell really broke loose and that's when I thought to myself that this could be the end. We stopped our road and bridge work for about two weeks. They wouldn't let us go out.

Airman 3rd Class **Frank Towns**, *Jet Mechanic*

During Tet seven C-141's took off one night from Cam Ranh Bay. I was in the second plane. With planes that big, when they took off the first would go to the right after takeoff, the second to the left, and so on. Four mortar rounds hit near the first plane as it went down the runway. All the planes got airborne but when that first plane reached Dover, they found that shrapnel had missed the fuel tank by less than an inch. If it had exploded, since we were right behind them we'd have gone up too.

Even though we were half way around the world from Vietnam when Tet started in February of 1968, there was an order issued to our unit that no one could be granted leave unless their mother or father died. For the next 72 days we worked 18 to 20 hours a day, or some days without sleep. Every plane that landed at Dover had to be re-fueled, and maintenance performed, and turned around to go right back to Vietnam. Working at that pace you get almost numb; it's almost like you're in another world. I had one date with a girl here in the States just before Tet; well after 72 days of no contact she's long gone! We were on tight security all that while. We received a Presidential Unit Citation for our efforts during the Tet.

*Hospitalman First Class **Alexander Phillips***

For us the Tet Offensive was all about the explosions at the Cua Viet River mouth. The *Cleveland* served as a helo haven during this time, embarking gunships overnight so that they did not get hit during the offensive. The danger that they faced inland was from mortar attacks.

*Sgt First Class **Jim Kuipers**, 46th Engr. Bn.,*

Tet delayed my arrival by two or three days. Nothing was going in or out of Vietnam at that time.

*Pfc **John Lawrence**, Crew Chief*

During Tet I flew thirty-one days straight. Our workload definitely increased during the Tet period. It was the busiest time I had over there. I didn't sleep in my bunk for a month.

*Spc4 **Ron Kappeler**, RTO*

We were supposed to go to a beleaguered outpost near the Cambodian border called Kham Duc. It was being overrun. As luck would have it I went on R&R and didn't go there. My friend Jerry Bodine tells me that this was a small camp with a tiny landing strip and about 200 men; it was the first time one of our jeep-mounted radio teletype units with a cryptographic encoder was put in harm's way. This equipment gave the headquarters company a secure line to their units. It was probably a good trip to miss; there were eleven marines from a nearby artillery unit that went missing, bodies not recovered. At Kham Duc Jerry said the NVA were running down one end of the runway and they were at the other end firing at them and trying to board a plane. The plane before his was shot down and his C-130 held the last fifty guys to get out of there. Some wounded were not found and had to be left. My replacement was shot four times in the leg and once in the mouth, but since he had no broken bones he earned the nickname "Swiss Cheese". Our 3-mode radio had to be destroyed.

At LZ Baldy, they sent RTO's into action one at a time, and finally they decided they wanted to send me back to LZ Bayonet. I stood on the landing pad that morning, looking for a ride to LZ Bayonet and that, as it turned out, was the first morning of Tet. There were no helicopters coming in. Finally one of those Plexiglas choppers came in -- a two-seater -- and I asked him where all the choppers were. He said on that morning nineteen choppers had been shot down in that area. He said he was going south. The pilot straddled the two seats of the chopper so I and another guy put our equipment inside and each of us stood on the skids, half in and half out, for a sixty mile ride to LZ Bayonet.

One morning while pulling the drums for shit burning detail, we found a hand grenade with the pin already pulled and the spoon held in place by masking tape. When the fire from the diesel fuel in the drum burned the tape off the grenade would go off.

Airman 3rd Class **Frank Towns**, *Jet Mechanic*

The morgue in Dover had a capacity of 3,000 bodies. That capacity was exceeded twice during my stint, both during the Tet offensive. I actually was pressed into work there for two weeks during Tet. It became almost too much, bringing them home to begin with and then working in the morgue itself, watching what goes on. It was almost a different world; those people had a strange sense of humor which they said was to keep them from going nuts! They would do things like moving an arm from one guy to another to make a whole guy. I don't know how I lasted two weeks on that!

Engineman **Jim Fritz**, *Mobile Riverine Force,*

Tet got our attention. We were on the Cambodian border and involved in numerous ambushes. We noticed a lot more enemy activity after the bombing halt.

Lt **Eric Dauphinee**, *Pilot*

There was a lot of traffic during Tet. We had observation aircraft working fire support. There were ARVN A-1's trying to drop bombs and napalm. Medevac and gunship helicopters were everywhere. All of us were trying to support the same units in close proximity while avoiding getting shot out of the sky or running into each other.

*Lt. Col. **George B. Gray**, CO 46th Engineer Battalion*

Just after the Tet (February 1968) offensive ended I was touring the outer perimeter of our base at Long Binh. I'm not exaggerating; there were many hundreds of dead VC outside our barbed wire. I asked my First Sergeant what we should do with them. "We're engineers," he answered. "We scoop out a big hole, throw them in there and cover them with lime." I agreed that it was all we could do. The other three engineer battalions at Long Bing were also involved in disposal of bodies. We were in the process of completing this task when I noticed a television cameraman behind me filming the work. He had a reporter standing next to him. I asked the reporter if I could help him. "We're going to bury **you** with this film," he answered. We kept on with our work and I heard no more about it. After Tet (February 1, 1968), bunkers were in great demand and a large reserve (400 plus) was stockpiled. The 1969 Tet again caused a run on bunker units.

The 1968 Tet, which US soldiers won decisively and the media awarded to the North Vietnamese, made impossible Task Force Builder #2 and sounded the death knell for Pacification. In 1965, had John Paul Vann's entire Pacification Program and US control of all US provided resources been fully adopted across all of South Vietnam, what would have happened?

General Westmoreland credited the Mobile Riverine Force with saving the Delta during Tet, and awarded them a Presidential Unit Citation.[lxi]

CHAPTER TWENTY

STRIPES AND MEDALS

1968

In order to help the transition to Vietnamization General Joseph M. Heiser, commanding general of the 1st Logistics Command, instituted the buddy system which had been successful in Korea. Under this plan ARVN troops were placed with U.S. units for direct participation and observation of engineering and logistical principles.

*Pfc **John Lawrence**, Crew Chief*

My Huey transported General Westmoreland around quite a bit. I landed on carriers at least twice with General Westmoreland. On one occasion Westmoreland forgot his briefcase and he went back to get it. I managed to push Westmoreland away from walking into the tail rotor of our Huey. I earned three Air Commendation Medals for service over there.

*Striker **Rick Dolinar**, Fire Control Technician*

My first class petty officer on the *Cleveland* was difficult. He was from Wyoming, and he disliked what he called "city boys." It was frustrating to work for him and work with him, but you just had to do it. However I was proud of my promotion from E-4 to E-5. I was also voted the Most Competent petty officer in the Deck Department. I felt good about that.

*Communications Technician **Dick Trimbur***

A marine sergeant (a lifer always complaining about getting "too old for this" was sleeping on the landing zone in his poncho while we were waiting for the chopper to extract us. We lit a can of Sterno and put it in his poncho and he got up screaming and swearing and here it was the 2nd lieutenant, not the sergeant. The shit hit the fan on that one!

*Pfc **Tom Petersen**, Radio Repairman/Tower Team*

In middle 1968 one of the old guys, Danny (Texas) showed up with Max. Max was immediately loved by all except 1st Sgt. Ragsdale. When Max was about six months old, Ragsdale told us (the Tower Team) to get rid of him. So we took our 3/4 ton about ten miles across a river and out of town and dropped Max off. Danny was bawling like a baby and we all felt kind of bad. We stopped off in town (Nha-Trang) for the afternoon before we headed back to Camp McDermod (the army compound in Nha-Trang). We arrived probably five hours after we had dropped Max off to fend for himself. There was Sgt. Ragsdale and Max waiting for us. We couldn't believe our eyes. We swore to old Ragsdale that we had dropped him off that morning at least ten miles away and across the river. Well, old Ragsdale relented but made it clear we were responsible for Max. We took him to the Vet on the Air Base for shots and fed him scraps from the mess hall. I've tried to find out what happened to Max after I left in April 1970 but no one seems to know.

*Engineman **Jim Fritz**, Mobile Riverine Force*

I transported three women from the USO show from Vung Tau to Dong Tam. I won the Bronze Star with V for valor for my actions during the December, 1968 ambush on the Vam Co Tay River during Operation Giant Slingshot.

*Spc4 **John Martin**, Radar Tech.*

Since we were supposedly behind the front lines we would hold daily formations; polished boots and the like. I had an M-14 with one clip of ammo. Often my calls to the field would require driving through two heavily ambushed passes, at An Khe and Pleiku. We were always happy to pick up hitchhiking Korean soldiers along that route so they could ride in the back of our ¾ ton truck for extra protection. Finally our warrant officer gave us his M-16 with a full bandolier of magazines. He was looking out for us and I felt better after that.

Pleiku Pass
Courtesy: John Martin

*1st Lieutenant **Edie Meeks**, Army Nurse Corps*

After three months in-country my roommate and I were promoted to First Lieutenant. It was the custom for anyone who was promoted to throw a party. We decided to invite everyone -- not just officers but corpsmen and people of all ranks – the people we worked with every day. We thought nothing of it since we worked so closely with these guys every day. We got in trouble for this since the officers and enlisted people were not supposed to fraternize. There was no way we would have left these other people out.

In Vietnam I saw what the will to live could do. You saw guys actually will themselves to live. You also saw guys who struggled and struggled, and then finally gave up.

In Saigon there were usually two RN's on, one for the recovery side and one for the ICU side. One night the gal who was supposed to be with me couldn't make it back from R&R, so I was alone. We weren't all that busy and I had a couple of corpsmen so I figured we'd be fine. Then we were told we were getting nine patients in. There had been an ambush. This was about 9:00 at night. I told one of the corpsmen that he was responsible for everyone in the ICU but that if he needed me to come change IV's or anything to call me. I would be on the Recovery side with all the guys coming in. As the evening went on a lot of the other corpsmen started dropping by -- just to say hello, they said -- and they started working. By the end of the rush around 2:00 the next morning these guys, who had probably worked all day, were all there. They "just happened to drop by" and they'd ask me what I wanted them to do. That was our camaraderie; they would back you up no matter what and we did the same for them.

We had a young patient with infected abdominal wounds. He got a letter; he was from a farm in Kansas. All my relatives from southern Minnesota were still farmers. This was in the Fall and his mother wrote that his father and some others had just returned from pheasant hunting with Spot the dog, and I related to that so much. And at the very end she wrote about how proud she was of him. I still think of that moment. And three days later he was dead.

Hospitalman First Class **Alexander Phillips**

We were executing a medevac of one of our injured sailors on the aft end of a PBR in the middle of a tossing sea. It was difficult to see as I wear glasses and the sea was whipped up by the helo's rotors, in addition to the rough seas. However with the cooperation of the PBR's CO and the expertise of the helo crew we pulled it off.

I served with a wonderful bunch of young kids, especially the crew of the Assault Craft embarked aboard the *Cleveland*. They worked hard and they played hard. One of the engineers was the first casualty we treated aboard the *Cleveland*; he was struck by one of the exploding shells at the mouth of the Cua Viet River and recovered enough to stay with the ACU. Dr. Michael J. Levine made several trips with us to the staging area of Dong Ha and he was also impressed with the professionalism of the ACU crew.

Sgt. **Floyd Jones***, Med. Admin. Spec.*

We had to inform the wounded servicemen what would transpire the day they departed Vietnam. It was like "overtime" for us as it was performed after dinner, usually around 8pm. Most felt it was a pain in the rear but I was touched by the response of the wounded so I asked for the job every night when I worked the day shift. Departing wounded were housed in a special ward. I would enter the ward with a large megaphone (battery operated) and give the following speech: "Ladies and gentlemen, I'm Sgt. Jones from the 100th Aeromedical Evacuation Squadron here at Tan Son Nhut AB. Tomorrow morning at 0600 you will be loaded on ambuses and taken to the flight line where our team will load you onto a C-141 aircraft for your journey to your assigned treatment facilities in the U.S., Japan or the Philippines." It never failed I would always be interrupted by applause and cheering. The joy and tears would rise up on many faces. "The plane has the best medical supplies, doctors, nurses and technicians to ensure you receive the best treatment. I will answer questions about your journey and what can and cannot be carried on the aircraft. Thank you!" I then walked the aisles with instructions and chatting about home.

Captain **Chuck Glazerman***, RF/PF Advisor*

My counterpart, a Vietnamese major, was killed. He was a proud man, who had fought with the Viet Minh against the French, and he certainly hated the Viet Cong, He was leading his guys and it just happened to be his day and he got shot. For his burial I was able to get a helicopter, put his body on board with his family, and took him to his final resting place. He deserved that. In a macabre way that was my proudest moment.

Courtesy: Chuck Glazerman

BMC *Don McMurray*, *Boat Engine Repair*

We wouldn't let sampans get near us. We even used water cannons but they always came up to beg, and one time the water cannon plan wasn't working. Our lieutenant took an M79 to scare them and it went off and killed a couple of people in the boat. Our government had to pay.

Sgt. *Floyd Jones*, *Med. Admin. Spec.*

On a seemingly quiet day we heard a "knock" at our back door. We found an Army Master Sergeant who was suffering from a venereal disease obtained on the local economy. He was married and wanted to keep it off his military records. He wanted to avoid a formal appearance at the clinic. The nurse authorized to administer penicillin was away. We agreed to help him but told him it was highly irregular and we could get in a lot of trouble. He said he would be grateful and promised to bring us a "case of steaks." We administered the shot and a few days later he fulfilled his end of the bargain. We decided to have a "barbeque" outside our barracks and charge $2.00 for a steak and San Miguel beer from the Philippines. The beer was flown in on our medical planes and cost us .10 a bottle; we always ordered ten or more cases. We also sold beer to other airmen for .25 a bottle and used the profits to buy more beer. We drank beer and ate steak free for a year. This deal went on for several years as I understand it. The Army MSgt continued to visit his girlfriend and show up at our tent right on schedule. Thanks to his appetite we all ate well!

Airman 2nd Class **Tom Emmons**, *Loadmaster*

My pilot, Major Diehl, was 55. He had a family. He took care of me like a son.. I flew with him for eight months unless he was on leave. Then I flew with some young gung-ho captain who wanted to make a mark for himself. The captain was "Hurry up, hurry up. We can get more missions in," whereas Major Diehl's approach was "This is a job. This is our schedule for today." I would see it and say "We got to do all that?"

Lt. Col. **Bud Might**, *Pilot*

The thing I'm proudest of is I flew thirty-five missions over Germany in WW II and for a year in Vietnam, and no one on my crew was ever hurt.

Lt. Col "Bud" Might
Courtesy: Shirley Bachus

U.S. troop levels fell to 495,000 by December 1.

CHAPTER TWENTY-ONE

HELMETS WITH BEER; THIMBLES WITH CHEER

1968

1968 proved to be the busiest year of the war including the siege of Khe Sanh, Tet, the My Lai Massacre and the start of Vietnamization. 1968 also saw President Johnson's exit and the relief of Secretary of Defense McNamara and General Westmoreland. NVA leadership remained unchanged. For the individual American, combat or support, 1968 would prove to be the hardest year to stay alive.

Airman 2nd Class **Tom Emmons**, *Loadmaster*

I had a man die on the tarmac. That was a damn shame. We had about a hundred guys on the plane. There were no seats. They were brand new troops. You'd bring the guys back to Cam Ranh Bay or Tan Son Nhut from out of the field, and they were dirty, then you got the new green troops who were scared shitless. They had no clue. They had duffel bags; they had a weapon. They looked like they came out of supply. We had to sit there that day and it was just hot. I could hear screaming in the back. There was a guy who went down and they were screaming for water. Heat stroke; he died right there on the plane. By the time I got water back to him he was gone. You talk about some freaked-out troops. Kids. Kids. And pissed. Pissed.

Another incident, it was probably the moment in Vietnam that made me the saddest. It was the night we were doing medevac right out in the field. They were carrying guys who were bleeding on stretchers, and loading up the plane and I was seeing people die on the airplane. There was blood all over the place.

Petty Officer 3rd Class **Vince Malaterra**, *Seabees*

We were sitting around somewhere and we had a bunch of body bags near us waiting to be transported to Saigon. Suddenly we noticed movement in two of the bags. Rats had gotten in there at some point.

Communications Technician **Dick Trimbur**

We had a spider monkey for a pet. This monkey liked to drink beer out of a helmet. After half a beer it would run around on the ground with the helmet on his head; you couldn't see the monkey only the helmet. It was hilarious.

Sgt First Class **Jim Kuipers**, *46th Engr. Bn.*

I had a stint as Sergeant of the Guard, supervising the perimeter defense. We had something like six or eight bunkers on the back side of Long Binh that were our responsibility. Normally the Officer of the Day and the Sergeant of the Guard remain back in the battalion area and don't go out there. But when I reported in for SOG duty the battalion XO or somebody told me that they were changing the procedure due to the fact that a sapper had gotten inside the perimeter and killed a few people the previous night. We had three men to each bunker, two of whom were to be up at all times. Up to that point the Rules of Engagement were that if someone wasn't shooting at you, you couldn't shoot. I told them that as far as I was concerned if they saw movement or hear somebody moving out there, open fire. Don't wait for permission. Because by God they got no business out there! I accept all responsibility. That's one of the reasons the battalion commander had me go out there was he didn't want any of his people getting hurt or killed.

The bridge over the MSR (main supply route) on the Saigon River had been blown. This was the road from Long Binh to Cu Chi. We were able to rebuild it **overnight,** and get it operational. This was on November 6, 1968. We were tasked to put an M46 aluminum bulk floating bridge across the MSR. This requires pontoons to be inflated, saddles put on them, and then you float them down and pin it together. C Company was on one side of the river and a bridge company was on the other side. They built from one side and we built from the other. It was about a 1,000 foot span right beside the blown main bridge. First we had to put in an approach and get it anchored, get it stable enough that you could begin floating the pontoons down. Delta Company was above us and they inflated the pontoons.

Initially I wasn't even out there, but Captain Phil Johnson, C Company commander called me and told me to get my butt out there. "Hell, Captain," I told him, "I don't know anything about bridges." When I got there they had the approach started. All I could see was a bunch of colonels and captains and majors standing around talking about how this bridge should be built. I asked a guy from the bridge company how this should be done and then I told Captain Johnson if he would get all those officers off the approach, I'd get this thing done.

We worked on that thing all night despite occasional sniper fire and a strong current. We had intermittent flares to illuminate the area. As the length of bridge grew out into the river we'd be driving one dump truck at a time onto the section to dump their loads of ten to twelve foot bulk for each section. As it worked out C Company built about 65% of that bridge, which is pretty good for a construction company that had never built a bridge before. That's because we had good men and we busted our asses that night. Around 0400 we came in contact with the other side of the bridge coming our way and a guy from the 65th told me, "You guys are done." It's tradition that the unit that builds the majority of the bridge doesn't have to get into the water to pin it at the end. So they had to get into the water and take their chances getting their fingers chopped off.

During the night, there were reports of VC floating down the river, hiding amongst reeds and brush, so we were constantly throwing grenades in the river. It was a pretty exciting night and I was very tired but I sure was proud of those guys for what they did that night. That's the only time I ever built that type of bridge. We had built bridges using cranes before where it took days and weeks to build but this was a new experience. And as often happens in a war we did it at night and under sniper fire. From the time the main bridge was blown until our replacement was completed was only twenty-six hours. And our bridge was only one-way but it would support a tank. The alternate route if this bridge was out was through VC-controlled territory and they sure didn't want that.

*Pfc **John Lawrence**, Crew Chief*

They were always trying to break our codes and they sent bombers against us from Burma. We had a lot of alerts where they picked up aircraft coming close to us. They shut off all the lights and electricity to make us invisible. That's when they started leaving alert planes on the runway with the engines running all night long.

My chopper broke down in Laos. A bolt broke off in the stabilizer. They told me I had to stay with the chopper until they could fix it. There were a few marines with me and some Laotians who didn't speak English. I had to stay with that chopper until they brought people from Danang to inspect it. It was two days before these people arrived to check out the chopper. They couldn't understand how the bolt could break but they drilled it out and fixed it. I didn't have those kinds of tools to do it myself.

I did a medevac on a red-headed kid from Philadelphia. He was begging me for morphine but I couldn't give him morphine because he had a head injury. Finally the kid croaked on me; he just passed out. So I gave him mouth-to-mouth and he came back. So when we landed we took him to the hospital. I went back the next morning and they told me he had passed. They said he had asked for me. He was just a kid. He was a red-headed kid from Philadelphia. And the nurse told me he was asking for me. The hard thing was when you tell somebody to hang in there, you're going to save them, and it's only a twenty-five minute flight, but sometimes . . . I did thirteen medevac's and that is the only time we lost a guy.

*Spc4 **John Martin**, Radar Tech.*

I usually rode in Hueys when I went on a call. Once I had to take a light observation helicopter. I tried to board it the same way I did a Huey, by walking around the back to get on. The exhaust blast from this chopper singed off one of my sideburns and half of my mustache. The pilot looked at me when I boarded but said nothing.

*Spc4 **Ron Kappeler**, RTO*

We were called out to an MP post that had lost communications. They had just killed a sniper in that area so we were advised to be cautious. On the way we saw a lot of anti-American graffiti on the quarry wall.

Propaganda circa 1966
Courtesy: Harley Brinkley

When we arrived I came up with the idea of a doublet antenna. This would allow us to avoid any sniper fire and still complete the job. The radio frequency was determined by the length of wire used. We tied a rock to each end of the wire and threw one rock over the crook of a tree. When we did this the rock pulled the wires up, raising the antenna.

*Pfc **Tom Petersen**, Radio Repairman/Tower Team*

We had a repeater site on Vung Ro Mountain that was taken out by a typhoon in November of 1968. All long distance communications north and south were lost. They loaded us up in a few vehicles with brand-new gear and we drove up Highway 1. The rain was heavy there and they didn't have any additional space to offer us, so we grabbed what we could -- blankets, sleeping bags, whatever -- and tried to make do on a warehouse floor. We had a new guy who was scared to death and he kept throwing his knife at the rats. We're lucky he didn't hit one of us. I'll bet he didn't sleep all night long.

*Spc4 **Ron Kappeler**, RTO*

I had duty one time to burn the waste from the latrine. We pulled the 55-gallon drums out from under the seats and poured some kerosene in. Just before the kerosene was lit I noticed a hand grenade with the pin pulled and held on with masking tape inside the drum.

*Lt. Col. **Bud Might**, Pilot*

One night we were up and our mission was scrubbed so we asked Saigon if they could use us. An army captain with a group of helicopter gunships asked us if we had any flares. We did. He said they had something going up the river and they couldn't identify it. He had eight choppers ready to go down as soon as we popped the flare. Our flare illuminated a bunch of heavily loaded barges. Anything moving at night was in a free fire zone and after they hit them there were secondary explosions rising higher than our altitude. The choppers were going down both sides of the river and I was in the middle. Anything that moved at night was fair game because our troops didn't move at night. A flare ignited on our plane once. The crewman shoved it overboard.

*Chief **Sidney Brown**, Hull Technician*

When we left Saigon for Vung Tau we got into an unusual tidal situation and we ended up high and dry at Vung Tau. We arrived empty and they started forklifting this steel matting for airfields into our ship. This stuff is 12' X 2 ½' and they had it stacked 18" high. This is the heaviest stuff you can carry on an LST. One stack of that stuff is all a heavy-terrain forklift can handle. The stevedores would stack it three high on the tank deck and up on the main deck. The tide never came back in. We sat there with no water around us for six weeks! They took the steel matting off to try to float us but it didn't work. We were sitting there drinking beer and barbequing steak and walking around the bank. You could squat down amidships and look under the ship from one side to the other. They decided that a tug from the Philippines would pull us off. They tied this 4" line onto the big chock on the stern and the tug boat got a running start and it ripped off the chock and everything off the main deck so you could look down to the mess hall like it was a skylight. The LST never budged. After six weeks, with the Seabees digging a ditch alongside and washing the sand and dirt out from under us and the tide coming in, we slid into the ditch and finally got our butts off the bank

We'd go down into the Delta around a village called Ben Tre and when you go up that river there are turns in it. And when the river turns left the sandbar will be on the left and the same when the river turns right the sandbar is always on the side of the turn. So if you're turning you have to bear as far opposite the direction of the turn as you can to avoid getting hung up on a sandbar. When you first start up that river it is about three miles wide. The further you go the more narrow it becomes. Where we would go to unload the river was about a quarter mile wide. They had tugboats pulling barges loaded with stuff. We hauled everything in the world; pallets of cement, generators, bulldozers, airplane parts, and we moved a team of guys who serviced helicopters.

Airman 1ˢᵗ Class **Bruce Quinlan**, *Instrument Repairman*

During September 68 I was in Cam Ranh Bay Hospital with a non-service related neck injury. I had been a springboard diver on my high school swimming team and I had an accident on the diving board; I hit the back of my neck and had a lot of trouble with it after that. While in Nam I was dropping tools and had numbness in my hands so I went to the dispensary and ended up in the hospital.

They put me in traction for a pinched nerve and I was in a ward with wounded soldiers. That was a real eye opener. Not being a combat soldier I had no idea what combat did to soldiers. It was horrifying seeing guys all shot up screaming and crying. A guy next to me had no right side of his head. He didn't make it. Once able to get out of bed I would go to the game room, passing a ward of guys locked up because they went crazy. I couldn't wait to get back to my unit. I saw and heard shit there I will never forget. It made me appreciate being a behind-the-lines troop. I cannot forget what I saw; in fact I have a disability claim with the VA for my ischemic heart disease due to Agent Orange exposure and for PTSD.

1ˢᵗ Lieutenant **Edie Meeks**, *Army Nurse Corps*

In Saigon at Christmas-time 1968 the CO decided we were going to display luminaries around the hospital sidewalks. So we had all these sand-filled bags with candles outlining our facility. I thought: Doesn't this just say, 'Here I am!' Some of us went to the roof of a Saigon hotel one night and you could watch the flares out in the night. It was fireworks to us but somebody was out there under those flares, fighting for his life.

We had a patient in the 3ʳᵈ Field Hospital -- around Christmas time -- and he had been shot in the chest; it had just missed his heart, and he arrived at the ER fast enough that the doctors were able to save him. We had him in the ICU. At this time every ward had some sort of a party going on and the medical staff would just go from ward to ward and each ward had to have some libation available. The ICU nurses kept ordering 180 proof alcohol from the pharmacy to put in our punch. It was wonderful but this fellow with the chest wound who was still in ICU asked us for a drink, since it was Christmas. We talked it over and decided to give him just a little thimble-full; just a little taste. After his Christmas cheer he broke out in a sweat and he turned gray and I thought we had killed him! He turned out to be okay. In fact he is the only patient that we ever found out about after he left us. He wrote to us from Walter Reed Army Hospital saying he was doing okay. He had stayed with us for about two weeks; usually guys were shipped out after three or four days.

FCTG *Rick Dolinar*, Fire Control Technician

While on the *Cleveland*, we never fired our guns in anger, although we often went to general quarters. By the nature of our duties, we were fairly close to shore, so as to deploy troops.

Best friends
Courtesy: Rick Dolinar

On the First Birthday of the commissioning of the *Cleveland*, April 21, 1968, we were off the coast of South Vietnam on a holiday routine. In that mode you could swim, sleep, or do whatever you wanted. They filled the well deck for swimming, baked a cake and grilled hamburgers and hot dogs. I chose to read and sleep. When I woke up, I went up to the mess deck to eat and a guy says "That was really neat, huh, about the downed pilot?" Apparently an F-4 had been shot down, and the pilots are trained to head out for the water where their chances of rescue were greater. Both pilots bailed out and one of them had to divert a bit to avoid landing on the ship. We picked him up and soon he was eating cake and hamburgers. After dining he was flown back to his carrier by one of our choppers.

As it turns out this pilot's hometown was Cleveland, Ohio. They sent this story out to a lot of the hometown newspapers and my mother sent me the article from *The Pittsburgh Press*. The way this story read I was the guy who pulled him out of the South China Sea, and I was sleeping at the time! I never bothered to correct the story in my mother's mind. Some years after the war this pilot attended a reunion of the *USS Cleveland* in Dallas, Texas. He gave a little talk about the incident and how thankful he was for our help.

*Engineman **Jim Fritz**, Mobile Riverine Force*

One time we lowered a drum into the river, to get water to use for showers. The drum came back up with a snake in it.

*Spc4 **Garry Ramsey**, Supply Clerk*

At a point out of Da Lat we were stopped and they were sweeping the road ahead of us. I climbed onto the top of my truck to get some C rations and I had my Polaroid camera; one of our choppers was coming in my direction so I took a couple of pictures and then a rocket hit the chopper. We went to the crash site to help. There were pieces of bodies that gave me nightmares for years. It never left my mind. Later we were driving past the Korean compound and we saw a bunch of VC heads on poles and other atrocities. I wondered afterwards if I really saw that. I was having nightmares about it and I wondered if it really happened; years later one of my friends assured me it did.

*1stLt. **David Cass**, Platoon Leader*

General Gus came out to visit our bridge site when his jeep was attacked by a water buffalo. His aide shot the buffalo with his 45 pistol. Later the General sent him back to pay the farmer for the loss of his buffalo but the farmer only laughed at him. The farmer showed him the buffalo calmly grazing in the rice paddies. Upon closer exam the buffalo was found to have a hole in its right ear and grooves on its forehead where the 45 rounds slid along its' skull temporarily knocking it out.

On a sunny afternoon in the summer of 1968, my driver, 21-year old Spec4 Larry Schue and I had just passed thru a masonry arch that marked the exit from the village of Long Hung, a small village adjacent to our base at Long Binh. As we cleared the arch we could see a Vietnamese woman with her back to us standing frozen in a ditch. She was clad in the black pajamas normally worn by the peasants in the area. The ditch was several feet below the level of the gravel road we were traveling due to the heavy rains of the monsoon. To her left was a cemetery similar to those here at home with various masonry headstones. A large black snake about twelve feet long was quickly approaching her at a high rate of speed. Her only option was to retreat and at a quick pace.

We had an M-60 machine gun with several belts of ammo, Larry's M-14 and the colt .45 my father had given me. I had a clip in the .45 but a round was not chambered. I stood 6' 2" and weighed 225 pounds. I had Larry stop the jeep and hand me his rifle. My intention was to expend twenty seconds butt stomping the head of the attacking snake with the M-14 and be on our way.

I was fast but the snake was faster. The butt plate did find the snake but several inches behind the head and with way too little impact. The 1 ½" to 2" diameter of the snake was pure muscle. The remainder of the snake caught up with and passed its' head in a flash as it wrapped itself around my legs. I realized I couldn't release one ounce of pressure off the rifle without the snake chewing a hole in my legs or feet.

I suggested that Larry exit the jeep, jump in the ditch, pull my .45 from the holster, chamber a round and ventilate the offending reptile. I cannot remember his exact response; something like "You got yourself into it and you can get yourself out of it" was the printable version, frosted with an expression of general dislike of snakes. Aren't officers supposed to lead?

As we exchanged verbal niceties, the snake increased its' efforts to be free of the constraining rifle butt. The rifle had ended up on my dominant right side and was trapped there by the snake's coils. Unfortunately my pistol was also on my right hip. I jammed the muzzle of the rifle in my right armpit and reached behind my back with my left hand and withdrew the pistol. I had learned to release some of the pressure against the slide by placing the hammer in the cocked position, which I could easily do with one hand. The next part was harder. To chamber a round in the .45 it is necessary to move the slide all the way to the rear and let it snap forward. I accomplished this with my teeth at the sacrifice of a chipped tooth. I had noticed that the snake frequently rested its' head on the metal sling fastener. I estimated where I could shoot and miss the sling fastener and put an end to this madness. I fired just as the snake cooperated and his coils and headless body immediately went limp.

I heard a spinning of tires in the gravel and looked up to see my driver taking off hastily down the road. I turned around and saw the mama san pick up the snake. Holding it up as high as she could with several feet of snake still trailing in the dirt she gave me a big smile with her betel-nut stained teeth and bowed several times at the waist. She then said "beaucoup chop-chop" (much food) and headed back the way she had come, dragging her supper with her. I could see my jeep and driver idling at the intersection about a quarter mile ahead. By the time I had walked there my temper and adrenalin rush had ended and I had calmed down. Larry knew me better than I knew myself.

*Hospitalman First Class **Alexander Phillips***

On April 10 I accompanied the ship's medical officer and another corpsman on a five-day Medcap visit in the village of Hua Cuong where we treated over four hundred civilians.

Bob Hope's 1968 tour started off in Tokyo, where his son was in the Navy. He then made two stops in Korea, where our manpower had increased fivefold since the Pueblo Incident. Ann Margaret was with him and entertained on Okinawa. Arriving in Long Binh the #2 engine on their C130 flamed out. They entertained 30,000 GI's. Hope admitted that he wanted to spend Christmas in the States, but "I can't stand violence."

The Hope Show traveled in flights of three into Cu Chi due to enemy activity. Hope mentioned that the Hong Kong flu was spreading in the U.S. "You're stuck here and the germs get back home!" Admiral McCain, whose son was now a POW, visited the show. At Chu Lai Bob entertained the Americal Division. They ended their Christmas Eve show at the world's biggest sand trap – Cam Ranh Bay – in the rain.

On the USS Hancock Hope made his first night landing then did his third show of the day. Some crewmen from the USS New Jersey were there too; this was the third war for the big battleship. Hope visited Danang (the R&R center for rockets) and then did their first show at Dong Tam, in the Delta. Gunfire interrupted the show. Then they visited Noc On Phnom, on the Laotian border. Bob was greeted with jeers when he kiddingly referred to this base as being "close to a neutral country." Hope next traveled to U-Tapao and then ended the show at Guam. Tet was never mentioned on this tour.

CHAPTER TWENTY-TWO

THE SNAKE ON A STRING

1969

Midway to the end of our Vietnam involvement the beginning was no clearer. Was this a war to stop the spread of communism or a rise of nationalism in Vietnam? Or both? Or neither? For the troops, both combat and support, those questions were often rendered moot by the frenzy of twelve and sixteen hour days and the lingering uncertainty of living through a tour of duty.

In the "world" increased antiwar protests and the February 1968 Tet Offensive helped drive President Johnson from office. Possibly due to his "secret plan" to end the Vietnam War, Richard Nixon won the White House; he authorized secret bombing of Cambodia instead. Ho Chi Minh's death on September 3, 1969 did nothing to derail the North Vietnamese efforts. In May of 1969 President Nixon announced troop withdrawals.

*1st Lieutenant **Edie Meeks**, Army Nurse Corps, 71st Evacuation Hospital, Pleiku, USA*

After six months in Saigon ICU I transferred to Pleiku. I was just getting so down with the work at 3rd Field Hospital. Also the fellow I was dating (who I later married) was in charge of ordering medical supplies and using the computer. After work he would want to go out to dinner. Well I had been dealing with guys that were blown up all day long and the contrast with having a nice dinner in downtown Saigon was too much. It was just too bizarre. I told him I just couldn't see him anymore. His life there was just so different from mine. You tended to stay with the people that did what you did and understood you. You didn't have to explain anything to them.

I just felt like a change of scenery would help me. Plus with the normal rotation of people many of those with whom I was working were going home. Since we didn't go over there as a unit you'd find your friends were going home and you still had six months to go. You didn't have that backup that you needed just to hold yourself together. So I transferred to Pleiku, to the 71st Evacuation Hospital. We wore fatigues there, in a bunker mentality. At night you brought your flak jacket and helmet to work because that is when the rockets came.

We worked six twelve-hour days. We rotated for both day and night shifts. We weren't staffed as well as night. When the patients got to us they had already been through the operating room and we would begin taking care of them. We would send our patients from Saigon to Japan or sometimes to the Philippines when they were stabilized, whereas at Pleiku we kept them longer. If they had malaria for example they were not going to be shipped out. I never got the feeling that we were shipping guys out of the hospital back to their units before they were recovered.

I was in ICU for about a month at Pleiku when I decided I couldn't do this anymore. I went to Medical ICU where you would get really sick, malaria-type patients. I wonder what ever became of those guys who suffered such bad bouts of malaria. In the Medical ICU we weren't dealing with guys who might bleed out, they were stabilized and we were dealing with things like getting their temperature down, etc.

Vietnam may have been the first war where we had ventilators in the hospitals in a combat zone. We had some in Saigon and one at Pleiku. These were big, cumbersome machines that you wheeled around, but they kept a person breathing if they couldn't breathe.

At Pleiku we lived in sandbagged hooches, six girls and a bathroom, with individual cubicles. The only air conditioning was in the ICU. We did have fans but it was so hard to sleep from the heat and the humidity.

*Spc4 **Tom Petersen**, Radio Repairman Tower Team*

Our squad leader went home in the spring of 1969, leaving us somewhat leaderless. There were five of us and we just did our own thing and got the job done. Around July of 1969, the other four guys rotated home; I was the only one who extended.

*Spc4 **Garry Ramsey**, Fuel Truck Driver*

I spent the remainder of my tour (ten months) as a fuel truck driver with the 61st Transit Company. One of the first things they did was try to make sure everyone knew how to drive a tractor. A sergeant would get up on the truck with the guys and watch as they tried to back the truck between some 55-gallon drums. He gave most of them a hard time. When my turn came I told him if he hollered and banged the side of the door, I was going to knock the shit out of him. He laughed but he didn't bang the door. I had experience driving trucks before the military so I knew what I was doing. After the "training" I hauled fuel every day.

Courtesy: Garry Ramsey

Our work at the 524th Quartermaster began at 0500 at the motor pool. We could work as late as 10:30 at night but no later, since the trucks didn't move at night. As a fuel truck driver I was out on the open road. An average trip would be to Phan Rang, about eighty miles. We usually spent the night at the compounds we serviced, including the Montagnard compound, and the Koreans. When we spent the night at a compound I usually slept under canvas in the tractor. I'd blow up an air mattress. At Cam Ranh Bay I slept in a barracks that held about twenty guys.

Spc5 **Bill Wyrick,** *Construction Engineer, 503rd Combat Engineers, 1st Air Cavalry Division, USA*

Between my first and second tours I spent two years at Fort Benning teaching camouflage and ambush techniques. I flew into Bien Hoa in September of 1969 and choppered to the 1st AirCav at An Loc. My duties were similar with the Cav as to what I did with the 46th Engineers, clearing landing zones in the bush. We were usually flown in by chopper with the dozer hanging underneath. Some guys actually rode in the dozers on these trips.

Spc5 **Frank Jackmauh,** *Surveyor, HQ Co, 46th Engr. Bn., Long Binh, USA*

Prior to entering the military I worked as a field engineer on a 16-story addition to the AT&T office building in Boston, Massachusetts. I also earned an associate's degree in civil and highway engineering. My AIT was at Fort Belvoir as a construction surveyor. From there I did four months of NCO training and emerged as a Spec5 surveyor. I landed by plane at Bien Hoa in early January, 1969. I was assigned to HQ Company, 46th Engineer Battalion.

I went over there as a surveyor but within a couple of months of my arrival the NCO that was running the Carpenter Shop returned to the states on some sort of personal matter and I was asked to step in. There were a couple of small hooches down there and a shower, and I was required to live down there to eliminate any theft of materials from the Carpenter Shop. Plywood and corrugated roofing were in great demand and I needed to keep an eye on these materials.

We received orders from units in the field (artillery, infantry, or whoever) as to their needs and we would prefabricate the modules. Once they received our product they would fortify it with sandbags for their protection against enemy fire.

After about ten weeks of Carpenter Shop duty a staff sergeant reported in and relieved me and I returned to my surveyor work. That is right when the survey work was beginning in the direction of Xuan Loc and I wanted to be a part of that. This was a stretch of road from the intersection of QL20 and QL 1 (Highway 1) through Xuan Luc to Gia Rey.

We worked seven days a week; one day was the same as the other. There was no day off. The Vietnamese at the Carpentry Shop worked about a forty-hour week. We tried to take one day off each week doing the surveyor work.

*LCpl **Alan Webster**, Military Police, 23rd Military Police, Chu Lai, USMC*

Like many somewhat rebellious kids I enlisted despite my parents objections. I always wanted to be a Marine and I wanted to have a choice in branch of service so I didn't wait for the draft. When my service was completed I told them "It's too late now, but you were right and I was wrong!" I flew into Danang, in February of 1969. The field was under mortar and/or rocket attack. I volunteered to help unload the plane if I could go back home on it. The officer in charge didn't find that amusing. I was briefly assigned to the 1st Marines for a day or so then flew to Chu Lai and was assigned to MAG-12.

In my two months with MAG-12 I worked as a grunt running perimeter sweeps both day and night. These sweeps were done to provide security for the choppers. I also manned a bunker on the flight line. This was about the time the Marines started to deploy back home and I ended up being sent to the Americal Division, United States Army, who eventually replaced the Marines at Chu Lai. One of my duties with the Americal was running convoys. I was only supposed to be temporary to the Americal -- about sixty or ninety days -- but I spent the rest of my tour with them. The Provost Marshal there, an Army colonel, requested that the Marine Corps let me stay with them. Later I was part of a hand-picked group of security guys (12 Army and 1 Marine) called the Strike Force. We were responsible for security issues at Chu Lai, both internal and external.

I worked security at the second gate at Chu Lai. This was the entrance for most of the supply trucks and we ensured that they were only carrying what they were supposed to have. There was a lot of pilferage coming out that gate so I made sure that the load on the truck matched what was on the chit the driver carried. I'd tear those trucks apart to make sure everything was correct.

The Strike Force ran both day and night patrols in the Chu Lai area. If we were running a convoy I was always in the second vehicle, a jeep, with an M60 machine gun. Every time. I would say, "Why me?" So they let me drive one time and I hated it. I'd rather be behind the M60. We'd go on a sweep into a Ville, and we'd check through the rice and find weapons or ammunition hidden there. Did the villagers put them there or did the

VC put them there? One thing I didn't agree with was torching the village instead of looking into how the weapons got there.

Spc5 **Tom Moschella**, *Vehicle Repair, 1st Log. Com., USA*

I was having trouble in high school so I went into the Army at seventeen. They assured me I could get into something mechanical, which I did. I flew into Cam Ranh Bay in February of 1969. I was processed and assigned to the 5th Maintenance Battalion, which was part of the 1st Logistics Command. I initially reported to An Khe in the Central Highlands. I was there for several months and then I ended up at Tuy Hoa, on the coast.

At An Khe (Camp Radcliff) we were right next to the 88th Transportation outfit. We had a shortage of engines for the trucks. They shipped us a hundred engines all at once. We were working around the clock to get these trucks up and running.

I was congratulated on my promotion to Spc5, and then they told me I was the only qualified repairman within 300 square miles. I was sent to Tuy Hoa where there were only two of us Track-qualified guys so I'd also deal with any track-related maintenance issues. I was working on tank-based artillery pieces such as the 155mm howitzer, with A, B, and C batteries of the 36th Artillery. I'd visit their firebases, assess the problem, go back for the tools and parts I would need, and return to finish the job. I put governors on them, injector units, everything. The thing I hated the most was when they threw a track and you had to fix that. They were a pain in the butt. When we worked on the big guns we had to build a platform to allow us to get under the vehicle. The whole job might take a week or more.

Once I got to Tuy Hoa everywhere I went was in a truck. I had my toolbox with me. If I was on a chopper, I sat on my toolbox for protection from ground fire. Once I was flying between two artillery LZ's in a chopper and we were clipping along at treetop level. We get some ground fire and the pilot quickly gained altitude and I'm thinking this is good, we're getting out of danger. He gained altitude then turns around and comes back with both M60's blazing. I just wanted to get the hell out of there and go fix my vehicles! He made a couple of passes and then we got out of there.

We worked two twelve-hour shifts but we also had guard and additional duties, so it was a very long day. And if you screwed up you would be assigned to the crap-burning detail. We had no hydraulic lift but we had a pit which allowed us to get under the trucks. Usually we pulled the whole pack (engine and transmission – about the size of a car) out when working on a truck. The most common problem on the trucks was the engines. Due to the tremendous wear on the vehicles the engines wore out fast.

*Engineman **Jim Fritz**, Mobile Riverine Force*

As part of Operation Sea Float we provided a floating naval support base for PBR (patrol boat river) and helicopters for brown water operations down in the Delta. Living conditions were poor. We had seven men trying to cram into a 50' ASPB (Assault Support Patrol Boat) barracks barge on Operation Sea Float. The barge was in the Song Cau Lon River.

Courtesy: Jim Fritz (3d from left)

*Capt. **Paul Kaser**, Admin Ofcr, 3rd Sec. Police Sqd, USAF*

I had a B/A in Journalism from Kent State University. With my background I wanted to be an Information Officer. I served almost two years at a base in Texas and then volunteered for Vietnam. I went to the Security Police at Bien Hoa in March of 1969. I spent eighteen months in-country.

When I got to Bien Hoa I expected to be an Administrative Officer but I did a lot of security work. I liked that because they were a good unit getting better at guarding the base. I went on perimeter runs and things.

The Security Police had K9 troops, ambush sites, lookout towers on the perimeter; they were more Army than Air Force. I was thankful for this activity because I didn't want to just sit in an office. The Security Police were also involved with Intelligence Reports. There were comments about arms caches and troop movements and occasional references to how many elephants the pilots killed. We knew our pilots were in Cambodia but that was never mentioned. There were comments about enemy cave systems but we didn't grasp how extensive they were. The caves had hospitals, machine shops, and everything, and not far away from Bien Hoa.

Sentry Dog at Work
Courtesy: Paul Kaser

I got to travel around the country quite a bit sometimes visiting other security units. I was up at Pleiku; I didn't get down to the Delta much.

In the Security role my office was down in the squadron area; since most of the rocket activity occurred at night we'd be up most of the night. I would check the perimeter to ensure that our troops were at their posts and make sure our mortars were ready. When we received rocket fire our mortar crews, with the aid of radar, would determine the location of the rocket site and provide counter battery fire. The VC countered this move by moving to another site very quickly after the first few rounds.

We would send out medical units from nearby Long Binh Hospital. These were called CAP's (Civic Action Patrols). My security guys would go out acting as guards for the medical people. I also went with Army guys on these missions. Also some of our NCO's would go to the villages; one time our guys went to a village to build a well. Another time they built a barracks for an orphanage.

One of the CAP's was by helicopter to a leper colony in the area. I also made a lot of trips to orphanages. I used to go there once a week. It was run by Catholic nuns. This place was actually quite isolated; I think it was near a village named Khe Sat.

Courtesy: Paul Kaser

I flew in there on a Huey along with our chaplain and some medical guys. A crippled kid from the colony ran up to me with a big can which had a snake in it. The kid had this snake on a string. I looked at the padre as if to ask "what am I going to do with this?" In the first place I was a little afraid of the lepers (I got over that) and now there is this snake. The colony people told me this kid was their best snake catcher and he was giving me this snake as a gift. This was right around Christmas so the snake was my first Christmas gift that year.

We made the rounds of the leper colony visiting the sick. One of the strange things was a lot of people were trying to get **in** there, even though they didn't have leprosy, because it was such a safe place. The VC left them alone. The VC did come in there occasionally to take their medical supplies. They made Ho Chi Minh sandals from old tires at the colony which they would sell outside the colony; the VC would take those too.

There was also a law enforcement aspect to our job. One of my jobs was to visit any guys we might have in the hospital and also go to the LBJ (Long Binh Jail). We did have some Air Force guys in there. That was a pretty gruesome place. I would go see our guys and interview them and see how things were going on with them. It was a very tense place because rockets could come in there too. The prisoners were really on edge because they couldn't run to bunkers when they were in LBJ.

Ship fitter 3rd Class Diver 2nd Class **Steve Doak**, *Harbor Clearance Unit #1*

I come from a Navy family and after high school graduation in a little farming community in Illinois my mother was steering me to the Navy. I went into the Navy Reserve and did an abbreviated boot camp at Great Lakes. I attended periodic drills with the Reserves for six or eight months while I was working full time and then I was called to active duty. I got orders to San Diego. When I got there I got a bunch of shots. Then they asked for volunteers for gunboats in Vietnam. I never told my mom this but I put my name down, but they didn't pick me for that. I got picked for an outfit called Harbor Clearance Unit #1. This was a diving unit that was over at Subic Bay in the Philippines. I initially went over there in the summer of 1969 as an apprentice machinist. After a month I told them I'd rather be working as a pipefitter so they switched me over to another workshop where I started welding and doing pipefitting. I was brazing, welding and arc welding and things like that. Some guys in my unit were divers so I got into that.

I was what they called an "89-day wonder." They would fly us over to Vietnam, put us where they needed us but at the end of 89 days, no matter what we were doing, they'd fly us back to Clark AFB in the Philippines so we wouldn't count against the manpower total in Vietnam. This was a common practice. The Air Force also did this for guys coming out of Okinawa and Guam. Once back from Vietnam they'd give us a couple of months to rest up before we went back over there.

As part of Harbor Clearance Unit #1 we would go over to Vietnam and try to salvage wrecks, mostly our gunboats sunk in the Mekong Delta. We had a map that showed where these boats had gone down. Once we located the wreck we would determine which way it was facing. Then we would come up with a plan to bring it up. When we pulled it up we'd try to patch it and tow it back to the facilities for repair.

We would fly to the job sites either by C130 or helicopter. Our mobile team might just consist of two of us, or a few more. There were salvage boats designed especially for this type of work; they had a crew of about five. There were covered sleeping compartments aboard, sometimes air-conditioned. They had a kitchen down below with an oven and hotplates. Some boats were larger with a crew of eight or ten. These boats could salvage larger craft. Our mobile team of two or more would go out with these salvage boats and work with them to complete the rescue of a sunken craft. On these trips we would do mostly demolition work.

In the Deltas where the rivers were maybe only twenty feet deep or so, we worked with what they call a Jack Brown rig; this was a triangular mask which fit across your forehead and came down around your chin. It covered your whole face so you could breathe and see. And you would get compressed air from the surface via a valve on your cheek that you could open and close. Most of the time we dove with just an old pair of cut-off shorts, maybe a long-sleeve sweatshirt as protection against cuts from sharp metal, and our combat boots. We didn't wear flippers. We would usually wrap an ankle or something around part of the boat to hold us in place while we worked. We didn't swim around much like you see in the movies. Even though most of our diving was done during the day it was so dark in those canals and rivers you couldn't really see anything. You could hold your fingers up against your mask and not be able to see them. It was so muddy everything we did was by feel.

A number of times we worked through the night. We changed divers occasionally not so much because of problems from the bends since the water was not deep, but you would just get tired and water-logged after a while. On most jobs we worked until the work was done. We didn't want to become a sitting duck for the enemy. It was: Get in and get out!

Spc4 **Noah Dillion***, Aircraft Mechanic*

When I arrived at Soc Trang Army Airfield I took a day time PE maintenance crew slot as a mechanic, declining to crew an aircraft. Later I chose to work on a night crew because the maintenance load required an additional PE crew. I felt safer working in the hangar at night when the worst might happen; Charlie was busy working his rice paddy's during the day time. Call sign for the 221st was Eyes Over The Delta "Shotguns".

The Soc Trang airfield was built by the Japanese during the early part of World War II. The French built concrete barracks after the war. In the late 60's the Americans added hot and cold running water; the VC provided the entertainment -- Soc Trang was known as "mortar alley."

At Soc Trang we had sixteen-man hooches built from 6" thick concrete half walls and a screened four foot section topped with a truss galvanized metal roof. They had divided up the sixteen man bay with mortar boxes wired into four man cubicles. The pilots got angry because our living quarters were better than theirs so we were moved to empty hooches. Top told us to move "everything" so we stripped the buildings and moved cubicles and all. We had wall lockers and metal beds just like in basic.

My work day was 1800 to 0600 but I often went in early. There were no days off unless you pulled guard duty. The 9th Infantry was our airfield security; when they shipped back to Hawaii aviation units took over.

On July 29th, 1969 I was promoted to Spc-5 and reassigned to the 114th Assault Helicopter Company located at Vinh Long Army Airfield as an OJT Aviation Electrician. Vinh Long is a large town located in the middle of the Mekong River in an area of the Delta known as the Plain of Reeds. The Army airfield there was taken by the VC during Tet (February 1968). Support troops were gathered and used to retake it. I outranked the Spc-4 running the PE electrical crew so I was made NCOIC of the electrical PE maintenance covering twenty-four slicks and eight gunships. Replacing someone who was doing a good job with a new guy who didn't know the ropes but had an extra stripe made no sense so I worked up a compromise with this other guy; I handled the office and bookkeeping chores and he stayed a productive crew member. Call sign for the 114th was Knights of the Air, Red Knights, White Knights and Cobras.

Courtesy: Noah Dillion

My Vinh Long work day was from 1800 to 0600 but I often I went in early to have a pass down from the day crew and stayed late that next morning to give the day crew their work assignments and a pass down. Lacking other diversions I spent most of my days at Vinh Long sleeping. Part of my job was retrieval of downed helicopters. When we couldn't repair it in place a Chinook would be called to lift it out. If Charlie arrived before the Chinook we sometimes had to burn the ship to keep it from falling into their hands. Hangar rats were not authorized flight pay for these trips. I feel this traced to jealousy between flight crews and maintenance mechanics; they felt we were not qualified to crew an aircraft. Late in my tour I convinced the hangar officer to put one of the electrical crew on flight pay; I declined the slot since I was "short".

South Vietnam's airports became the busiest in the world. The number of Army aircraft rose to 4,200.[lxii]

*Spc4 **Larry Gombos**, Quartermaster, 43rd Field Service Co, Bien Hoa, USA*

I flew into Bien Hoa in September of 1969 with orders to the 43rd Field Service Company. I figured it was a supply depot since that is what I had been trained to do. I spent the first night there and then they pulled three of us aside and told us we were TDY (temporary duty) to Personal Property Depot, Saigon. The three of us got into a truck bound for Saigon. We had three other guys with us -- in body bags.

CHAPTER TWENTY-THREE

VIETNAMIZATION

Vietnamization was announced on June 8, 1969. U.S. engineer units began shifting their equipment – usually their best equipment – to ARVN units.[lxiii]

Chief **Sidney Brown**, *Hull Technician*

When we would go places to offload cement the forklifts would tear the paper cement bags open. That cement would get six to eight inches deep down in the tank deck. They would waste a third of the cement tearing those bags open. Those guys didn't care. In January of 1969 we were in a local Catholic orphanage run by some Vietnamese nuns. They always had two or three men there that did maintenance for them. We'd tell them with very bad, broken English, that we had cement available for free if they wanted it. And they would come down and clean up all this stuff in the tank deck; they'd get a broom and sweep it up. You'd see these nuns in their black habits that would end up gray when they were finished. And they would cement playgrounds and parts of sidewalks; cement was like gold over there.

Spc5 **Tom Moschella**, *Vehicle Repair*

We had a lot of Vietnamese running the tool room at An Khe. We also had Vietnamese cleaning the hooch. They were very poor and they were in a hell of a situation over there. They were okay. They adapted; whatever they had to do. I felt sorry for them because they were in a situation where they had to hustle to get by.

*Spc4 **Tom Petersen**, Radio Repairman/Tower Team*

I was fluent in what I call "marketplace" Vietnamese. I could count to ten and I could haggle a bit over prices. I could also talk to the girls. There was an orphanage in downtown Nha Trang, operated by Catholic nuns, and I spent a lot of time there. All the kids seemed happy, the facility was very clean and I never saw prolonged crying, angry outbursts or conflict of any kind. What I did see was devotion, contentment and a lot of laughter. The older girls took care of the younger kids and babies under the watchful eye of the nuns. The kids had great fun when they did laundry and if anyone, including the nuns got too close, they were splashed with lots of giggles and I dare-you-to-get-closer! One thing I never asked was where the boy orphans were; I never saw one over five or six, while the girls were there well into their teenage years.

The Orphanage in Nha Trang
Courtesy: Tom Petersen

There was a young Vietnamese girl there that just devoured everything we could teach her. My predecessor had books sent over to give her. I carried on with that. I missed my big family back home. I went there and helped out including changing diapers and holding kids and playing with the older kids. My aunt back home kept a box in the church basement for people to put extra clothing in and I'd get that box every month or so.

*Engineman **Jim Fritz**, Mobile Riverine Force*

We passed a Vietnamese boat while going up river during Sea Float. On that boat a Vietnamese lady was holding a baby. Our boat bumped their boat and she dropped the baby into the river. I still feel badly about that.

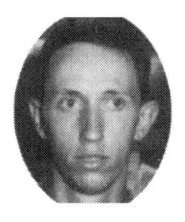

*Pfc **Garry Ramsey**, Fuel Truck Driver*

Vietnamese girls cleaned our barracks and worked at the mess hall. At Bien Hoa we would pick them up in a cattle truck to bring them to work. One of our barbers was caught with an AK-47 behind our outhouse. We had a mama san who would warn us of impending VC activity. When I told my first sergeant and captain what she said they thought I was crazy but it turns out she was right. I had a touch of malaria while I was there and one of the girls kept supplying me with cold towels for my forehead.

Courtesy: Garry Ramsey

As we passed the starving Vietnamese on a convoy I would give them a lot of my C rations, it just hurt me so much to see their faces.

*Captain **Paul Kaser**, Admin Officer*

One of my frustrations was working with the Vietnamese Police. One time we had a rocket alarm and we had gone out to make sure we were ready for a ground attack. The First Sergeant called me and asked me to stop by the barracks. He said we had a problem. They had caught one of the Vietnamese going through their barracks looking for watches and stuff.

Courtesy: Paul Kaser

*Spc5 **Frank Jackmauh**, Surveyor*

In the Spring of 1969 I was asked to run the Carpenter Shop. We were building prefabricated modules to bunkers and other things and I had 200 Vietnamese working for me. I also had an interpreter who spoke English very well and he helped me communicate with the chief Vietnamese foreman who ran things. Very few of these Vietnamese had any carpenter experience; they were villagers who just came in from the outlying villages. The plans for our modules (bunkers, latrines, showers, etc.) were drawn up in English but they understood them. Most of the specs were in meters. They did a wonderful job. Every now and then we'd get visited by various higher ups and I'd tell the interpreter to have the workers bang their hammers and saw wood to impress them; just make a lot of noise!

Briefing a new officer
Courtesy: Frank Jackmauh

I made some good friends at the Carpentry Shop; I got along with the Vietnamese people very well. I got a lot of visitors at the Carpentry Shop.

Moving a completed pre-fab bunker out into the yard
Courtesy: Frank Jackmauh

Visiting ARVN's would be looking for scraps of wood. One time I befriended a Vietnamese Army captain and he wanted some scraps to burn fires. I was invited to his home in Saigon one Sunday and he took me to the zoo with his wife and two children. I was an honored guest and the meal was chicken. Chicken over there was considered more expensive than beef. Some of the hors' d'oeuvres his wife served were a bit unsettling, sitting on a platter as they were with little feet sticking up, but I wasn't brought up to be rude so I indulged.

The Australians were also quite friendly people. We traded food with them for their gin and tonic.

*LCpl **Alan Webster**, Military Police*

There was a Vietnamese family living in one of the hooches outside the Chu Lai gate. This was down by the area where we had a dump. I befriended this family because they were a great source of information. The fact that I didn't take advantage of the papasan's daughter may have helped me get information from them. They invited me to eat with them one time. I was hesitant to do this but I finally relented. They served me a bowl with noodles in it. I just looked at it and finally asked him to eat it first. He grinned and took a bite. Then I ate. He started giving me information. He said "Big gun hit Chu Lai tonight." It turned out that he was right. We got hammered. And he started giving me intel.

I had an aunt that was sending me Care packages. I would give the candy to the kids. They were a good source of information. It's probably an indication that I was doing this stuff right that the VC put a bounty on me.

*Captain **Paul Kaser**, Admin Officer*

I spoke a bit of Vietnamese and we had a well-educated Vietnamese guy who was our translator. We worked with the QC (the Vietnamese Police) from time to time, which was not always easy. I got to know the translator quite well; he had kids and he lived just off the base, which was kind of dangerous for him. I would take him home sometimes and I ate with him a few times although I was told not to do that. He introduced me to some Vietnamese journalists . He was one of the northern refugees that had traveled down to South Vietnam. Most of the refugees from the north were Catholics. In a way it was bad to get to know these Vietnamese because so many of their stories were very sad. I never did find out what happened to the translator when I left. Most of the guys that went into the "Re-education Camps" never came out. After the Fall of Saigon the nuns weren't even allowed to wear their habits.

Ship fitter 3rd Class Diver 2nd Class **Steve Doak**

One of the things we noticed was if an Army base was closed down, within a couple of days it would be stripped clean. They'd take all the metal and everything and either use it for themselves or sell it on the black market. When we turned our boats over to their navy we'd sit by the docks and watch them take all the supplies we had just given them, and we heard they were offloading that stuff into their cars! Whether it was food, gasoline, anything, they'd just take it for themselves.

Spc5 **Tom Moschella**, *Vehicle Repair*

There was an ROK compound near our base. I used to travel between An Khe and Qui Nhon all the time to pick up vehicles or whatever. Cook and I were traveling down the road and there were three or four ROK Marines on the side of the road. They flagged us down and asked us if we were busy. They wanted to go up on the mountain to collect some firewood so we took them up there. The wood collection took several hours and by the time we unloaded it at their base we had to spend the night there. They fed us steaks and it was great. In the morning we were preparing to leave and we saw the ROK's in a formation. The commander called out the four guys who collected the wood. I figured he was going to congratulate them for collecting the wood. Instead he started whipping their asses for kidnapping us like they did.

On another trip to Qui Nhon, going down Highway 9 through the An Khe Pass there was a stretch of road that had been blown out. A sixty foot stretch of road was just gone and the remaining roadbed was taken down to the level of the nearby rice paddy. They had a detour set up so I went on to Qui Nhon and on the way back they had the bridge closed. We had to drive down an embankment and through a creek and up the other side. The reason the bridge was closed was the ROK's had bodies lying from one end to the other. They had thirty or forty VC bodies on that bridge; they went out and found the guys that mined the road.

1st Lieutenant **Edie Meeks**, *Army Nurse Corps*

I loved dealing with the Montagnards because they were short! Diane and I went into the town of Pleiku to see what it was like. We went to the local hospital. The Vietnamese nurses at the hospital worked just during the day and went home at night because it was dangerous to be out at night. We were told, and I don't know if this is true, that if a patient was scheduled to receive for example three liters of fluid during twenty-four hours, they'd give all of it to them during their day shift. So a lot of the families came to take care of the patients because there was no one else to take care of them at night. And they would bring their children and their animals because if they left their animals back at home they might never see them again.

CHAPTER TWENTY-FOUR

SITTING ON A MINE

*Spc5 **Frank Jackmauh**, Surveyor*

In February of 1969 during the Tet (a year after the big Tet) I remember being in my bunk and hearing this artillery fire and realizing that it sounded differently than the normal outgoing artillery fire. Two minutes later lights went off alarms went on and they said we were getting hit. I grabbed a flak jacket and a steel pot, still in my underwear, and ran to a bunker.

We seldom took fire as we were standing in a road doing our surveying. Sometimes when we were pounding stakes in the ground or whatever, we'd pick up sniper fire. But I enjoyed the work I was doing so I went along with that.

Surveyors at Work
Courtesy: Harley Brinkley

*Sgt. **Floyd Jones**, Med. Admin. Specialist*

We had four rocket attacks during my year at the base. One rocket reached the airfield but hit unoccupied land and no one was injured.

*Spc4 **John Martin**, Radar Tech.*

We were hit three times with rockets during my tour. We were never mortared. The big rocket attack during Tet 1969, blew up one of our outhouses and hit our barracks. We had shrapnel holes in the roof and they knocked my wife's picture off the wall, busting the frame.

Rocket Damage
Courtesy: John Martin

Another time we had small arms fire and we thought the VC were inside our perimeter, but it turned out to be a few of our guys on dope shooting at each other.

*Chief **Sidney Brown**, Hull Technician*

We had a load of Air Force helicopter guys that were being shifted from Cam Ranh Bay to the Delta to build a new airstrip. The ship was crowded and we're transiting up the river with everybody up topside. Some of the Air Force guys are sitting in jeeps up on the main deck listening to Armed Forces radio and telling jokes and having a good time. Well you hear the rounds go by before you hear the pop. And when they hit the LST it was like putting marbles in a fruit jar and shaking it. It was metal against metal. Everybody started running for the ladder. Most navy men go down a ladder in times like this without putting feet on the rungs; you just grab the outside and slide down. Well the Air Force officer ahead of me was taking his time climbing down rung by rung. General Quarters is being sounded. The Air Force captain stopped in the middle of the ladder and I landed feet first on his chest. It knocked the breath out of him. I apologized but told him not to stop on a ladder during an attack.

Courtesy: Sid Brown

A couple of weeks later we got stuck on a sandbar on a turn in the river. We were standing topside watching some of our jets really pounding something. Then we heard a whooshing noise from an RPG (rocket propelled grenade). It hit right near me against the edge of one of our lifeboats. The force of the explosion moved in the opposite direction from me, fortunately, and exploded into an armored bulkhead of Radio Central.

Airman 1st Class **Bruce Quinlan**, *Instrument Repairman*

One night I was working in the shop checking an air-speed indicator when the radio announced a Red Option. I grabbed my weapon and I could hear mortar rounds hitting. They started getting louder and louder. The enemy sappers were trying to get inside the base to destroy our repair shops and the C123's. As I was running for the crow's nest the mortar rounds were landing behind me and one of them actually knocked me down. I took a quick assessment of my body and realized that I was not hit. I jumped up and climbed the thirty feet into the crow's nest. When I got to the top all hell broke loose. There were flares all around the perimeter; illumination flares, and red flares. I knew there was imminent danger for an invasion. The Army, the Air Police, the Koreans and Australians; we had a lot of people running around. We heard small arms fire going out but nothing coming in. There were a lot of explosions all around the perimeter. I was told later the explosions were the VC sappers being hit by our small arms fire. All this excitement was very new to me. I was just out of my mind seeing and hearing all these explosions. Once the All Clear was sounded I came down from my crow's nest and I saw that a mortar round had actually landed on my shop. There was shrapnel all through the shop; nobody was hit but some of our equipment was damaged.

LCpl **Alan Webster**, *Military Police*

We had constant incoming mortar and rocket fire at Chu Lai into the early part of 1970. Sitting in my bunker at the front of the base you could hear the rounds going past and you'd wonder if they were going to hit your bunker. The rounds would march their way around the base. It was probably observed fire.

We were out on the road and we drove over something and I heard a click. I told them to stop. I radioed back that we were sitting on a mine. They said they would get somebody out there to deal with it. The guys they sent knew what they were doing and they defused the mine. But that upset me. They were supposed to clear the mines before the convoys went down the road each day.

1st Lieutenant **Edie Meeks**, *Army Nurse Corps*

At Pleiku our hospital was near the Air Base, which meant that we were rocketed fairly frequently. And the plan was for you to put the patients under their beds during a rocket attack or, if you couldn't move them, put a mattress on top of them. One night part of the ER was blown up, and one night the CO's house was blown up. He was thirteen days past his rotation home date and he said "That's it. I'm out of here."

The danger in Saigon when I was there (this was after Tet) was more the drive-by bombing kind of thing. You always had to be on guard. But in Pleiku you expected to be rocketed almost every night. In Pleiku when the first rocket attack came I started to take care of my patients and the soldiers in the beds would say "Now Lieutenant, it isn't going to be that bad." And they started telling jokes so that I wouldn't be afraid. I thought that was the sweetest thing.

Captain **Paul Kaser**, *Admin Officer*

We had some Army guys staying in the transit barracks waiting to go home, and during one of the first rocket attacks I experienced we had to drag them out of the bunkers. They had been drinking and it was hard to get them to move. At least one of them was killed during that attack.

*Spc5 **Tom Moschella**, Vehicle Repair*

We got hit a lot at An Khe; a lot of mortars and sappers. The mortar attack in June of 1969 took out half the choppers that were there and they moved the rest of them down to Tuy Hoa. I guess they got tired of taking these attacks so they sprayed Hong Kong Mountain with Agent Orange and then they bulldozed the mountain bare. They sent half of the MP's at our base down there.

Attacks at An Khe were common. They blew up stuff in my maintenance compound on several occasions. The sappers came through the wire and through our maintenance depot and blew up vehicles as they went through, then blew up the ammo dump, and then went up to the POL and blew it up; the flames from that fuel going up climbed about 500 feet in the air; lots of smoke. On this occasion my buddy Cook and I were out on the Green Line on guard duty. They called and told us to keep an eye out for the sappers coming back through our area. I was watching to our front and Cook was watching out the back and he shook me and said there were people coming our way. We went out and captured two sappers, one of whom was wounded in the neck as they came by. We called it in and the MP's came and took them away.

Courtesy: Tom Moschella

Another time we were on the Green Line at Camp Radcliff (An Khe) and we knew there was a bunch of VC up on the mountain. Our choppers arrived and one of them hovered about thirty feet in the air right above my bunker and let loose with his rockets. My life definitely passed in front of me for a second and I couldn't hear a thing for a week!

One night we received a ground attack; maybe eighty or ninety VC coming across this creek at us. We had two 175's, two 8" guns, and a duster. I was really worried but they lowered a 175 and put a flachette round in it. One minute those guys were there and the next minute they're gone. It just vaporized some of those guys.

Spc4 **Noah Dillion**, *Aircraft Mechanic*

I experienced routine mortar harassment mortars but I never fired my weapon at the enemy. Soc Trang was a free fire zone so I enjoyed firing the "mad minute" but Vinh Long was a no fire zone and I never fired my weapon there.

When I arrived at the 114th I was put in charge of removing the tops of two dozen 55 gallon drums that were going to be used to build the bunker. One of the men on the detail was a kid from Texas with a handlebar mustache. We were told to turn the barrels upside down the evening before because these were empty JP-4 drums. Someone failed to turn one of the drums over and when this kid chiseled the lid loose it dropped to the bottom and the sparks ignited a small amount of JP-4 which flashed off, shooting the lid to heaven knows where. The kid was just standing there dazed from the explosion. It singed his eyebrows and mustache off and he had a soot face like Alfalfa usually had on *OUR GANG*.

CHAPTER TWENTY-FIVE

FRUSTRATIONS AND THE TRADING GAME

1969

Spc5 **Frank Jackmauh**, *Surveyor*

One of my frustrations was that some of the officers went by the book. You could actually discern between OCS candidates and military school graduates and ROTC grads. In 1969 our XO came to the Carpenter Shop and noticed that I had the Massachusetts State flag flying beside the stars and stripes. The governor of Massachusetts had sent me that flag. The XO ordered me to take it down.

Courtesy: Frank Jackmauh

1st Lieutenant **Edie Meeks**, *Army Nurse Corps*

It started raining while I was still in Saigon and was still raining when I got to Pleiku. I remember one whole one wall of my hooch was mildewed. If you tried to wash it off it still came back. So I wrote to my mother and asked her for a shower curtain. When I put it up the mildew was still there but at least now I couldn't see it.

Spc4 **Tom Petersen**, *Radio Repairman/Tower Team*

There was a famous hunting lodge in Ban Me Thout. It was called the Bungalow. Teddy Roosevelt had been there. The Army took it over and made it a signal site. Somehow it had burned down around the beginning of December, 1969, including the whole base and our tower. The story they told was that an army lifer accidentally burned it down while heating his food with a can of Sterno. Of course the wood was old and went up like a match stick. The guys from this base were demoralized that their lovely base was ruined; it was really frustrating and depressing to witness. They were even upset that we were coming in there to get them back up on the air. The captain there was not very successful restoring a positive attitude to the place.

Sgt First Class **Jim Kuipers**, *46th Engr. Bn.*

The seasonal change was from six inches of dust to six inches of mud. Rain or shine, that was your choice. The monsoon did make things rough if you were trying to build a road; if you put dirt down it was washed away. At the Motor Pool we had three bays in a big, tall building with a metal roof open on one side. You could only work on wheeled vehicles although we could get a grader or a dozer in the shop, but doing so might tear up the concrete. One of my bays was a pit. You could work on some tracked vehicles inside but usually you just worked on them outside.

Spc5 **Frank Jackmauh**, *Surveyor*

The monsoon is when our four inches of dust became twelve inches of mud! You could practically set your watch by when the afternoon rain started each day. Monsoon rains were very dangerous when we were constructing a stretch of road involving descent into a valley then up and with a curve in the road also. Tracked vehicles operated on these roads a lot better than wheeled vehicles. But once we got a base down and asphalt poured the road was completely safe.

*Spc4 **Noah Dillion**, Aircraft Mechanic*

I always wondered why they would tape off the windshield and chin bubbles of the hueys. I went to Vung Tau to deliver a damaged aircraft to Bell Helicopter for overhaul. On the way back in a gaggle of three choppers, the rains started as we gained 200 feet. One pilot landed because he wasn't instrument rated, one tried to land on a barge – he missed and went into the drink -- and we kept flying. Our pilot made it back to the airfield on instruments alone. My question was answered the hard way.

*Spc5 **Tom Moschella**, Vehicle Repair*

The monsoon gave you no reason to try to get dry. Our living quarters were up off the water but our junk yard area was under over a foot of water. We rigged up a pallet with some ropes and towed ourselves around like we were water skiing.

*LCpl **Alan Webster**, Military Police*

Why give us rain gear in the monsoon? You were never dry and it was a biting cold. We were escorting a flatbed trailer down towards Duc Pho and they got two flat tires on the trailer. We were stopped and we told the captain we would stay with the trailer. The captain said he was freezing. I told him I carried a bottle of Jack Daniels in my jeep. We stood in the rain getting warm with the Jack Daniels and another flatbed came to take the load off the first truck. It was getting dark so we were hurrying.

1st Lieutenant **Edie Meeks**, *Army Nurse Corps*

We didn't need a neurosurgeon in Saigon because we were able to ship patients out so quickly. But in Pleiku, in the central highlands, we had a neurosurgeon. We had a patient one time with brain damage and after his brain surgery he appeared to be getting better. For me, even as a nursing student, neurosurgery was the toughest because you could fix so little. I had high hopes for this patient but one morning I came to work and they told me he had spiked a temp during the night -- the temperature in his brain was off and he died. It was such a blow.

Ship fitter 3rd Class Diver 2nd Class **Steve Doak**

There was some frustration getting spare parts since most of our repair work was done in the middle of nowhere. We simply had to make do. When we pulled the Zippo boat up the whole side of it was almost gone. This is the boat that had hit a mine. We had some sheet metal flown in by helicopter and we had cutting torches and welding torches and I welded for eighteen hours straight. I was the only welder on that crew. Night, day, overnight. Every time I'd strike an arc I'd get shocked since I was standing in the water. I had welding spark burns on my ankles where the sparks would go down into my combat boot. I still couldn't patch it up like I wanted; I didn't have the time or the equipment I needed. We patched it the best we could and got it pulled off the bank and it just barely floated. The water came right up near the top of the patch but I didn't have any more materials to patch. We hoped that if we went very slowly we might get it back. We threw off machine guns, ammo, anything heavy. We got it about three miles away and water started to come in over the patch. Within ten minutes it was listing and we cut it loose in the middle of the canal. We did get it away from the firebase, which was the plan, but we hoped to get it all the way back to the repair shop and we couldn't. Seeing that boat go under was hard to watch.

LCpl **Alan Webster**, *Military Police*

I stayed in my bunker on the Chu Lai perimeter when I had pneumonia and they took a stripe away from me for that. They said I should not have been there. That did not sit well with me.

*Spc5 **Tom Moschella**, Vehicle Repair*

While at An Khe I was on guard duty. We were under orders NOT to fire our weapons. This one time I heard noises and thought I saw something and I fired. In the morning there was a blood trail where I saw something, and some satchel charges. But they still made me pay for the ammunition I expended!

*Airman 3rd Class **Frank Towns**, Jet Mechanic*

We never knew what our mission or our return cargo would be until it showed up. One time we had eighty to one hundred officers' show up in full dress uniform. They boarded the plane, folded down the seats, and I gave a puzzled look at the cargo master, then I asked the pilot if these guys were going home. "No," he told me, "They're re-enlisting." These officers had come from all four branches of the service -- and they were not combat-types -- to fly in a combat zone **above** Vietnam, to re-enlist in the military. By re-enlisting in a combat zone they received a combat re-enlistment bonus! We went up, circled, stayed up there about 45 minutes and then landed. They all re-enlisted in the air. You will never find that flight on a manifest or on any records. The lowest rank I saw was a major. There were even some generals.

*Spc4 **Garry Ramsey**, Fuel Truck Driver*

Many times on a convoy they wouldn't allow us to go back to the water trailer to refill our canteens. When it is 110 outside it is even hotter in the cab of a tractor. When the monsoon started the roads became seas of mud. Often a truck would slide off the road into a rice paddy. We had to have choppers pull the truck out of the paddy. I saw that happen at least three times.

The mess hall at Cam Ranh Bay was fair. The bread had bugs. When they issued us our seven-day supply of C rations, I held on to my beanies and weenies but I gave a lot of the rest away to the Vietnamese. Coming off guard duty one time we went in to eat. I told the cook I'd have a couple of scrambled eggs. When the cook dipped into the can of grease for the grill there was a big old dead rat in the can. Somehow the rat had worked his way into the can and drowned. I think that was the last time I ate any eggs or anything else in that mess hall.

Communications Technician **Dick Trimbur**

We would always take a medic with us; we never went anywhere without a medic. A couple of times we went in there and the medic would tag and bag something, and a minute later you would see a little movement in the body bag. The overall frustration was in going into harm's way, getting on the ground, and there was nothing there. When you go into the LZ the choppers drop you and they're gone. They don't sit around waiting for you to do your job. Now you have to radio in to get the extraction. The hardest part was watching the choppers leave you not knowing how long you're going to be there.

Spc5 **Frank Jackmauh***, Surveyor*

A mess sergeant from the other side of Long Binh would come to the Carpentry Shop and he would want to borrow four or five of my people. The Vietnamese were anxious to work for him because he would feed them. There was a lot of trading going on. I traded an Omega divers watch to a MACV advisor for a camera once; one guy drove up in a deuce-and-a-half and I didn't see anything in the back of the truck. I didn't understand what he wanted to trade. He pointed to the front seat of the truck where there was a Vietnamese girl sitting. He said "Her, you can have her for a couple of days."

Another guy wanted to trade me a small Cuyese Light Observation helicopter. All I had to do was assemble it. I told him I couldn't do anything with that. I was starting to feel like Monty Hall on Let's make a Deal! My consolation prize was I did receive a couple of Army Commendation medals over there.

CHAPTER TWENTY-SIX

CRONKITE SURRENDERS

After a post-Tet visit to Vietnam CBS newsman Walter Cronkite went on the air to declare the Vietnam War "unwinnable." "If I've lost Cronkite, I've lost Middle America," President Johnson concluded. And so he had.

Newly-elected President Nixon met with South Vietnamese President Thieu on June 8, 1969, on Midway Island where Nixon announced the withdrawal of 25,000 American troops. This announcement also created a de facto change in the goal of each soldier from winning to surviving.

1st Lieutenant **Edie Meeks**, *Army Nurse Corps*

The people I worked with were some of the angriest people I've ever seen; those of us working in the hospitals never saw the victories, all we saw was what was left over. Day after day we would see the bad news. It didn't make any sense because we didn't seem to be going anywhere with the war. There were too many rules for our troops to operate under while the other side could do anything they wanted. It just wasn't fair.

I don't think I felt proud; I concentrated on the losses. Could I have done more? What did I miss? And most times I didn't miss anything. The ones that really stuck in our minds were the ones we couldn't do anything for. But I did appreciate the sense of teamwork among the staff. If you had a busy night and you thought a patient needed some blood you would just order it and the doctors trusted you to do that. I had absolutely fabulous corpsmen. If you told those guys that you needed something all of a sudden it would appear. They'd say, "Don't ask," and I didn't. We never asked and we didn't care as long as we had it there for our patients.

Ship fitter 3rd Class Diver 2nd Class **Steve Doak**

Every time we got a boat up and towed it back for repairs was a proud moment.

*LCpl **Alan Webster**, Military Police*

We were out somewhere and the Army officer told the men to break down their M16's and that I would supervise them doing it. This caught me by surprise but the Marines know their weapons and these Army guys were not as proficient. Anyway one clown didn't listen and he lost the sear off his M16. So now he had a rifle that would only fire one round at a time. And the armorer didn't have any replacement parts.

The Army put me in for a Silver Star for my service under them but the Marine Corps wouldn't let me have it.

*Chief **Sidney Brown**, Hull Technician*

I was awarded the Combat Action Ribbon meaning you were shot at and returned fire.

Courtesy: Sid Brown

*Spc5 **Frank Jackmauh**, Surveyor*

I had no girlfriends or wife when I went over there and while I missed my family and my dog I just accepted my task and got on with the work.

*Airman 3rd Class **Frank Towns**, Jet Mechanic*

On any given day, there might be about 300 hearses lined up to pick up a body for transportation to another location. There was a transient barracks there at Dover for the escort, who would arrive a day early to accompany the deceased to his hometown. One time I was going somewhere off base, and I was pulled over. In fact all the cars on the highway got pulled over. The FBI, MP's and the CIA were swarming all over the place. They were investigating a guy that was transporting drugs from Thailand via military aircraft, in caskets. A second guy had been transporting cigarettes. We had to prove who we were. They made a movie out of the guy shipping the drugs. He said he was making a million dollars a day.

Engineman Jim Fritz

I had numerous combat missions in the Delta and won the Navy Achievement Medal and a Bronze Star.

Courtesy: Jim Fritz

*Spc5 **Tom Moschella**, Vehicle Repair*

We were changing the transmission on a small tracked vehicle. There was an E-7 there pretending he knew everything. I had just been to school for some of this stuff but he wouldn't let me near him so I just sat and watched him try to put it back together wrong. After he left, with the work unfinished, I got three or four guys from the gun crew and put it back together correctly.

**8" Self-propelled Howitzer Engine
Courtesy: Tom Moschella**

*Spc4 **John Martin**, Radar Tech.*

One of the guys in our barracks was a drug user. Somewhere he had inherited a puppy, and he found it amusing to give the dog drugs just to watch it stagger around. Shortly after the staggering began, the dog would lose control of its bowels. Eventually some of us tired of cleaning up after the dog and I complained to the barracks sergeant. He told me to take the dog with me on my next trip on the road, which I did. I let it out in one of the villages. When I returned the drug user had found out that I had taken the dog and he was preparing to pummel me. The barracks sergeant stopped him and told me to "go find his dog."

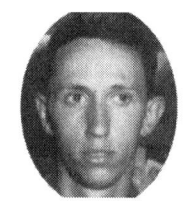

*Spc4 **Garry Ramsey**, Fuel Truck Driver*

I was maybe one of the few not into smoking pot. One time I walked into the head and the nine or ten guys in there all ran out the back door. I guess they figured since I wasn't into pot I must be an informer on those who were!

One morning I came in from guard duty and our Platoon Sergeant, Sergeant Brown, asked me to go talk to Bobby Mitchell and Owens. These guys were both big drinkers and they were going at it pretty good this time. The sergeant wanted me to tell them to go down to the motor pool. When I got there they were still drinking. I was getting nowhere with them so I pretended to see Sergeant Brown coming. They both pretended to be asleep but Mitchell forgot he had a burning cigarette between his fingers which gave them away. Mitchell was not a positive influence on Owens and later they transferred Mitchell to another unit. At his new location he held an M16 up to his captain's chin and demanded a transfer. He got his wish; a one-way ticket out of Vietnam.

*Spc4 **Noah Dillion**, Aircraft Mechanic*

A damaged helicopter was making a final approach. Our fire and rescue trucks raced with the chopper as it moved from the end of the runway to the hangar. The wounded pilot landed near the front of the hangar, which was against regulations, and shut the engine off. The main rotor and tail rotor were still spinning. A crowd of men raced to help remove the wounded. One of my friends went around the back of the chopper to get to a buddy; he realized his mistake too late and he raised his arm to deflect the blade heading for his head. He was struck on the forearm and as he fell the trailing blade hit him again, which broke his arm and caused a serious cut on his forehead. He was put in the ambulance with the man he was trying to help but he was still a lucky man that day. We hangar rats are a close knit group and we were treated like trash by the door gunners and crew chief cliques. We were a very dedicated bunch of young men who grew old way too fast.

Courtesy: Noah Dillion

*Spc4 **Tom Petersen**, Radio Repairman/Tower Team*

I had to go check out a tower on Lang Bian Mountain, near Da Lat, sometime in late 1969, because some dummy drove his truck into the supporting guy wire for the tower. This guy got the wire snagged on his truck and he kept gunning the engine on the truck, not understanding why he wasn't going anywhere. They feared that he twisted the tower. Anyway I got up there pretty late in the evening with a pinnacle helicopter landing on the mountaintop. The Montagnard girls that lived there took me to the mess hall. It was a small base with only one cook; all he had was leftovers and I said that was fine. About six or seven of the Montagnard girls were just sitting there watching me eat these leftovers. They were laughing at my attempts to speak their language.

**Towers on Lang Bian Mountain
Courtesy: Tom Petersen**

Cooks always get a hard time from the troops and this guy was the only cook on this small base. After I'd polished off the leftovers he said he had a peach pie that nobody wanted. He gave it to me and I ate the whole thing over the next half hour. I thought it was pretty good. The next night

I showed up at the regular chow time. Toward the end of the meal the cook shows up with another peach pie. I shared it with the rest of the guys at my table.

I returned a week later for a check on the tower and one of the girls saw me and ran up to the mess hall. When I got to the table all that was sitting there was a peach pie!

*Sgt. **Floyd Jones**, Med. Admin. Specialist*

Nothing made me prouder of my country than the night an Australian flare dropper called in an emergency. These flares were very powerful -- one million candle power. One of their flares had jammed in the launch cradle. With no regard for his personal safety the Australian airman physically grabbed the flare and dislodged it, freeing it from his aircraft in a matter of seconds and saving the lives of his crew members. He had third degree burns over half of his body. His pilot landed at the closest medical facility, who notified us of his emergency. We called Clark AFB in the Philippines and within two hours a C-141 was dispatched to Saigon to pick him up and transport him to Brook Army Burn Center in Texas. Within twenty hours the Australian hero was being treated by the best burn unit in the world. Sadly, he passed nine hours after arriving but the crews transporting and caring for him during those twenty hours did the impossible keeping him alive. His burns were so severe he could not have survived had he been injured in the immediate area of Brook Burn Center.

My pride still swells today knowing that the United States of America would dispatch a single C-141 aircraft configured for "one patient" and more importantly, a wounded soldier from another country. No expense was spared to ensure that we make the best effort possible to save a life. The USA takes care of its own and its friends. I am proud to be from a country with this philosophy.

During my tenure, August 1968 – August 1969, over 17,500 wounded GI's were moved through my unit. Many of these men recuperated and returned to the field. There were two other units like ours: Cam Ranh Bay and Danang. The Navy and Marines had facilities which moved the majority of their wounded.

Captain **Paul Kaser**, *Admin Officer*

After a rocket attack some of the nearby Vietnamese houses were on fire. Some of the Army guys were out there fighting the flames. A reporter was standing there watching. I got to where I hated to see reporters talking to our guys. And I was a journalism major! When Walter Cronkite announced that he didn't think we could win, American support for the war was over. But I think we were starting to learn how to fight and win that war.

CHAPTER TWENTY-SEVEN

SPARE SOCKS

*Sgt. **Floyd Jones**, Med. Admin. Specialist*

As I walked the aisles giving instructions to the wounded about to be sent home one soldier touched me more than any. I approached his bed and he had just finished opening a present. It was in April of 1969. I asked him if it was a birthday present and he said, "No sir, it's a Christmas present that's just caught up with me!" Lying on his stomach were tee shirts, socks and underwear. He looked up at me and said, "Sarge, would you like some socks? I only have one leg now so I'll only need one of each color!" I had to hold back the tears but jokingly told him, "Look at it this way. You know how easy it is to lose a sock? Just think how lucky you are to have "spares" when that happens! You have twice as many as the rest of us for the same price!" He quickly responded saying I was right and that he had to start thinking differently about shoes and socks. This young man was an example of the character I witnessed while meeting with these men and women. With over 17,500 moved in my year of service, I never once heard anyone complain or bitch about their injuries or condition. We truly have the best fighting soldiers and support troops in the world.

*Spc4 **Garry Ramsey**, Fuel Truck Driver*

One of my friends, John Cardwell, had a pet spider monkey named Cherry Boy. John's monkey -- maybe all monkeys in Vietnam -- disliked Vietnamese people, perhaps because the Vietnamese people ate monkeys. Anyway John's monkey would attack the hooch girls. He would jump on them from the rafters and bite them in the neck. We had to restrain the monkey when the girls arrived for work.

*Spc5 **Tom Moschella**, Vehicle Repair*

I was on guard duty at An Khe on one of the towers on our perimeter. The tower is situated about halfway up the mountain and it is a few hundred feet above the road on one side and about five feet from the mountain itself on the other side. We actually had a couple of guys thrown out of the towers by the apes that lived on the mountain. It nearly killed one guy. So when you were in the tower one of you watched the Green Line and the other watched the mountain.

Courtesy: Tom Moschella

*Spc4 **Garry Ramsey**, Fuel Truck Driver*

Most of my problems with rats occurred when I was on guard duty. When you opened your food they'd smell it and come crawling up your legs. There was also a big bug there, like a cockroach with big pincers on it. I was bitten a few times in the back by those bugs.

Driving my fuel truck back from Da Lat the bridge we used had been blown. We did not know the bridge was out and we were going about 30 mph. The trucks ahead of me pulled off the road to the right and when I pulled off the trailer almost flipped on me. In that area there was a lot of high elephant grass growing near the road. I saw something big moving through the grass and coming right at me. I got my truck stopped and a big bull elephant ran right past me.

Ship fitter 3rd Class Diver 2nd Class **Steve Doak**

On another occasion we did a job for the Coast Guard. One of their cutters had run across a Chinese trawler in the middle of the night and when it refused to stop when they fired across its' bow they sank it with gunfire. They wanted us to determine what the cargo on this trawler was. There were four or five of us for this mission. This job was in the South China Sea not some little canal. On the way out I got very seasick. I was almost incapacitated the whole time.

The cutter showed us where the wreck was and we made a series of dives down there to check the cargo. The Coast Guard guys were great hosts and they invited us over for dinner, showers and movies. We determined that the trawler was full of AK-47 ammunition hidden under the nets of the trawler. We also found the crew members of the trawler underneath the nets, dead of course. And one by one during the course of our search they started popping to the surface. The bodies were bloated and the fish had down their work on them as well. The Coast Guard was very pleased that we confirmed their actions with this enemy supply vessel.

Chief **Sidney Brown**, *Hull Technician*

Up near our fuel farm there was a big black panther hiding behind the 55-gallon drums. About the time we were getting ready to shoot the thing we realized we would be shooting into all those oil drums.

In August of 1969 we were ordered to Japan for much-needed repairs. We broke down in the South China Sea, far too close to North Vietnam. The problem was our fuel pump and we had to make a part to fix it. In the meantime we were without power and fresh water. So we drank warm beer and started to hand-make a part. In the meantime, being sailors, we welded some pipes together to make a mast. We rigged a sail for the mast and put a second sail up by the gun mount.

The LST Luzerne County as a Sailing Vessel
Courtesy: Sid Brown

We raised the anchor ball although the water we were in was far too deep to drop anchor. We dipped the anchor. Then we see a ship on the horizon that turns into a Russian freighter bound for North Vietnam, its' decks bristling with artillery. The Russian ship passed us and then slowly turns and comes back. Using a megaphone and in perfect English, the Russian captain asks us if we need any help. "No thank you," our captain replies, "we're just swimming and drinking beer." And so endeth the appearance of the U.S. sailing fleet during the Vietnam War.

*LCpl **Alan Webster**, Military Police*

We were ambushed while on a convoy south of Chu Lai. This occurred during the day. We were on QL1 with a mountain off to one side and rice paddies on the other. The fire was coming from the rice paddies. We took cover behind a log. Then I see a Vietnamese man walking towards me. He was wearing a white shirt and white shorts. He was looking at me and grinning. There was a line of black clad VC behind him in the rice paddies. Then further back in our convoy a captain pulled up and started blazing away with a quad .50. The VC took off. The two Army guys I had with me were new in-country and one of them jumped up and saluted the captain. I told him he shouldn't do that. I told him he just targeted that captain and by right the captain could have shot him. Then the captain came up and got on him. I looked for the guy in white clothes and he was gone too. I don't know who he was. I don't know if he was with them or was being made to go with them or what. I don't know. Afterwards I thought maybe I should have shot him but I didn't. Looking back I guess I'm glad I didn't. But I'll never forget that grin.

A Marine General came to visit Chu Lai. I pulled the security detail at the chopper pad. The general arrived on one of those two-rotor helicopters and he went about his business. About the time he was going to leave the door gunner on his chopper kept motioning to me and pointing downward. This went on for half a minute or so and we couldn't talk because of the propeller noise. Finally I realized that he was pointing to a phone on the outside of the helicopter! I picked it up and it was the general thanking me for providing security for him. Who knew there would be a phone on the outside of the helicopter?

I was sitting in front of the perimeter bunker as dawn was approaching and it was very foggy. I'm just sitting there, no weapon or anything, and the fog is lifting and I see this pair of black pajamas walking toward the base. Charlie is coming in through the fog! I couldn't yell. I couldn't speak. I couldn't move. I could see him and the fog kept lifting. And then it started to lift faster and Charlie booked it out of there.

There was a small island off the coast of Chu Lai and they took me and a sergeant out there one time in a mike boat to see what was going on. They dropped us off with a plan to come back later at a designated time. I didn't like this because there were just the two of us. I saw a Vietnamese guy eat an egg that was just about to hatch; he ate the baby chicken. He just sucked it out. I couldn't do that! If there was anything going on out there besides eating chicken hatchlings the people weren't talking.

I went through the back of the village one time with my interpreter. The interpreter told me the VC would be in the village that night. So I told my guys they should just drive up to the bridge and back all night and avoid the trouble that was waiting in that village. I found a captain and a sergeant in the village that night. I nearly shot the sergeant! The next day I was questioned by the Provost Marshal and a major. They wanted to know what happened last night. I told them nothing happened. They finally told me they knew what had gone on but I wasn't going to squeal. .

I got my military driver's license in Vietnam. We were supposed to chain and lock our vehicles when they were parked to prevent people from stealing them. It was easy to steal unchained vehicles since they didn't need a key to start them. Part of my job was to check vehicles to see that they were secure. One day a sergeant and I found a jeep that was not secured and we drove it up to the motor pool and they issued me a military driver's license for driving in the jeep. Then we found a ¾ ton truck and did the same thing. They noted that on my license too. Then I drove a deuce-and-a half into the motor pool and finally a 5-ton truck. At that point the Motor Pool captain told me not to drive a tractor trailer in there next! I had to break the law, stealing vehicles, to get legal on driving the vehicles! Meanwhile, the drivers of those vehicles would have to go to the motor pool and explain why they hadn't secured them.

*Chief **Sidney Brown**, Hull Technician*

Our drinking water came from machines called edulators, which we obtained from the US Army. The process spins the water around like a centrifuge and with the addition of chemicals purifies the water. It does not extract Agent Orange however. After you have seen dead water buffaloes in the river it is hard to be enthusiastic about drinking the "purified" water, or bathing in it, or doing anything with it. Our edulator broke once in March, 1969, and I was sent with three other guys to get some fresh water from the Air Force at their water purification plant. When we arrived at their location they told us to take all we wanted but that we should get out of that spot about a half hour before the sun went down. We were seven miles up the Basaac River, in a bad place. It was after dark when we left the place with only half the load of water we hoped to get. We came across a mass of military vehicles blocking the road ahead of us. There were tanks, APC's, halftracks, just about everything. They were manned by the ARVN. "What are you doing here?" they asked us. We told them. They thought we were crazy. "There is going to be a war here in a minute," they told us. We pressed on for the ship. After a while we could hear a lot of shooting behind us with red (us) and green (VC) tracers filling the air. Back at the ship one of the officers insisted we go back for more water. We asked him to look at how the sky was lit up in that direction. "You can court martial me, lieutenant" I told him, "but I'm not going back there." He went to discuss it with the captain and we heard no more about it.

Ship fitter 3rd Class Diver 2nd Class **Steve Doak**

I got into a fire fight one time and earned my Combat Action Ribbon. There were a bunch of our boats -- all types and sizes -- on an operation, including a boat with a 30mm cannon, and a zippo boat, which shot flames, and another boat called the Monitor, that had a 60mm cannon, a couple of 50 calibers and a mortar pit on it. Our objective was the salvage of a Monitor that had been sunk. These boats are very expensive and we wanted to retrieve it if we could.

Knowing that the wreck was in a hot zone of the delta we went in with over fifteen boats. Many of the boats were manned by Vietnamese. We started receiving fire from the shore the night before. The next morning they spread out all the Americans amongst the boats. My boat was the last in line going in. I felt vulnerable. We were not in a canal; it was more of a river tributary. We were zigzagging. Our boat kept steering into the banks of the river, then backing out, and then repeating this move. The other boats were just losing us since they were not over-steering as our boat was. We found the wreck and we were diving over top of it. We had Vietnamese soldiers on one bank and they choppered in some ARVN to protect us from the other bank. Helicopter gunboats were above us for additional protection.

We dived on this wreck for about a day; at one point VC started walking mortars toward us on the river. We had a guy in the water and we pulled him up so he wouldn't get his eardrums burst. We cut our anchor line and all the other attached ropes; all the other boats had taken off and there were just two boats, including us, in the middle of the river. Each of us left in a different direction.

The next morning we returned but we were hit with small arms and P40 rocket fire from the bank. We had been authorized to spray the shoreline on our way in so there was a high volume of fire from our fifteen boats. Then we heard a different sound which we identified as P40 rockets from the shoreline coming toward us. My boat was again toward the rear of the column and I saw the rounds spraying the boat in front of us and I figured we'd be next. Another American, a chief petty officer, was with me in the boat and he and I were firing our M16's toward the shore. A P40 round landed just short of our boat and threw shrapnel all over us. Both of us were knocked backwards into the boat. When I turned to look at him I saw he had taken most of the shrapnel in his left arm. His flak jacket had protected him from greater injury. He had a big tattoo of a leopard that he was very proud of on his arm. Half of it was gone. I had a little bloody string down the inside of my forearm. I dropped what I was doing and started bandaging his arm. A lot of firing was still going on but our ship was finally able to get out to the main river where we could lick our wounds and get organized. Medevac choppers were called for the chief petty officer and some Vietnamese guys in some of the other boats.

The medic was looking at the chief and he asked me if I got anything. I showed him the little trickle of blood on my forearm and asked him if it deserved a Purple Heart. "Nope," he answered. The chief told me if I got a Purple Heart he would kick my ass! "But I'm wounded," I laughed.

Spc5 **Tom Moschella**, *Vehicle Repair*

At Tuy Hoa I'm coming back from an LZ. I'm in a chopper and everything was normal until we got close to Tuy Hoa. The pilot was flying about twenty feet above the beach and he swings out over the water and he buzzes the Air Force base and he does the same thing at the Army base. When he gets to our landing area he zooms up several hundred feet and swings out over the ocean, and he's flying sideways. Since all the seats were taken by other guys I was sitting in the middle of the floor. I'm sitting on my toolbox with the strap of my M16 in my hand. When he turned sideways I dropped; I was floating in mid-air. I was still in the chopper but my toolbox, helmet and M16 all went to the bottom of the South China Sea. My nipples are on the deck of the chopper but the rest of me was hanging out the open door of the chopper. One guy grabbed the back of my uniform and held on and I grabbed a pole on the bottom of one of the seats. I'm flapping in the air. He lands the chopper and while the blades are still rotating the pilot and co-pilot exit the chopper and take off, so I didn't kill them. And I had to jump through hoops to get a new rifle.

Working on a big gun at an LZ one time I was taking the unit apart and they got a fire mission. Those guys were waving at me to get the hell off the track. I was going to change the governor and the crew was responsible for the fuel cutoff. But they hadn't tightened the cutoff switch. When I started it up it started to run away. All of us jumped off the track and the motor's just running away. So I grabbed a 9/16 socket and got back on and shut each fuel injector down, one at a time. When I had the motor shut off I'm standing there as happy as hell and the gun in the next pit goes off and it blew me about fifteen feet away. I couldn't hear a thing for ten days. The fun part was after I got it all put back together I took it out for a test drive. This is an M60 base with a 175mm gun on it and I'm tooling down the road at 35mph. I hit a bump and the gun barrel starts rocking up and down. I thought I was going to lose the damn thing.

*Spc4 **John Martin**, Radar Tech*

I was making a call at a firebase and needed to go to another base for a part. My jeep was stopped on a bridge due to VC activity. It was a long delay and night was falling. The tankers guarding the bridge invited me to spend the night in their bunker but due to all the rats I saw walking around the bunker I declined and slept in the jeep.

*Engineman **Jim Fritz**, Mobile Riverine Force*

We had two empty mike boats tow an empty barge down the river to the South China Sea for purposes of loading the barge with JP-5 diesel fuel. Chief Towery was in charge of this and there were about six of us with him. We recognized if we were hit on the way down river the barge would blow up due to the gas fumes; on the way back loaded with JP-5, the barge would just burn.

Spc5 **Frank Jackmauh**, *Surveyor*

Six or seven of us from the surveying team bought a pallet of beer from the Long Bing PX. There were 72 cases but within three weeks it was gone. We didn't turn anyone else away so we did have some help.

Captain **Paul Kaser**, *Admin Office*

The monsoon created lots of flooding. The road between Bien Hoa and Saigon was a problem. I think it messed up our water supply on the base since we were using the old French plumbing system. The monsoon also brought out a lot of snakes. I got a call that the guys had grabbed a very large constrictor snake. When I got out there they had already killed it. I was disappointed; I thought maybe we could make it our mascot. But the sergeant said he wanted to make a belt out of it.

Spc4 **Noah Dillion**, *Aircraft Mechanic*

I was on guard duty one night, and I heard a boy yelling out *Choi Hoi*. He had his hands on top of his head. I told him to lie down in the road in my beam of light. I called the OD and several guys came down the road in a jeep and stopped. One of the interrogators found a live mortar round on the side of the road. I was later told the kid had been recruited by the VC against his will; they were holding his older brother as leverage.

Courtesy: Noah Dillion

When I made E-5 I was Sergeant of the Guard when I pulled guard duty. One night a guard complained about a pain in his hand. The hand was swollen to the size of a football. This man was medevac ked. A week later another guard on this bunker called to tell me that a snake was crawling toward his position. I identified the sand cobra with the STARLIGHT on my M-14. I told the guard to keep an eye on it; seconds later he stood up and shot the snake with his rifle. He made his shot from the hip without taking aim. The OD pulled up in his jeep with three other men. Vinh Long airfield was a no fire zone. One of them found the snake and verified that it was a cobra. I concluded that the bunker was a snake pit and asked that we abandon it. My request was refused but they allowed the guards to stay up top on the tower. In the morning engineers lifted the top of the bunker off and found the floor crawling with baby cobras.

CHAPTER TWENTY-EIGHT

THE END OF THE MIDDLE YEARS

The dress rehearsal for the 1969 Hope Show was held at the White House. General Westmoreland was in attendance. From there Hope entertained soldiers in dress uniforms in Berlin. It was easy flying into Berlin, Hope mused. "You just stay between the tracers." The troupe then flew to the USS Saratoga, off the coast of Italy "I was piped aboard. They used a real pipe!" Next stop was a base in Turkey and then Sharia, in the Persian Gulf. Was Hope getting a head start on the next war?

Bob landed in Bangkok and then went to Lai Khe; his fifth visit there. "It's one of my favorite swamps." At Long Binh he observed that "all the big brass are here. It's like a slow leak at the Pentagon." At Nakhon Phanom, four miles from the Mekong River, Hope told the troops that if they listened carefully they "could hear neutral troops carrying neutral ammo down neutral trails." At U-Tapao he did a night show and had some negative comments about the Paris Peace talks.

Admiral McCain and Cardinal Cooke visited the show at Cu Chi, and they hit Chu Lai "mid-monsoon." They did the USS Ranger and the USS Sanctuary, and a Christmas Show at Camp Eagle, near Hue, for the 101st. Next they visited Khorat, then Danang, where Neil Armstrong received a big hand. They landed on Taiwan on their return trip to the States.

Was it the best or worst of times? By the end of 1969 troop reductions had begun but activity in Laos and Cambodia had increased. Ho Chi Minh was dead, President Johnson, Robert McNamara and General Westmoreland were no longer in charge, but the killing continued. More Americans were killed after Paris Peace Talks began than before.

As part of the price paid for our naval bombardment of the North Vietnamese coast during the Middle Years twenty-nine of our ships were hit by counter-battery fire. No ships were sunk, but five sailors were killed and twenty-six wounded.[lxiv]

For Support Troops the grind continued. Engineering efforts had shifted from base construction to roads and bridges by 1968 and would ultimately result in 3,000 miles of new or improved highways.[lxv] By late 1967 attention was directed to the secondary road network and by mid-1970 75% of the scheduled work was accomplished. Due to the importance of jungle clearing to combat operations the *concept of "dozer-infantry teams" was developed wherein bulldozers equipped with Rome Plows became part of the assault force.[lxvi] Much of the road and bridge work was done for military purposes but a secondary issue was the development of the South Vietnamese infrastructure.[lxvii] Pacification difficulties were also lessened. Secretary of Defense Melvin Laird limited new construction to things which "Vietnamized" the war effort.*

To handle an army in battle is much less difficult than to bring it on to the field in good condition.[lxviii] By 1967 a million ton of supplies were coming in averaging one hundred pounds a day for every G.I. there.[lxix] Management of everything required automation. IBM 7010/1460 computers replaced the UNIVAC 1005,[lxx] port facilities were enlarged[lxxi] and the average waiting time for a berth improved from twenty days in 1965 to two by 1970. By 1969 the 1st Logistical Command had grown to over 10,000 men and the 34th General Support & Aviation to 7,000.[lxxii] The introduction of several shallow-draft ports increased annual shipping tenfold. The DeLong piers were very effective.[lxxiii] By late 1967 McNamara initiated action against excess materiel.

The 1st Signal Brigade was activated in April, 1966 and numbered over 20,000 men a year later.[lxxiv] By summer 1968 dial telephone exchanges, secure voice terminals and message and data transmission facilities were in every major logistical installation.[lxxv]

By 1968 all helicopter-evacuees were within thirty minutes of hospital care.[lxxvi] Over half a million casualties were picked up by helicopters during the Middle Years alone. U.S. personnel were the top medical priority, followed by U.S. dogs from the Canine Corps. The next priority was NVA, then VC, then our allies, the ARVN. They were last because they had no particular intelligence value. Civilians were at the bottom of the ladder.[lxxvii]

MASH units became MUST units[lxxviii] (Medical Unit, Self-Contained Transportable), but the inflatable units were easily punctured by shell fragments.

AN-TPS-25A Ground Surveillance radar became a critical item. Production of this item had ceased in 1959 so requirements in Vietnam were found at Reserve units in the U.S.[lxxix] By early 1967 APC's were converted from gas to diesel and the overhaul of all USA river craft was begun.[lxxx]

In May, 1967, the existing mortuary facility at Tan Son Nhut was deemed to be inadequate and a new mortuary was constructed on the air base in September, 1968.[lxxxi]

In June, 1969, our engineers began turning their equipment over to the ARVN. During 1968 and 1969 the following structures were built:[lxxxii]

Schools	1253	*Churches*	263
Hospitals	175	*Dispensaries*	422
Marketplaces	153	*Bridges*	598
Roads (km)	3154	*Dwellings*	7099

*Some portions of the American public were mollified by the troop reductions and Vietnamization, but more surprises awaited them in the 1970's. Vietnam was not the "war to end all wars," as Woodrow Wilson described World War I; by 1970, people would settle for the end of **this** war.*

PART THREE

SNIPPING THE TAIL

LATE YEARS -- 1970 -- 1975

By 1970 the word quagmire was synonymous with Vietnam. But the work went on; many of the career military men – known as "lifers" – embarked on their second or third tours, while the recently drafted marched into uncertainty, perhaps fearful that they were merely reinforcing defeat

*In Vietnam it was War As Usual. Westmoreland was gone but his Search and Destroy policies lived on, still guiding the combat troops, albeit with lessened enthusiasm. By this stage of the war the support troops had something the combat troops lacked – **purpose**. They just kept going to work, either supporting the combat troops or building the Vietnamese infrastructure. By late 1969 Vietnam's secondary roads were receiving more attention from Army engineers.[lxxxiii] By spring of 1970 nearly half of the US Army Engineer Command was working on highway construction. These efforts helped to revive the local economy. In the Delta, a clay-lime stabilization process was developed to offset the shortages of rock. The new roads required the construction of 250 bridges,[lxxxiv] fifty of which were built by the newly-formed ARVN engineering units. Engineers also led the way into Cambodia, using Rome plows and flying cranes to carve out Landing Zones and firebases.[lxxxv]*

While prosecuting the war was still a full time job the work of shutting it down began. Processing material for the retrograde movement – leaving Vietnam – required three times the effort as our arrival.[lxxxvi] Equipment was prepared for return to the U.S., given to the South Vietnamese, or destroyed.

CHAPTER TWENTY-NINE

TOO MANY PEOPLE, NOT ENOUGH WAR?

1970

Although U.S. troop strength had been reduced by a third since 1968, Vietnamization and reduced roles for Americans sometimes resulted in a condition that did not exist in the earlier years of the war – boredom.

Spc5 **Frank Jackmauh**, *Surveyor*

When I extended my tour in Vietnam for six months I was given a thirty day leave anywhere in the world. I was planning to go to Innsbruck, Austria to visit a friend from my basic training days but my folks hadn't shipped my winter clothing so I went back to Boston instead. I stayed there eight or nine days and this was in February of 1970 and, since I had come out of a warm climate I just got on the plane early and returned to Vietnam. Boston was just too cold.

I spent most of my remaining Vietnam time in Xuan Loc. I also had a 40-day TDY to Ham Ton (on the coast) to look for potential rock quarry sites. I surveyed the "new" QL-1 (Highway 1) between QL-20 and Gia Rey. This was a stretch of about 32 kilometers. It was somewhat up and down but not mountainous. There were gradual slopes, probably no more than two or three degrees. All the drawings were done in France and everything was in metric units. This work was actually begun back in 1969 and spilled over into 1970. When I left Vietnam in November of 1970 this work was ongoing.

We worked ten to twelve hours a day, seven days a week. We worked all the time but there was nowhere for us to go. I was surveying, or what they call "laying out the road." We would be driving in elevation stakes every 25' or so along the road.

Ambush Alley in Background
Courtesy: John Freemyer

Being engineers we brought a pre-fab hooch to Xuan Loc. At Gia Rey I slept in 3' wide culvert halves. I slept in the culvert, under the culvert, or in jungle hammocks, depending on where we were. We only stayed there a few times. At Ham Ton we stayed with the 25th Division Artillery.

Bosun Mate Chief **Don McMurray**, *USS Askari ARL-30, Dong Tam, USN*

Between tours I was stationed at Willow Grove, Pennsylvania. I went back in June, 1970, again to Dong Tam, which was growing by the day. We repaired, replenished and serviced the whole river craft, not just the engines like on my last tour. On the first tour we were inside the basin, this time we ran with the *Askari* from Saigon to Cambodia.

USS Askari ARL-30
Courtesy: Don McMurray

We had a 72,000 ton A-frame lifting capability. We used a big hook; the boats either had river damage or shrapnel. We had two big ammis tied alongside the ship and we would put a 30 degree list on the boat to return them to an even keel. We would swing this ammis underneath it and sit the damaged boat down on railroad ties and the mechanics would do their thing, change the screws or whatever. We'd work ten – twelve hours then every two or three days we would move. This ship was self-propelled so we had to man our stations and move up and down the river so they couldn't zero in on us.

*Lt. Cdr. **Paul Gesswein**, Deputy Commander, Giant Slingshot, USN*

Courtesy: Paul Gesswein

On my second visit to Vietnam I flew into Long Binh in September, 1970. I was issued equipment there and met my boss, (who was in the hospital recuperating from a gunshot wound), the people to whom I would be reporting, and then I went up to Ben Luc to begin my job with Operation Giant Slingshot. Ben Luc was an intermediate support base for Giant Slingshot containing probably less than two hundred men, including Navy, Seabees, Seals, ARVN, dust offs, sea wolves, psyops guys; a real military melting pot. I lived in a two-man hooch. I had a dog and a jeep.

I was the Senior Advisor to a CTG (Commander Task Group) stationed in the so-called Parrot's Beak area, the triangle between the Vam Co Dong and Vam Co Tay Rivers jutting into South Vietnam west of Saigon and east of the Cambodian border. The Parrott's Beak geography harbored significant NVA infiltration routes into the Mekong Delta, the breadbasket of Vietnam, and efforts to deter this infiltration had begun back in October, 1968.

We had five ATSB's (Advanced Tactical Support Bases) under our supervision. There were four on one river, and one on the other and they had PBR's going out on patrol. The Vietnamese, under the Vietnamization Program, were in charge. I was the Senior Advisor to them. I helped them plan the operations. I had a counterpart who was in charge of the security of the base, the supplies, the repairs, that sort of thing.

*Petty Officer 3rd Class **Vince Malaterra**, Engineer Aide, MCB-3, Seabees, USN*

After my first tour in Vietnam, I went to Guam and was working on the air base there. They were gearing up for the use of B-52's there. My job was to set up the coral crushing plant. They mixed crushed coral with asphalt for the runway. That's when the government found out that working with coral seemed to create all kinds of sores and eye and lung irritations from the dust of the coral.

I returned to Vietnam for my second tour in September, 1970. We came in at Bien Hoa and from there we went to Ca Mau. From there we went to Chow Dunk; there we erected some sort of barracks which they planned to turn over to the South Vietnamese at some time for use as a school, housing, or whatever. But that never happened.

On the second tour, we built LZ's (landing zones). We would take in our team of fourteen and in a week we would have everything plowed under, air matting put down, fuel bunkers put in, ammo bunkers installed, generators ready to go ahead to rearm these choppers to get them back in the air. They were air dropping us all the machinery we needed to get the work done -- earth compactors and things -- and I'm watching them parachute this heavy equipment out of the back of a plane.

*Engineman **Jim Fritz**, Mobile Riverine Force*

My final five months in Vietnam were spent on Operation Sea Float down at the southern tip of the Delta. The camp was Nam Can and we had about a hundred guys there.

Ship fitter 3rd Class Diver 2nd Class **Steve Doak**

Shortly after we started the Vietnamization Program I lived on a boat. We were training Vietnamese to learn the salvage procedures and they would be given the boats when we left. We kept a couple of the old Mike boats (LCM's) for ourselves and the living quarters on that thing were just bolted onto the deck. They had canvas tops to keep the rain off us. Two of us built plywood hooch up by the wheelhouse and we lived there on cots. Our shower consisted of dumping a bucket with a rope attached into the river or canal. We used that bucket for soaping and rinsing. That is the same water where you would see the floating dead pigs and things. I never pulled up a snake or anything in the bucket but one time I'm rinsing off and I notice an old mamasan over at the bank taking a crap in the canal. We also lived in the barracks at Cat Lo, down near Vung Tau. There we had regular beds, bathrooms and showers.

1stLt **Dick Immes**, *Pilot, 90th Attack Squadron, Bien Hoa, USAF*

I arrived at Bien Hoa on Christmas Eve, 1969. The Air Force had about 10,000 people there at that time. I flew the A37, which was derivative of the T37 trainer plane the Air Force used. This plane was used primarily in ground support operations. It was well suited for this type of work. We had a very stable bombing platform and we could lay our bomb within fifteen feet of the target or the smoke grenade. Every time. We were as accurate as the A1's but we were faster and could get on and off the target quicker. You had to do the calculations in your head since it was a manual sight, sort of like Alvin York in WW I.

The A37 was a two seater, but you rarely flew with the second guy unless you were doing some photo work. When Cambodia opened up there were not enough photo planes so we filled in and took some of those missions. We did a lot of checking on the bridge locations in Cambodia to see if there were any changes. We were photographing those sights almost daily. We also had a 70mm camera in the belly of the airplane and we were taking a strip of pictures for the intelligence people, but most of what we did was close air support.

*Captain **Paul Kaser**, Admin Officer*

In May of 1970 I was made adjutant to the base commander until my departure for home in October. During that period I was Chief of Administration for the 3rd Tactical Fighter Wing and commander of the Headquarters Squadron section of the Group. This period was mostly spent in the commander's office.

*SSgt **Allen Thomas, Jr.**, 124th Signal Battalion, 4th I/D*

After my second Southeast Asia tour I went to the 3rd Armored Division in Germany. From Germany I flew into Danang in May of 1970. From Danang we were on a truck convoy to An Khe. I reported to the 124th Signal Battalion, my old unit, part of the 4th Infantry Division.

On this tour I didn't have a job! When I arrived they were supposed to have five staff sergeants in my MOS; they had fifty or sixty. I kept looking for something to do and I finally became an assistant to the battalion sergeant major. He called me his technical assistant and he used me to talk to people he didn't want to talk to. After a while I morphed into being a career counselor trying to talk to people about staying in the army. That work lasted until I took the seven top E-6's in the battalion out of their job. I guess I was too good at this job! These guys weren't ineffective but they wanted out of our unit; they wanted to go to a better place. They wanted a place where they had beds, lights and hot food; no mud.

By October the 4th Infantry Division shut down; they were on their way home and I was sent to the Americal Division at Chu Lai where they had replaced the Marines. I would have preferred to chopper to Chu Lai but we drove. After hitting two land mines I was not anxious to be behind the wheel again, but we were short on drivers. That was a very long drive.

We got there right after a typhoon so they needed us; communications were out. So for a month I was doing what I was trained to do. After things were up and running I was out of work again. This time they had more than one hundred E-6's so we just sat around with a lot of food and a lot of booze. I worked in the NCO club when I was off duty although I was never really "on" duty. I finally went out and **found** a job. I went to S-3 (Operations), The Operations group had a lot of communications issues and no one to resolve them, and so I fit right in. I ran S-3 commo.

Both at the 4th Infantry Division and the Americal Division, I was putting in time because they had too many people. The war was winding down. I just went out and found myself something to do to keep me occupied.

Living conditions at An Khe were okay; we had wood huts, but they were crowded. At Chu Lai, we were in an nco quarters with wood hooches, beds with mattresses, and fans. One good thing about having so many people around doing nothing is that we were able to keep the bases very clean.

*SSgt **Jack Stroud**, Commo Chief*

After my second tour in Vietnam, I was assigned to Ft. Bragg, NC, but ended up sleeping in the streets of Baltimore! I was with the 4th Bn., 74th Artillery and we had riot duty. From there I went to the 3/17th Combat Engineer Group in Eschborne, Germany.

For my final tour I flew into Bien Hoa in June of 1970 and was stationed at Ban Me Thuot. I was the Commo Chief for the 2/17th. This was the HQ Battery for the 17th Artillery Regiment. There were six rooms down there that the guys stayed in. My job was sending SitReps every night! I would get the SitRep set up on the teletype and ready to go and my operators would send it. It was their job to get the entire SitRep sent. These things were usually ten or more pages long. Being in charge, I had a 24/7 responsibility.

I started my first tour in Thailand, living in a hotel. On my second tour we lived in hooches, although our work space was a hotel. On my final tour, home was a bunker surrounded by sandbags.

*Pfc **Bill McGonigal**, Fuel Handling Specialist, 114th Assault Helicopters. 1st Aviation Brigade, USA*

I landed at Tan Son Nhut airbase in September of 1970 and was choppered to Binh Long. I was sitting in the door gunner's seat and when we hit Binh Long, the pilot turned the chopper on its' side, and there was nothing between me and the ground. It was awesome. After that I went up every chance I could get. He did that to scare me but it didn't. I enjoyed it.

I received a degree in mineral economics from Penn State. My draft number was 44; I graduated on Sunday and the notice to report for my physical was on Monday. I enlisted to get the MOS I wanted. The nearest thing I could find to my college background was fuel handling specialist. I think my mechanical ability was of more help than my degree.

My duties included supplying fuel **to and from** helicopters. I worked 12/7 and by the time I left Vietnam I was the ncoic of refueling helicopters. Once the commanding officer's helicopter had some contaminated fuel. They came and got me out of bed because I was the only one that knew how to take the fuel **out** of a helicopter. They occasionally had to work on a helicopter and this required taking the fuel out of it also.

We lived in a single floor hooch. No a/c or fans. We had spiders and mosquitoes. Spiders were our best friend because they provided the cobwebs to catch the mosquitoes. When you first get in country the first thing you do is tear down all the cobwebs. And you find out that that was a big mistake. You learned to live with the spiders.

*Electricians Mate/Fireman **Bob Miller**, USS George K. MacKenzie DD-836,*

I was raised in Chicago. My dad was a WW II vet (Pacific) and he agreed to pay for my college if I maintained a 2.5. I got a 2.2 and a letter from the Draft Board, so I joined the Navy Reserves.

Courtesy: Bob Miller

I did two years Inactive and then went on Active Duty. I actually flew over to join my ship at Subic Bay, in the Philippines. On the way we landed on Guam. We saw rows and rows of B-52's but were pointedly told there would be "no pictures taken." I was an electrician's mate/fireman aboard a WW II tin can. My battle station on this tour was the forward 5" gun mount.

Hull Technician Chief **Jim Sooy**, *USS Samuel Gompers AD-37, USN*

I entered the navy in 1957. I was a diver at one point and then I went into nucleonics, which is the testing and evaluation of metals. Eighty-five percent of nucleonics is math. You're taking metal apart, examining it with high power microscopes, ultra sonic sound waves, radiation, cobalt 60 and iridium 195.

The *Gompers*, affectionately known to the crew as "Fat Sam," was a Destroyer Tender – a floating repair shop. The *Gompers* had a hospital on board, and seven complete repair shops, and could literally build a new ship. We had metal smiths, machine repair, electronics, radiation, weapons, etc. Up to seven vessels could nest alongside the *Gompers* while being repaired. We always had three or four ships tied alongside.

Four destroyers "nested" alongside "Fat Sam"

March 13, 1970 *Gompers* deployed to South Pacific. Our first job was to deliver some dependents to Yokosuka, Japan. The *Gompers* had its' 5" gun removed, and had only four .50 caliber mg's, and was never supposed to be put in harm's way, but everything around Vietnam was in harm's way.

Pfc **Bernie Wright**, *Wireman/Switchboard Repair, 79th Maint. Bn., USA*

I flew TWA into Bien Hoa in April of 1970. As I was being processed in I commented on a terrible odor. The clerk told me they were burning the shitters, and he told me I'd probably get to do some of that over the next few days, but then a colonel told the clerk they needed my MOS at Long Binh right away and I was on my way. The colonel told me I was needed to repair switchboards. I told him I was a wireman. He said "you're a switchboard repairman now." It sounded better than frying shit!

Courtesy: Bernie Wright

I had no training for switchboard repair, either in the States or in Vietnam. They pointed me at one and they were very surprised when I was able to figure it out. I was always good at tinkering. We worked a six day week, 0730 to 1630 day but sometimes you had to work more. I was sometimes choppered to remote locations to repair their switchboards. I went to a number of bases in the general vicinity of Long Binh and I went down to the piers at Saigon a time or two. We lived in screened-in hooches. We had no problems with rats, maybe because our chow was so bad.

*2ndLt. **Jane McCarthy**, Nurse, 95th Evacuation Hospital, Danang, USA*

I had completed two years of nursing school and it seemed like I was constantly traveling back home to my small town of Cohasset, Massachusetts to attend the funeral of a friend that had been killed in Vietnam. So the Vietnam War was bothering me before I even got into it! I made yet another trip back there for a funeral during Tet of 1968 and I felt like I had to do something. At that time our little town had lost eight boys. I talked to an Army recruiter in Boston and was inducted into the Army Student Nursing program. They paid me for my last year in nursing school and then I owed them two years of military service as a commissioned officer in the Army Nurse Corps. After nursing school I went to basic training in Texas and then I spent ten months at Walter Reed Hospital working in the ICU recovery room there. I got orders to Vietnam in September, 1970.

I flew to Oakland, California and from there to Hawaii. I was the only female among a couple of hundred soldiers on the plane! I remember thinking "Now Jane, don't let this go to your head. You're going to think you're pretty special here!" Somebody on the plane said "Look to your left and look to your right; one of you isn't going to come back!" I spent time looking out the window and crying about every fifteen minutes or so of this long flight. After Hawaii we landed briefly on Guam, and then we arrived at Tan Son Nhut, in Saigon. I spent three days there living in a small quarters with a few other females that reminded me of a hut like we built as kids growing up, except this place had concertina wire all around it with a guard walking the perimeter. Then they took me down to meet with the chief nurse of the Army and she told me she was going to send me to Danang.

I flew on a C130 to Danang with my usual two hundred GI companions. There were no seats and we crammed our duffel bags into the plane. They strapped eleven of us in at a time. We flew to Chu Lai first and we pulled off all the duffel bags when we arrived, so they could remove the bags of those who were staying there. We landed somewhere else on that trip also and at each stop all the duffel bags had to be pulled off, and then reloaded.

We finally arrived at Danang in the evening and they took me to a place where there were some Donut Dollies, and I spent the night there. I was taken to the hospital the next day. I met with the Chief Nurse, who said "I don't know what I'm going to do with you." She told me to go find my hooch and to come back in three days when I was settled. When I reported back to her a few days later she put me in the ICU where I worked for just a couple of weeks. Then I was moved down to Pre-Op & Receiving.

We were a typical ER and we treated walk-in problems. I dealt with a lot of drug overdose and drug withdrawal. Heroin was the worst. Some of those on heroin that were due to rotate home soon knew they had to get off that stuff. And we also had malaria and we delivered babies for Vietnamese civilians. We had an OBGYN doc. And the hospital wards wouldn't take Vietnamese women who were about to deliver so we had to do it.

Courtesy: Jane McCarthy

My duties at Pre-Op were to meet the incoming casualties, put them on gurneys, begin a chart on them, get their blood pressure, get some history, assess their wounds, and start IV's; I got really good at starting external jugular IV's and this was a very important part of my job. I would get them to X-ray if necessary, determine their blood type (to do this we used a syringe and a stick in the femoral artery -- we didn't rely on the blood type that was on their dog tags), call the surgeon that would be needed for this type of wound, and prepare them for surgery. We would also get the necessary blood from the blood bank. If the guy was in shock we would get two liters of O neg blood right away. O neg is kind of a universal blood type. I would start pumping the O Neg in -- we had blood bags we used -- and by the time I had the O neg used up the blood bank guy would be back with his specific blood type. We also had to assess their air way; if the guy was asleep we would bring someone in to intubate them. All this was done to stabilize the patient. But sometimes we didn't have time to get them to X-ray; we moved them straight to the OR.

Courtesy: Jane McCarthy

We were right down the road from Camp Kenshaw. I looked east over the South China Sea. Of course you could not have walked to the ocean because of the concertina wire and the perimeter guards. On the other side of the perimeter was a Vietnamese fishing village. We were at the base of Monkey Mountain. Our living quarters for officers (doctors and nurses) consisted of three two-story barracks, A, B and C. A was women only, B was women on the bottom floor, and C was all men. I had my own 8' by 8' room with a cot, a very thin mattress and folding chair. I also had some shelves. We had a mamasan that we paid $4 to do laundry, iron fatigues, polish boots and clean the room.

Spc4 **Larry Gombos***, Graves Registration, Personal Property Depot, USA*

For the first few weeks of my Graves Registration duty I had to go by lots of body parts and sights that were hard to look at. Later I was responsible for the removal of jewelry and the packaging of personal items such as stereos for mailing home. After that I had the job of going through letters and personal items to determine what should be included in the shipment to next-of-kin. Finally I boxed additional things for shipment home. All of these tasks were done after the remains were identified, sometimes by forensic anthropologists.

There were about eighteen guys working in Graves Registration. We saw about forty-five dead a day. In my view some of the body counts were definitely understated. We also received coordinates on where the KIA fell. Some of our dead were coming from places we "weren't supposed to be" like Laos and Cambodia. I worked ten hours a day, six days a week. I caught guard duty about once every three weeks. The weapons were locked up until then.

*Spc5 **William Wyrick**, Construction Engineer, 503rd Combat Engineers, 1st Air Cavalry Division, USA*

We used dozers with twelve foot blades to carve LZ's out of the jungle. Sometimes we lined up two or three dozers side by side to carve out a clearing. We would have guards sitting beside us because we couldn't hear shooting above the noise we were making. We also had a machine gunner on the site with us. There were a number of occasions when the guy sitting beside me tapped me on the shoulder to tell me to seek cover due to enemy fire.

*Cpl **Mike Holz**, Counter Intelligence, 5th Bn., 525 MI Group, USA*

When my draft notice appeared, I volunteered at the last second. I was a lawyer before the Army claimed me so it was difficult taking orders from idiots! I flew into Tan Son Nhut via Pan Am, I think, in January of 1970. Our compound was about a kilometer from the air base.

Courtesy: Mike Holz

I was part of Detachment B, Counter Intelligence. We were like the FBI. My duties involved running background checks on the Vietnamese working for the Army, or girls that were planning to marry a GI. Our work schedule was 6 ½ days per week; I had Saturday afternoons off. Among my duties was traveling to the nearby Army bases to ensure that they were following the correct security procedures. I had a Top Secret security clearance for this job. We didn't have to deal with the usual Army BS; no formations, inspections or drills.

1stLt **Frances Janki**, *Nurse, Tachikawa AFB Hospital, Japan, USAF*

I had finished nursing school and eighteen months of work in the hospital I had graduated from and I just needed a change. I decided to join the Air Force. I worked at Moody AFB in Valdosta, Georgia from February of 1969 and then we heard that they wanted volunteers for Japan. They wanted two nurses to go together under the "buddy system." One of my nurses and I volunteered and flew into Yokota AFB in December, 1969. This was only ten or fifteen miles from Tokyo. I bought myself a small Christmas tree to decorate.

I worked on an all-male surgical/orthopedic floor. Our patients were from Korea, Japan, and of course Vietnam. There was a "clean" ICU and a "dirty" ICU, distinguishing between wounds and no wounds. I worked in the clean ICU. The patients in the "dirty" ICU were isolated to prevent germs from spreading. I did work there a few times. It was all about routines: Come in to work, look at the paperwork, collect the medications, etc. We worked eight hour shifts five days a week.

Patients capable of being transported to the States would leave but if not, they would stay with us for a month or two. Some of our patients did go back to Vietnam when they were ready. We had one Marine with broken bones in casts for quite a while. Some of our patients had malaria. The psychiatric patients went to another area.

CHAPTER THIRTY

VIETNAMIZATION CONTINUES

1970

The ultimate NVA goal of Tet was a revolution among the South Vietnamese population and a conversion to their side. This did not happen. The biggest revolution to hit South Vietnam during the war was the consumer revolution felt mostly in the cities. Saigon, for example, overflowed with American cigarettes, hair spray, guns and other niceties, mostly stolen from our warehouses.[lxxxvii]

Spc4 **Larry Gombos**, *Graves Registration*

We had Vietnamese women that processed the paperwork, we had a mamasan cleaning the hooches, they did our laundry, and we saw the Vietnamese in the restaurants. At one of the houses near our Saigon base the mamasan had her kids rolling joints. The kids were very good at it. They would finish with a pack of twenty and it looked like it came off the shelf at a supermarket in the states.

Captain **Paul Kaser**, *Admin Officer*

Courtesy: Paul Kaser

I volunteered to teach a class at night at Bien Hoa High School. That was a strange experience. I thought I was there to help the Vietnamese teacher with pronunciation and stuff and when I walked into the room there were forty-five Vietnamese kids. He said "Okay, the class is yours." He walked out!

2ndLt. *Jane McCarthy,* Nurse

About fifty percent of our casualties were Vietnamese. Most of those were civilians, women and children. And babies with frag wounds. I can remember holding a baby that came in dead with frag wounds. And we had a lot of kids running around. They'd come in the morning with hand lacerations or an infected foot. So a few of us nurses started what we called the Pediatric Clinic. These are the days before nurse practitioners. We were not nurse practitioners! We didn't ask any doctors or anybody about this, we just started doing it. And I've got some very precious pictures of those kids. I don't think we ever started a chart on them or anything but they'd come in and we'd just do the best we could.

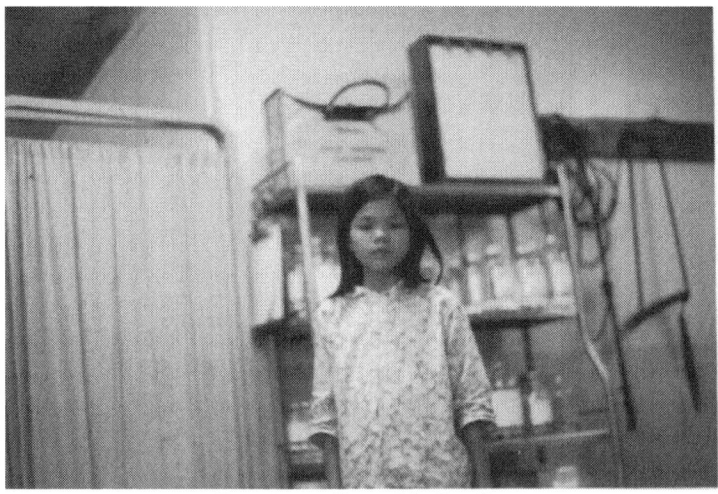

Courtesy: Jane McCarthy

*SSgt **Jack Stroud**, Commo Chief*

My contact with Vietnamese on my last tour was solely with the Montagnards. I found that the Montagnards were very strict with themselves. I thought they were a very nice people. They worked to make sure that everything was right. They would take anything you'd give them but they were happy with what they had.

*SSgt **Allen Thomas Jr**, 4th Infantry Division*

We had an ARVN Battalion assigned to us at An Khe. This was during the Vietnamization period and we were supposed to be showing them the ropes. Every section chief, first sergeant, and supervisor had an ARVN counterpart with him all the time. Most of our work with the Vietnamese concerned technical stuff and they were bright. They were also cordial and we would share pictures of our families and things like that. Most of them spoke English very well.

The Vietnamese we were dealing with were pretty educated and pretty well trained. They had been around a while. Some of them had trained in France or the United States. Most of those people wound up here.

*Cpl **Mike Holz**, Counter Intelligence*

I was in frequent contact with Vietnamese. I worked with their interpreters and we also had house girls. Most of the guys I worked with were pretty good guys. The maids were all poor people from awfully poor families. But it seemed like everybody else was trying to hussle; money changing, selling their sisters and stuff like that. Nobody tried to sell dope to me though. I think you had to go looking for that.

Spc5 **Frank Jackmauh**, *Surveyor*

We had mamasans working for us at Xuan Loc but we had no Vietnamese on the road crews. Back at Long Binh we had one Vietnamese working for us as a surveyor and he did very well. We trusted him with his readings.

Every now and then when we ran low on lumber we'd get a couple of planks cut by a local Vietnamese sawmill. These planks would be cut from rosewood, a hard, sturdy wood. This sawmill was run by a Vietnamese family and their band saw was run off an old jeep engine. We'd agree on a price with them and then bring the wood back to our carpenter shop to use for custom projects. I learned about this place from the sergeant that I replaced at the carpenter shop before he went home on emergency leave.

**Assembling a pre-fab bunker
Courtesy: Frank Jackmauh**

There was a Vietnamese man who was like a woodcarver. I have a desk plaque and a wall plaque with the engineering symbol on them that he made out of rosewood. We would pay this man for his work. We collected money for things we asked him to carve.

Lt. Cdr. **Paul Gesswein,** *Deputy Commander*

Among the other functions at our ISB (Intermediate Support Base) we had repair facilities for the PBR's. The Vietnamese were taking over the repair function for the boats and they were rather proud of themselves for doing this. They were pretty good with the mechanical stuff, although they were a bit behind on the electronics end of things.

**Island Harbor Marina
Sketch by Paul Gesswein**

Ship fitter 3rd Class Diver 2nd Class **Steve Doak**

I worked mostly with their military guys and I had mixed feelings about them. When we first started sharing our boats with them during

Vietnamization down at Cat Lo we'd be out there sweating and working all morning, and we'd go to chow and they'd be standing there in line. They hadn't done anything all day and they're ahead of us in line in their clean uniforms. There would be a hundred of them waiting for the mess hall to open. This went on for a couple of weeks. We almost had a riot on that one. They finally decided to put two lines together. The guys that were training as divers were pretty motivated and they were hard workers. The rank and file navy guys were not very motivated. The impression I had was they figured that if they stayed out of trouble for a while they would survive the war. They knew it was ending.

Cook 3rd Class **Vic Griguoli**

Sentry Duty
Courtesy: Vic Griguoli

We were training ten Vietnamese officers on our LST in my final days. These officers got off the ship just prior to an incident we had and it is always possible that they passed the word to the enemy. The plan was for them to take over the LST when we exited as part of the Vietnamization Program. The ship was to be theirs come July 31. But when the time came the LST was not given to the Vietnamese; it was instead sold to somebody in Europe for use as scrap metal. I didn't trust any of the Vietnamese.

Spc5 **Bill Wyrick**, *Construction Engineer*

In 1969 and 1970 I was stationed north of An Loc and security was tight out on the Fire bases. There was no contact with Vietnamese people. They caught one of the houseboys at An Loc stepping off the distances from the water tower to the CO's hooch. I think that is when they discontinued use of domestic help. As the job foreman I would see to it that we gave any excess food to the Vietnamese kids.

1stLt **Frances Janki**, Nurse

Some Japanese worked in the hospital. They were very good and helped us learn Japanese so that we could purchase things in the marketplace. Sometimes the male Japanese didn't like to lose face taking orders from a female. I found a seamstress I worked with. Sometimes the cab drivers would drive off rather than deal with someone who was using a book to try to translate where they wanted to go.

At the end of the runway at Tachikawa was a Japanese shrine. That is why we had to land at Yokota when we arrived; the Tachikawa runway was closed because they built a shrine just off the end of the runway.

Pfc **Bill McGonigal**, Fuel Handling Specialist

We had a hooch lady that did our clothes and shined our boots. Once we had some money stolen and the hooch lady took MP's to where the stolen money had been stashed. I spent a lot of time at the motor pool; we had Vietnamese mechanics there helping on the helicopters. We had Vietnamese women that helped out in the mess hall and I ran into a lot of people when I got into downtown Binh Long. We'd go down to the fruit and vegetable market and sometimes buy a watermelon for the kids. The people that I met were extremely nice, especially our hooch mate. She took extremely good care of us. I didn't know of anyone that had a problem with her. They treated her with utmost respect.

I think the town of Binh Long was there before the base. That was not always the case, but I noticed some of the buildings looked to be old. There was an old Catholic church; there was a nun stationed in this church and she was from Ireland. She talked to us about the problems they were having in Ireland between the Orange and the Green.

Petty Officer 3rd Class **Vince Malaterra**, *Seabees*

On the second tour we were usually with the 101st Airborne. We would get loads of gravel from riverboats and the Vietnamese would unload it by hand. We used the gravel for runways and for foundations of buildings since the water level was only about a foot beneath the ground.

Some of the Vietnamese we were in contact with were Chieu Hoi's and they really made me nervous. And we were around a lot of civilians. Every place we went there were little villages. Some seemed friendly to us and sometimes not. We used the Vietnamese to fill sandbags, burn the shitters and things like that.

CHAPTER THIRTY-ONE

EVIL SPIRITS, POTHEADS AND THE DEATH OF SGT. PEPPER

1970

Those who entered the service in the late 60's and early 70's had grown up watching student protests on television. They had seen the rancorous debates and rising body counts on the nightly news. And the coup de gras was when Walter Cronkite, our most trusted news anchor, declared the war unwinnable. Flavor this with soaring drug use among draft age men and you have the perfect recipe for morale, drug and racial problems in 1970's Vietnam.

Among U.S. personnel there were 46 deaths from fragging in 1969, 209 cases in 1970, over 215 in 1971 and 551 by July of 1972. Ninety percent of the perpetrators of fraggings were intoxicated.

*Spc5 **Tom Petersen**, Radio Repairman/Tower Team*

As I was preparing to leave Vietnam I came across a citation that they had prepared recommending me for the Bronze Star. I noticed that they had misspelled my last name, which happens frequently, and I pointed that out to them. This happened only a week or so before I left country. But that is the last I ever heard about that Bronze Star.

*SSgt **Allen Thomas Jr.**, 4th Infantry Division*

Six months can be a long time when you don't have anything to do. Time just worked on you and you could get into a lot of trouble. We had a lot of people who drank too much and did a lot of things that they shouldn't have done. Guys were just bored out of their skull. Once you've been in the service that long and always had something to do, boredom was a real problem. It really tears you up to sit around and do nothing.

SSgt **Jack Stroud**, Communications Chief

When I arrived there was no Commo officer, no commo anything. They threw me to the wolves. They gave me a bunch of potheads, a big bunker with a lot of radios, a repair position in the bunker; that's all we had down there was repair and supply. Just after I arrived they came in and wanted to swap out the old CRC46's, which they replaced with GRC106's. These new radios were better – better range and clarity -- but they were also harder to operate. But the guys caught on pretty quick.

Cook 3rd Class **Vic Griguoli**

On the *USS Meeker*, we hit a typhoon in the Gulf of Tonkin. We would normally make about 14 knots at sea but during the typhoon we did about 2 knots, and we lost an anchor, chain and all. We were lost and you could see Chinese boats in the water, we were that close to China. We steamed to Taipei to pick up an anchor because it was unsafe to be without it. We stayed three days in Taipei and then steamed to Subic Bay, which was nice. The *Meeker's* home port was Guam, which has little more than a few gooney birds, so the Philippines made a nice departure for us.

Spc4 **Larry Gombos**, Graves Registration

Some of the anthropologists screwed around with the bodies, posing them with cigarettes in their hands, drinks, things like that. I saw that seven or eight times.

Because Saigon was a "rear area," there was a bit of spit and polish.

*Spc5 **Frank Jackmauh**, Surveyor*

I was somewhat upset by the captain who commanded B Company. I think he had been downgraded from his job as Brigade Aide-de-Camp. One of my fellow surveyors had a pet dog, a yellow lab named Sgt. Pepper, and the previous owner of the dog had taught the lab to discern the difference between lifers and enlisted men. The dog would always bark at lifers. Somehow Sgt. Pepper learned to accept our master sergeant, who we worked with every day, but the captain didn't like that dog and he told one of us to take him out and destroy him. That didn't go over well.

Some of the hippie types, California guys, bothered me a bit on my last tour. It was a clash of folk music and heavy metal. They were draftees with a different point of view. They weren't college guys, as I was.

**New alignment over hill to bypass Ambush Alley – March, 1970
Courtesy: John Freemyer**

The monsoon was pretty bad. We were working on a section of road between Xuan Loc and Gia Rey, and there was a small, vertical curve combined with a horizontal curve. This curve in the road required some fill to build up elevations. Surprisingly French engineers did a good job because they actually put in proper banking on the turn, both for drainage and stability. The monsoon would wash off some of the fill when we put it in, but if we compacted it well most of it held. The soil engineers were responsible for determining what was needed.

As surveyors we needed paint brushes to paint our stakes for the road crews. We couldn't seem to get them so we ended up whacking branches off a nearby tree to do our painting.

I received an Army Commendation Medal for the Ham Ton recon. They gave me another one before I left. I'm also proud of all the people that I served with. And I'd do it again at the drop of a hat. We didn't lose anybody while I was there.

Spc5 **Bill Wyrick**, *Construction Engineer*

When they started winding down the war it was very difficult to get replacement parts for the equipment. We had to cannibalize a lot of our equipment. We had .50 caliber machine guns with us when we carved LZ's out of the jungle but because the drawdown was going on, ammunition for the .50 caliber was not made available to us. It was available for the ARVN so we went through MACV to get it. There was no paperwork involved. It usually involved a trade for beer or something.

Spc4 **Bernie Wright**, *Wireman/Switchboard Repair*

We learned that our cook was selling our fresh fruit on the black market.

Ship fitter 3rd Class Diver 2nd Class **Steve Doak**

In the 70's we had more guys that had come out of the fleet. Their mentality was still fleet sailor ("Keep your mustache trimmed, keep your hair short"). We weren't used to that. I ran into problems with some of those old timers late in the game. By then I looked like a pirate; my hair was long and I kind of clashed with that new generation of nco's that came over and wanted to straighten things out. Our guys were hard workers. And they played hard. We had a reputation for hard drinking, womanizing and partying. We enjoyed that moniker.

*1stLt **Frances Janki**, Nurse*

We were very well stocked and had everything we needed. Food, medicine, whatever; we were very well supplied. Sometimes an older patient, a master sergeant or whatever, would have a tough time responding to me. I would talk to my head nurse and everything would be taken care of.

*Bosun Mate Chief **Don McMurray***

The Viet's had weird ideas. Down in the delta, say if your boat was going left to right, and their sampan was going at you, what they would do was cut just behind your wake, as close as they could get to your stern, to get off any evil spirits they had on their sampan. And you weren't supposed to touch a Viet kid on the head because the evil spirits would be transferred to him. That was a no-no.

Aboard the Askari
Courtesy: Don McMurray

U.S. troop levels fell to 335,000 by mid-December

CHAPTER THIRTY-TWO

ON TO CAMBODIA

1970

President Nixon ordered the invasion of Cambodia on April 30, 1970. "This is not an invasion of Cambodia," Nixon explained. He had ordered a "secret" bombing of Cambodia a year earlier. The bombing backfired when it encouraged the NVA to move west toward the Cambodian capital of Phnon Penh. Allied troops entering Cambodia in 1970 found most of the NVA bases along the border abandoned. In June of 1970 the U.S. Senate repealed the Gulf of Tonkin Resolution. Ohio National Guardsmen killed four war protesters at Kent State on May 4, 1970.

Cpl **Mike Holz**, Counter Intelligence

One of my proudest moments was when Detachment A of our unit broke the story about the Cambodian coup against Prince Sihanouk before the CIA knew about it. If my group, Detachment B, was like the FBI, Detachment A was like the Army CIA.

1stLt **Dick Immes**, Pilot

We flew into Cambodia officially in May of 1970. The ARVN had a mission of using a bridge to get to their objective; they had armor with them and didn't want this bridge destroyed. The ARVN were taking mortar and machine gun fire from the other side of the bridge and they requested air support. The first planes in was a flight of F4's and they were told NOT to hit the bridge and NOT to crater the approaches. The first bomb hit right on the approach to the bridge. The ARVN were upset. The next planes in were A37's and they took out all the enemy mortars and machine guns. The F4's were sent home.

Another time the Army was dealing with a bunker system on a mountain; it was pretty inaccessible for them. The terrain was very difficult for infantry. We were diverted to this area but we were armed with slick bombs, which were not ideal for this type of job. We needed the ground commander's approval for this job since we were within minimum safety standards for the type of ordnance we were using. The F100's went in first and did their job, and then we came in and got a lot closer to our friendly troops. The Army was in danger of being overrun so they had little choice but to call us in on top of them. Our A37's were so accurate we got a nice letter from the Army after that episode.

Spc5 **Bill Wyrick,** *Construction Engineer*

Some of our people were called on to support the move into Cambodia but I was not directly involved.

U. S. Army engineers led the way into Cambodia using flying cranes and Rome plows. They built 56 kilometers of roads and 23 bridges. Among the support troops involved in the Cambodia foray seven engineers were killed and 132 wounded.[lxxxviii]

Sgt **Bill McGonigal***, Fuel Handling Specialist*

We were headed west (towards Cambodia), with a load of aviation fuel in drums. I was riding shotgun on a deuce and a half and I had been given some directions as to which way to turn on the roads. There were three guys in the back and two of us in the cab. We really didn't know where we were other than we were heading towards Cambodia. Three rounds went over our heads and we're sitting on a load of aviation fuel. One of the guys in the back had his M-16 on full automatic instead of safety. He had sent the three rounds over our heads. It was an interesting moment.

Spc5 **Bill Wyrick,** *Construction Engineer*

One of the enemy tricks was to plant mines at night after we had finished smoothing out the road. They would place an unexploded 105mm artillery shell under the mine. When the mine was driven over it would detonate the much bigger 105 round.

At An Loc they were trying to mortar the helicopters but they always overshot and came near us. The fire bases were hit a lot. One night we lost 66 killed and 40 wounded. The company commander was one of the men killed. They breached our wire, killed the guards – they went to sleep or something – and were throwing grenades and satchel charges into our hooches. Our hooches were out on the perimeter at this time.

I received a Technical Service Vietnamese decoration and the Cross Palm from South Vietnam's President Ky in 1970. The Technical Service medal for excellence, as I understand it, was only given out six times during the conflict. I was recently advised that this medal is being placed in the Army Museum at Fort Leonard Wood, in Missouri. The other award was for saving some people during that big March 19, 1970 attack at An Khe. We had an armor outfit in with us and they had been our security. They pulled out that day and ARVN troops were moved in to be our security. We were overrun and I saved some Vietnamese women and soldiers during that attack and won the Bronze Star and Purple Heart for it.

Spc5 **Tom Moschella**, *Vehicle Repair*

We got hit at Fu Tai one night late in my tour. We were picking up mortar and small arms fire. Our automatic weapons in the towers were not responding and I was told to go "straighten them out." I got up to the towers as a trip flare went off so I knew there was something out there. I cleared the jams on the machine guns and noticed enemy soldiers on the roofs of the nearby buildings. It was a hectic night made worse by the fact that I was close to going home.

Courtesy: Tom Moschella

*Cpl **Mike Holz**, Counter Intelligence*

On one occasion we found a SECRET memo in the desk drawer of a Brigadier General. We had to write him up for a security violation.

One Saturday afternoon I hitchhiked about twenty miles outside of Saigon just to take pictures. I did that on a lark; it was dumb. I didn't take pictures of anything that special; rice paddies and things like that. While I was out there these combat guys picked me up. One of them had a 1,000 yard stare. He asked me what I was doing out there. I told him I was taking pictures. He said, "You'll die out here." I got the hell back to town!

*Spc4 **Bernie Wright**, Wireman/Switchboard Repair*

One night on guard duty I heard a scuffle out in front of our bunker. With my night vision equipment I could see it was a cobra and something else, which my partner identified as a mongoose. He said we were in for a show and he was right. The battle lasted for about thirty minutes. The mongoose won.

*Captain **Paul Kaser**, Admin Officer*

There were thirty-three attacks on our base in the eighteen months I was there. This would include rocket or mortar attacks (what we called "standoffs") and also sappers infiltrating the perimeter.

*SSgt **Allen Thomas Jr.**, 4th Infantry Division*

On my third and last tour I had too much time on my hands. I saw all the USO shows. We were shot at when I went from the 4th ID to the Americal up at Chu Lai. They hit the front of our long column; I wasn't even aware of it at the back of the column. Unlike my first two tours of Southeast Asia I didn't drive over a land mine!

*Engineman **Jim Fritz**, Mobile Riverine Force, USN*

We ran a number of ambush patrols on a small boat out of Nam Can. There were three of us on the boat and we were looking for sampan activity. We'd cut the engines and hope to find something, but we never did.

*Bosun Mate Chief **Don McMurray***

A lieutenant got in trouble and our government had to pay: We wouldn't let sampans get near us. We used water cannons to keep them away but they always wanted to come up and beg, and this time it wasn't working. He took this M79 to scare them, and it went off and killed a couple of people in the boat.

Cook 3rd Class **Vic Griguoli**

We were not supposed to be in either Laos or Cambodia, but our LST took supplies to bases in both countries.

The *Meeker* navigating the rivers
Courtesy: Vic Griguoli

I was on the *Meeker County* in June of 1970 and they sounded General Quarters at 0240 hours. We were tied up at the Vung Tau pier. Although it was night time they had so many lights around it was like daytime. My battle station was in the captain's cabin, wearing headphones. We started to hear concussion grenades going off in the water. I was due to rotate home in three days (July 1) and this was making me very nervous. A voice from the pier came over the headphone telling us they had something under the ship and they didn't know what it was. I kept announcing that I had just three days left. No one seemed to care. They kept trying to rig some lights to look under the ship but they call it the brown water for a reason; it was very muddy water and difficult to see.

One of my friends (a new guy just aboard two weeks) had the watch on deck and he noticed that there was a light colored rope coming from a telephone pole on the pier to under our ship. All the other ropes around our ship were bigger and dirty like the water. He had noticed this difference and it was him who sounded the alarm; the older guys on the ship may not have noticed. Divers went into the water and they felt something underneath the ship but due to the murky water they couldn't determine what it was; it had a Vietnamese timer on it for certain. The speaker from the pier told us to be patient. Then they told us to get all non-essential personnel off the ship. I asked the captain what all this meant and he told me that we apparently had a 40 pound metallic charge attached to the hull of our ship. This news caused me to remind him that I had just three more days' in-country. The next thing I know someone is slapping me and taking the headphones off me.

The divers couldn't de-activate the bomb because they couldn't see the timer in the murky water but they finally de-magnetized it and got it off the ship. They put the bomb in the captain's gig and steered it out to the mouth of the river. I was starting to cook breakfast when there was a mushroom cloud in the water; a huge explosion. Hiroshima-like. A few minutes later our ship was bouncing like a cork against the pier.

I think some of our guys must have blabbed something the night before while they were on liberty in the bars about how we were going to be taking this big load of supplies, ammo and fuel up river the next day. Loose lips **do** sink ships! They found a plastic bag and a plastic pop bottle that they figured the sapper must have used to allow him to swim under water to attach the bomb, but thank god for the young man that turned in the alarm. His alertness may have saved over one hundred lives! For some reason the after-action report recorded just one stick of dynamite in that satchel but we knew it was forty pounds.

*LCpl **Alan Webster**, Military Police*

We were outside the base one time and we saw a motorcycle driven by a Vietnamese with an American on the back. We chased them and I told the sergeant driving our jeep if he could catch them I'd get them off the motorcycle. The motorcycle turned into a sandy field and lost his advantage in that terrain. We caught them and I dove at the motorcycle and took the American off. I asked the American what he was doing and I learned that he had opium in his canteen. I looked around and saw that there were a lot of large rocks in the area and I could have killed both of us when I dove at this guy. I realized that it was stupid to dive at him.

Hull Technician Chief **Jim Sooy**

When we were anchored in Danang Harbor we would see rockets flying over our heads from Monkey Mountain to the air base at Danang

Spc5 **Frank Jackmauh***, Surveyor*

One time on the Ham Ton recon we were in a remote area with a jungle canopy over us and we saw a group of Vietnamese approaching; about six of them carrying firearms. We didn't know if they were ARVN, VC or NVA. We just stayed quiet and let them go by. We didn't recognize them and they didn't see us. It was frightening.

I had an R&R trip in August of 1970, to Hawaii. My brother was visiting a college friend there so I went to see him. We had a good time and before coming back I bought two pilsner glasses. When we finished our work each day it was nice to sit out on the ground and drink a beer out of my pilsner glass, sipping it in front of people as they walked past.

We had lots of rats in the perimeter bunkers at Xuan Loc and we did see an occasional cobra. We used to trap some of the rats. We used to find humorous ways to destroy them. We didn't like rats because they were snake food. I was reprimanded by the B Company commander once for spraying compressed air on a rat we had trapped in a cage. He didn't like that but he's the guy that destroyed our dog because he didn't like him.

We were harassed occasionally during our work and we'd find mines in the road. Sometime you would be standing out in the middle of the road silhouetted against the skyline while doing your surveying and we'd get plunked at now and then. Thank God they were bad shots. The road we were working on had been cleared at least 100 meters on each side so the sniper had to hit us from that distance, but I hit the dirt more than once.

Airman 3rd Class **Frank Towns**, *Jet Mechanic*

On July 1, 1970 I participated in the maiden flight of the C5 Galaxy, from Dover, Delaware to Cam Ranh Bay. This was a test flight and it was like flying on a cloud. I had flown this mission for years on the C-141 and although the C5 and the C-141 both had four engines, the similarity ended there. When the C5 arrived they asked me to check the oil and things, and I told them I didn't have a tech manual; I didn't know where the oil was! Believe it or not you needed a Top Secret Security Clearance to change the oil on the C5.

There were other classified aircraft around Dover in those days. I saw a major take off in a twin-engine fighter-bomber, a very small plane. I saw him later that day on the base, and I asked him how high that plane went. He told me "The logbook will show 73,000 feet but I was at 84,000 feet." That is like being on the edge of the earth; that's over fifteen miles up!

The C5 could be loaded from both the nose and the tail while the C-141 only had one load entrance. The C5 had sixteen tires, twice that of the C-141. The fuel and cargo capacity of the C-141 was 318,000 pounds, while the fuel capacity alone of the C5 was 318,000. I took pictures of the plane at Cam Ranh Bay. They told me I couldn't take pictures. I said "bullshit!" After that flight I came back and was discharged in September.

2ndLt. **Jane McCarthy**, *Nurse*

They would sometimes call Red Alerts and we were supposed to put on our flak jackets and helmets and go into bunkers. I was sitting in the bunker one time and no one else showed up and I thought "What would happen if they had a Red Alert and no one came?" "What if they had a war and nobody showed up?"

We had a mortar attack one night. The mortar rounds landed near the helipad, by the ER where I worked. I was not working that night; I was in my hooch. Another time I was visiting some friends in C hooch and some small arms fire entered the perimeter. The guys went and got their M16's, and I thought "Boy, this is dangerous!" I said many times "If I get killed over here, I'm going to be really pissed!"

When I went arrived in Vietnam I found out that eight nurses had been killed. I looked into it and found that seven of them had been killed joy riding on helicopters. I made a very clear decision that I was not going to go on helicopters unless it was a good reason. I didn't hang out with the dust off pilots or go off with them on a Sunday tour.

Courtesy: Jane McCarthy

*1stLt **Frances Janki**, Nurse*

One body bag in the morgue was moving. The guy was alive. He had been found face down in a puddle of water. This guy spent a lot of time with us and he was a lot of fun. He was fine. He was an Army guy. We saw Army, Marines and Air Force guys, but not many from the Navy.

A young man came in with shrapnel in his left arm. He was on our floor. The problem with shrapnel is that it moves. This patient had a sharp piece of shrapnel close to a nerve or artery so they left him with us so we could observe him. It did move and hit an artery but we were just a few feet from ICU so we whisked him in there and he made it.

We tried to do a lot of support for these guys knowing that it was not easy to communicate back to the States. We could use the MARS system or help them use my tape recorder. I would ask them "How would you like to make a tape message for your family?" And we would mail the tape for them. My fiancée was flying for the Air Force in Vietnam while I was in Japan. We used to communicate with the MARS (Military Air Radio

Service) system when we could. Everybody was in on your conversation. We said "over" a lot. We also used the reel-to-reel tape recorders. We also wrote letters but the reel-to-reel was more fun.

We were everything to these guys when we had them. Some of the Marines may have had a tough time dealing with me; I looked like I was seventeen years old and they were right out of the jungle! Some of these guys thought "I can't take orders from this lady." A few times I had to call in the Marine liaison officer and tell him I was having trouble with one of his people. As an officer I was the person in charge and it was a problem if they were not following my orders. The Marine officers always straightened them out.

We were supportive of the war. As nurses our goal was to take care of the patients. There wasn't really a lot of talk about the war. The only newspaper we got was the *Air Force Times*. The patients didn't talk much about the war either. They were just kind of glad to be out of it, away from it. A lot of them just needed the rest. Our patients were more than just guys from Vietnam. We also had guys from Korea, Japan and other places. If they were there long enough guys could get a pass for a few hours.

The doctors and surgeons were good. I didn't get much recognition. We were so far removed.

Bosun Mate Chief **Don McMurray**

A lieutenant got in trouble and our government had to pay: We wouldn't let sampans get near us. We used water cannons to keep them away but they always wanted to come up and beg, and this time it wasn't working. He took this M79 to scare them, and it went off and killed a couple of people in the boat.

They had big water snakes. One was trying to get in the vent of one of the ships, and it was 7' long, and I pulled out my gun; I was going to shoot it but then I realized there was metal behind the snake. I thought better of it.

Ship fitter 3rd Class Diver 2nd Class **Steve Doak**

Almost all of our work was done in the rivers and canals of the Delta. We did have two missions that were not down in the Delta. Two of us flew over to the western fringes of South Vietnam, near Can Tho and Ben Tui, to do a demolition job in support of one of the Vietnamese villages. There was a major ferry crossing used heavily by both military and civilians in that area and their ferry had hit a mine and sunk right there at the ramp. They wanted us to clear it out of the way so they could move a new ferry in. We did a series of demolitions on the sunken ferry and dispersed it.

Courtesy: Steve Doak

Lt. Cdr. **Paul Gesswein,** *Deputy Commander*

We did get a couple of mortar rounds at least once. We were exposed to fire when we drove through Indian country once a month to our staff meetings, but I don't recall any problems.

Courtesy: Paul Gesswein

Bob Hope's 1970 Christmas tour started off with a dress rehearsal at West Point, attended by then Army Chief of Staff William Westmoreland. From West Point to England – a joke about warm beer – then Germany, then to our newest aircraft carrier, the John F. Kennedy, and some of the Sixth Fleet in the Mediterranean. Hope called the JFK "the biggest bird sanctuary in the Navy. I didn't know Texas would float."

From the Mediterranean to Bangkok, a 7,000 mile flight, with shows at U-Tapao and Ubon. In Vietnam, shows were held for the 101st Airborne at Camp Eagle, near Hue, with Marshall Ky of South Vietnam in attendance, and for 26,000 at Danang, where it somehow wasn't raining. Hope described Danang as the only place in South Vietnam with rapid transit – "there's a rocket going any place you want." They also visited the hospital ship USS Sanctuary.

On Christmas Day the Hope crew entertained a mostly shirtless crowd of 25,000 at Long Binh. "Long Binh -- that sounds like Dean Martin's wine cellar. With all the troop withdrawals I'm surprised to see anyone here." Bob also made a sarcastic remark about the Paris Peace talks. After a quick stop in Korea they ended the tour at Elmendorf AFB in Alaska, "where men are men and women are women, but it's too cold to do anything about it."

In summary, Bob Hope noted that "this most unpopular of wars has lasted too long." Bob mentioned the "light at the end of the tunnel," and then called for a "little more patience and unity here at home."

CHAPTER THIRTY-THREE

THE WELL-OILED MACHINE

1971 – 1975

After more than five years of war the routines and procedures were well organized. Living accommodations, food and medical care had improved each year since 1965; South Vietnam was no vacation spot but efforts were made to bolster morale.

Petty Officer 3rd Class **Vince Malaterra**, *Seabees*

I landed at Danang In October of 1971 on a commercial Pan Am airliner. We ran off the plane with the ground rumbling under our feet, grabbed our duffel bags, and were directed to a bunker. The airfield was receiving an attack of B40 (rocket) rounds. Welcome to Vietnam.

Guys would come to Bien Hoa for steam baths and other things, but outside Bien Hoa it was very remote. We had to drive through some unfriendly villages to get to a job site. It was the first time I saw a guy's head up on a pole. Scared me to death.

When the monsoon hit they offered us ponchos. What good was a poncho? We were soaked through and through but we had work to do. I ended up with pneumonia. I was pretty sick. I went to a temporary field hospital; I thought it would mean leaving Vietnam, but it didn't thanks to antibiotics.

The monsoon would flood the roads. The VC would mess with the water flow, building dams and things, and then the water would wipe out the bridges. We found lots of snakes then too.

Bosun Mate Chief **Don McMurray**

I flew over for my third tour in August of 1972. The *Lawrence* was a guided-missile destroyer My job was at the starboard port wing, at the

Polaris (compass). As a support troop repairing river boats on my previous two tours I was always on the receiving end of enemy fire. Now I had a chance to be on the shooting end.

CWO "Woody" Woodruff, Maintenance/Pilot

After my tour with the 1st Cavalry Division in the mid 1960's I worked as a helicopter instructor for a year. I also attended Army Maintenance School in Virginia and returned to Vietnam to do maintenance work. When they learned of my flying background it wasn't long before they had me flying Hueys and Cobras, mostly Hueys ferrying troops.

*SSgt. **Jack Stroud**, Commo Chief*

Around March of 1971 I was sent over to Charlie Battery. My job was to get them shut down and ready to move back to Cam Ranh Bay. I knew when I got over there in June of 1970 and they didn't have a Commo officer that there was something going on. Anyway my job was to get the equipment ready to go and get the radios mounted back on their ¾ ton trucks. I also prepared equipment and paperwork for destruction with thermite grenades. In April we convoyed down to Cam Ranh Bay with our guns and everything else. As soon as we left the gates the Vietnamese raced in to get at anything left behind. It was like a land rush in the old west. Once we got everything back to Cam Ranh Bay we horsed around for a week or so, then they loaded us on a plane and we were gone.

*Spc4 **Les Daulton**, Truck Driver, 198th Brigade, Americal Division, USA*

I was going to college and over a short period of time my girlfriend dropped me, and my grades dropped, so I dropped out of school, for a while I thought; I was drafted ten days later, at age 21. I had experience driving a semi so that determined my job in the Army. I flew to Cam Ranh Bay, then a bumpy C-130 flight north. I spent my first four days helping retrieve a semi that had gone off the road. Then I went to Chu Lai.

When I first got to Vietnam (March 1971), we drove supplies from Chu Lai to Quang Tri, Da Nang, Duk Pho, etc. In October 1971, we started to close down some of the outlying bases, turning them over to the ARVN and I pulled guard duty two or three times.

In October of 1971 the Americans began to phase out of the landing zones and withdraw back to Chu Lai. Then in January of 1972, the Americans pulled out of Chu Lai and withdrew to Danang. The war was winding down so an everyday work routine was not in place. We would go days without driving anywhere. When we were loaded we might be gone for two days. It took a full day to go from Chu Lai to Danang (about sixty miles). We had to spend the night there. Same thing from Chu Lai to Duk Pho -- a full day getting there. The roads were, well, they weren't there. There really wasn't a road between Danang and Chu Lai. The road to Duk Pho was just a dirt road, a country road.

Courtesy: Les Daulton

We got whatever was left over after everyone else left. We lived in hooches. We did have some issues with rats. I only saw one movie while I was over there and there was a rocket attack while it was going on. I never did see the end of that movie.

I never ate in the mess hall. Why would I? The drivers would bring back something from their runs each day, be it canned bacon, fresh bread, produce, canned goods, or whatever. We had hot plates and refrigerators in our hooches and we would fry up some BLT's. Or we ate peanut butter and jelly sandwiches. We ate pretty well.

*Pfc **Rich "Saw" Negich**, MP, 101st MP Co, 101st Airborne Division, USA*

I arrived by plane at Bien Hoa in August, 1971. We flew from there to Danang on a C-130 and took a Chinook helicopter way up north to Phu Bai; Camp Eagle. I Corps was once the domain of the Marines but by the time I arrived all the Marines were gone. The war was winding down.

MP's worked the three gates at Camp Eagle. The two secondary gates (Jollee and Rear Gate) were in a Free Fire Zone; you didn't have to ask permission to return fire. But the Main Gate was not a Free Fire Zone which is why the mortar attacks always came from that direction. We also conducted patrols inside and outside the camp, we manned certain bunkers, later I did convoy escort, and we also escorted prisoners, both enemy and American.

Courtesy: Robert Negich

*1stLt **Claude Roberts**, Rescue Pilot, 39th Aerospace Rescue & Recovery Svc, USAF*

I arrived in May of 1971. We had both ground and flying duties. Both were mostly done during the day. We flew a C-130 out of Cam Ranh Bay. Our rescue missions were mostly done over the Ho Chi Minh Trail in Laos.

We flew up and down the Trail at high altitude (20,000) waiting for beepers to go off or forward air controllers signaling a pilot down. We organized and directed almost all the air rescues.

Once a pilot went down then virtually all the air war stopped and everything was turned over to us. In discussions with the FAC (forward air controller) we would determine what types of ordnance we needed to suppress whatever antiaircraft fire or enemy ground units were in the immediate area of the downed plane. If possible we also tried to establish communications with the downed pilot. The rescue choppers would be on alert, usually on the ground in Thailand waiting for the word from us. After the rescue chopper went in and made the pickup we would then refuel them. We would descend from our normal high altitude to about 4,000 feet to do that. The choppers always went in with a small amount of fuel so they needed us after the rescue. Our C-130 had a pod under each wing that the helicopter could access for refueling. Some of these complex rescue operations took several days, or at the least many hours. The choppers often got shot up pretty well.

The majority of the days we were up there no one was shot down and we had a relatively easy day. We spent about three days a week in the air and as much time with duties on the ground. My ground duty, due to my history degree, was squadron historian. As historian I would compile a quarterly report on the rescue mission activity. These reports were classified and sent on to higher headquarters and never seen again, at least by me. In addition we practiced on a mission communications simulator, primarily working with the new guys on the vital communications piece of a rescue operation. There could be dozens and dozens of people we had to talk to during a rescue mission and the training helped the news guys learn the ropes. These rescues were extremely intense communications problems and you had to know who to call at each step.

We had it pretty good because we were air crew. Air conditioning was required. We lived two pilots to a room, with a television, in a Quonset hut with a cement wall for protection against shrapnel. There was a common living area with a television for some of the rooms and a common shower. We had no rats; some roaches and large bugs. There was an outdoor movie which I went to a time or two. The war was kind of a well-oiled machine by the time I got over there in May, 1971.

*2ndLt. **Jane McCarthy**, Nurse*

If there was a backup in the OR the patients would stay with me for a while. I would sometimes medicate them with morphine, but I didn't do that too much. For head wounds the neurosurgeon would look at the patient and if he couldn't help that was what we called an expected patient. I would set up an area in the back and sit with him until he died.

We also had to inspect the KIA's in their body bags to look for ID and ensure there were no live grenades still on them. We tagged them. Then they were taken to our morgue. I don't know if they did autopsies over there or not. We worked twelve hour shifts. We had one day a week off.

*Electricians Mate/Fireman **Bob Miller**, USS George K. Mackenzie DD-836,*

As an electrician my main job was to replace lighting and wiring damaged from all the heavy firing. My battle station on the first tour was the twin forward 5" gun mount. Our ship operated on what they called the Gun Line, which meant we patrolled the Vietnamese coast providing gun support for our troops inland or targets identified north of the DMZ. Our captain volunteered us quite a bit for this duty since we had a dual propulsion system, like all WW II destroyers. If gunfire knocked out one of our propellers we could still operate. Newer destroyers had just one propulsion system. On my second tour in 1972 I was still an electrician's mate/fireman but my battle station was the After Steering compartment.

Courtesy: Bob Miller

*SSgt. **Jack Stroud**, Commo Chief*

Around March of 1971 I was sent over to Charlie Battery. My job was to get them shut down and ready to move back to Cam Ranh Bay. I knew when I got over there in June of 1970 and they didn't have a Commo officer that there was something going on. Anyway my job was to get the equipment ready to go and get the radios mounted back on their ¾ ton trucks. I also prepared equipment and paperwork for destruction with thermite grenades. In April we convoyed down to Cam Ranh Bay with our guns and everything else. As soon as we left the gates the Vietnamese raced in to get at anything left behind. It was like a land rush in the old west. Once we got everything back to Cam Ranh Bay we horsed around for a week or so, then they loaded us on a plane and we were gone.

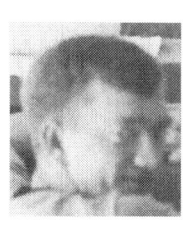

*Sgt. **Don Wilson**, Aviation Supply*

A few months after I left Recon and Vietnam I went to Memphis for three months of aviation supply training. Then I returned to Vietnam as part of the 31st Marine Amphibious Force in February of 1972. Our squadron rotated every six months with another squadron so I did two six-month tours in this capacity. My first time was on the *USS Tripoli LPH-10* and the second tour was on the USS *Okinawa LPH-3*.

The plan was to organize a helicopter squadron around a Marine BLT (Battalion Landing Team) and station them on an LPH. We had some Cobra helicopter gunships (CH-53's) and some medium transport helicopters (CH-46's), and a few light helicopters for this mission. We were all up and down the coast of South Vietnam.

I worked about four hours a day doing my supply job, ordering spare parts and replacement parts for helicopters, and then I spent the rest of the day flying on helicopters inside South Vietnam, dropping off mostly South

Vietnamese recon patrols at various landing zones. I flew on every type of helicopter; when somebody needed a rest they called me. Virtually all of my work was done during the day.

Petty Officer 3rd Class **Charlie McDonald**, *Gunner's Mate*

I enlisted in the Navy in March of 1970. Our arrival in the South China Sea on my first Vietnam tour came in January of 1972. We had three captains on my three years on the *Strauss*. The first was a great guy, a full commander. When we finished firing we threw the empty brass shell casings overboard. Not all of them would sink. The CO would fire at them with a rifle to hole them.

My job and my battle station was Mount 51, the forward 5" 54 gun mount. I did the maintenance on Mount 51.

Anti-sapper Watch – Danang
Courtesy: Charlie McDonald

I also stood anti-sapper watch when we were in Danang Harbor, patrolling up and down the lifelines and watching for bubbles. In port your watch was four hours. At sea we stood port and starboard watches, twelve-hour days. During battle stations it was all hands on deck. Like most sailors we slept three high. I got seasick quite often.

Bosun Mate Chief **Don McMurray**

I flew over for my third tour in August of 1972. The *Lawrence* was a guided-missile destroyer   My job was at the starboard port wing, at the Polaris (compass). As a support troop repairing river boats on my previous two tours I was always on the receiving end of enemy fire. Now I had a chance to be on the shooting end.

CHAPTER THIRTY-FOUR

WORKING WITH THE VIETNAMESE

1971 – 1975

The big story for ARVN combat troops in 1971 was the attempt to duplicate in Laos their successful Cambodian foray of 1970.[lxxxix] Their goal was to sever the Ho Chi Minh Trail. Better late than never? The recent Cooper-Church amendment limited U.S. involvement; the resulting ARVN venture turned into a 7,700 casualty disaster. Despite the limited U.S. support over 1,000 Americans were killed or wounded during this Laotian adventure, the majority of them Support Troops.

Spc4 **Rich "Saw" Negich***, MP*

We had Vietnamese civilians cleaning our hooch and they did our laundry. They did not work at the mess hall. The Vietnamese prisoners we took were all North Vietnamese; there were no VC around anymore. The NVA were either happy to be out of the war or they were surly and defiant.

Convoy Duty
Courtesy: Robert Negich (Irish Powered)

Bosun Mate Chief **Don McMurray**

We had worked for 48 hours with Vietnamese advisors on a riverboat of theirs that was in a scuffle. The boat had holes in it and the Vietnamese said "Bad boat!" So they opened the sea strainers and sunk it. The water was 12 – 15 feet deep. We had to pull the ship up, position ourselves, get the ammis in place, put divers in the water – it took two days for the divers to finally get belly straps around it – then we had to lift that sucker out of the water, all because they said it had bad spirits. That's some of the things we had to deal with.

1stLt **Claude Roberts***, Rescue Pilot*

We had a maid that came in once a day or so to clean the place up. Air Force personnel were not allowed off the base at Cam Ranh Bay so we did not get into "town" to see the locals. We made up for that on our occasional forays into Thailand.

2ndLt. **Jane McCarthy***, Nurse*

When we worked on the Vietnamese casualties it was our job to stabilize them and then they'd be transported by bus down to the Vietnamese hospital. It was good for me to see what the Vietnamese hospital looked like so we would know where we were sending them. Their hospital wasn't much. As a result I tried to keep the Vietnamese kids as long as I could to give them a better chance to live.

My best Vietnamese friend was a nurse. Her name was Minh. She worked with me there as a nurse and an interpreter. She would log in all the Vietnamese patients and get their names. She was an RN trained in Saigon. Her husband was a minister and a lovely, lovely person. She wore her white uniform to work. And Sgt. Krang was there with me too. He was our liaison with the Vietnamese Army. If we received any ARVN casualties he was the liaison back to their unit.

Petty Officer 3rd Class **Vince Malaterra***, Seabees*

The damn ARVN soldiers were just a pain in the ass. In many cases they had better equipment than we had. Once I saw they had brand-new deuce-and-a-half trucks.

Spc4 **Les Daulton**, *Truck Driver*

We did have Vietnamese girls cleaning the hooches and working in the mess hall. One guy married a Vietnamese girl and moved off the base to live with her. Whenever one of our guys got ready to go home we had a local Vietnamese guy make up a nice plaque for him with the Americal Division logo and everything. We would take up a collection to pay for this plaque. The idea occurred to me to go to the px and buy a pallet of coke and beer, which we could then sell for .25 or .50. I approached the lieutenant with this idea, explaining that we would use the profits to pay for the plaques. I told him I would give him 50% of the profit (about $200). He thought it was a great idea and he gave me a letter authorizing me to make this large purchase (our beer and coke purchases were rationed at this time). We bought the pallet and I gave him his money right away. He thought that was awfully trusting of me. But shortly after this we were moved to Danang and I lost track of the pallet. I never got a plaque either!

Ship fitter 3rd Class Diver 2nd Class **Steve Doak**

If an Army base was closed down, within days it would be stripped clean. They'd take all the metal and everything and either use it for themselves or sell it on the black market. When we turned our boats over to their navy we'd sit by the docks and watch them take all the supplies we had just given them, and we heard they were offloading that stuff into their cars! Whether it was food, gasoline, anything, they'd just take it for themselves.

*Spc4 **Bernie Wright**, Wireman/Switchboard Repair*

We had Vietnamese civilians doing our laundry and housekeeping work. We'd go out periodically to check our wires on the perimeter and the people would come up and try to bug you. Sometimes our wire got snipped and once we found a tunnel. We had to call the tunnel rats to go down there. The ones that did our laundry were nice enough but I really didn't like being near these people.

When I was due to rotate home they told me they wanted to send me to Fort Gordon, GA to train Vietnamese on switchboard repair. I told them I didn't like the Vietnamese in Vietnam and I sure didn't want to work with them in the United States.

*Lt. Cdr. **Paul Gesswein**, Deputy Commander*

The first guy I had over me at Ben Luc was a South Vietnamese. He was kind of a plump, happy-go-lucky sort of guy who was not all that aggressive. He was fired about halfway through my tour. His replacement was from North Vietnam and he was a real go-getter. What a difference between the two. He stepped up the patrols and the ambushes. And he chewed ass.

Courtesy: Paul Gesswein

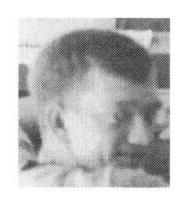

*Sgt. **Don Wilson**, Aviation Supply*

Our choppers hauled more Vietnamese troops than we did Americans. I thought the Vietnamese Marine Corps was very efficient. I had the feeling that the commanders of the regular ARVN had to watch their troops very carefully. Once in a while we had somebody that wouldn't get off the chopper; most of the time we shoved him off.

CHAPTER THIRTY-FIVE

DRUGS

1971 – 1975

By 1971 large scale U.S. operations were avoided. In May, 1971, two congressmen (Robert Steele from Connecticut and Morgan Murphy of Illinois) came back from Vietnam with the disturbing news that 15% of our troops were actively addicted to heroin. Those addicted were kept in Vietnam until they dried out.

Spc4 **Rich "Saw" Negich***, MP*

Drugs were really bad when I was over there. Every company had a drug counselor. Ours was a heroin addict! They used to do urinalysis tests. The guys knew I didn't do any of that stuff so they were getting me to piss in bottles for them. They'd put a little bladder under their arm and use my urine out of that to pass the test. I feel bad about it now because the fact is they were killing themselves. We had one California guy who could have been a movie star. He wanted to try heroin in Vietnam. After two or three months of that you wouldn't even recognize him. Some of those guys ended up in LBJ (Long Binh Jail). Some of those guys told me they'd do anything to get high. They'd smoke toothpaste, the brown stuff on the inside of peanut shells, just anything to get high.

One guy dumped a couple of caps of heroin down into the coffee urn. Anybody drinking that coffee was going to test positive for heroin. This guy was ensuring that everybody would look bad and he might slip by with the rest of them. An ingenious junkie!

SSgt. **Jack Stroud***, Commo Chief*

The guys were all strung out. The only thing is I got them to where they respected me. They didn't do their drugs while they were on duty. They did that stuff on their own. I respected them for that. I asked them "What would you do if we were overrun like Delta Battery?" We had lost D

Battery while I was there. They were located on the other side of the airfield. That was not a fun thing to clean up; I went over to see what was going on and it was a real mess.

"They didn't do their drugs while on duty" -- Jack Stroud (right)
Courtesy: Jack Stroud

I did notice quite a bit of difference in the way people reacted to things versus my earlier tours. You could just tell that there was something different by the way they reacted. A lot of it could have been the drugs. One guy brought me his drugs one time. He said "Here, you need these more than I do." I told him I didn't want to use them and I just burned the damn things.

*Spc4 **Les Daulton**, Truck Driver*

At Chu Lai I had to pull guard duty two or three times. We were manning this huge guard tower, about one hundred feet in the air. There were eight of us there for a 24-hour period. There was supposed to be one of us at each window looking out over the ocean. I had to pull the 24-hour duty by myself because the other seven guys were shooting up! Another time in a Quonset hut I pulled guard duty with a guy. First he took a tablet of Orange Sunshine. I asked him where he got that stuff. He told me he got it from the Air Force. He said "the pilots fly it in and bring it over here to sell to us." Then he had to snort heroin to come back down. I asked him why he would take a tablet to get high, and then take a snort to come back to where he started from. And then he's puking his guts out. Naturally I had to stand his shift that night too. I couldn't trust him.

The Quiet Side of Chu Lai
Courtesy: Les Daulton

In the morning we had a sergeant who was on the ball. He called us together and told us we had a problem. He had noticed some bare foot prints in the mud around the motor pool. So we had to pull the gas tanks off all the trucks and drain them out. And it's a good thing we did. Somebody had put grenades into some of the gas tanks, with rubber bands wrapped around the spoons. As soon as the diesel fuel ate through that rubber band it would explode. They caught the kid; he was only fifteen years old.

Electricians Mate/Fireman **Bob Miller**

One of our sailors had been taken off our ship and was headed home on emergency leave. Waiting for his flight in a bar in Saigon he talks to a guy (Australian) who identified himself as a spotter. There had been a time when the *Mackenzie* was lobbing shells and they forgot to lock in the computer. So when the order to came to "fire for effect" they were shooting all over the place. The spotter didn't know which way to run.

The Australian asked Hank what his call sign was: "Tempest," Hank answered. The Aussie knocked him off his bar stool. He said he had nearly been killed.

On my second tour we had a change of command. In between Hawaii and Nam there was a lot of smoking marijuana on the fantail. At either Guam or Midway, at muster, all doors were locked and a Navy investigations unit came on board and went locker to locker. Any vegetable matter resembling marijuana, you got busted. It could have been overlooked but later, in retaliation, somebody threw a sonar target used for chasing submarines over the side. That was one black mark against the new captain and when we came home his new sports car had some compound put in it which blew his engine out. He lost his command. He was the first lieutenant commander to captain a ship.

Lt. Cdr. **Paul Gesswein,** *Deputy Commander*

All servicemen returning from Vietnam had to undergo drug tests. I failed mine due to the cough medicine I was taking. I was really upset and went to see some bigwig on the MACV staff and he got me on the plane.

Courtesy: Paul Gesswein (front left)

Petty Officer 3rd Class **Vince Malaterra**, *Seabees*

The Marines and the Screaming Chickens (101st Airborne) were great guys. I really admired the Koreans and the Australians too. The Australians loved the Seabees because they could always get something from us; a generator, ammo, or whatever. Everybody did the best they could with a view toward getting home safely. I didn't think much of the ARVN.

I lost some friends on my second tour and my life changed; I decided not to get close to anybody after that. Those feelings took a long time to go away but it's getting better.

Spc4 **Rich "Saw" Negich**, *MP*

It was a brotherhood being over there. You did what you could for your friends and they did what they could for you. I had a lot of good friends. Most of them were from the Midwest; Illinois, Iowa, Michigan, Wisconsin, but my best friend was from New Jersey. He had Agent Orange cancer and died two years ago.

Electricians Mate/Fireman **Bob Miller**

Chief Lopez was a WW II vet. He had three ships sunk under him. Everybody respected him. We respected him more than we did the captain. There were some rules that were tough to take; if you were caught taking a "Hollywood shower," wasting the fresh water, you showered with salt water for the rest of the cruise.

Our ship got a fleet commendation and extended for two months because we were so effective. We had battle stars and an E for Excellence.

1stLt **Claude Roberts**, *Rescue Pilot*

Successful rescues were the cause of much celebration back at the bases. The pilots always felt kind of sorry for the ground personnel who were restricted to base at Cam Ranh Bay. The extreme tedium of their everyday work had to be tough to bear.

We had married men and bachelors among the pilots. Many of the men freely indulged in the delicacies of Thailand, and a few did not. One of those who abstained told me he thought it would "ruin his marriage." Those who indulged implemented a PCOD (a cut-off date) about two weeks prior to their DEROS. This was a precaution that they would not bring home an unwanted disease.

It was the navigator's job to keep us from flying over danger based on the intel he was receiving. Specifically he picked the holding points for our aircraft (supporting fighters and helicopters), air refueling points and tracks for the refueling tankers. Our navigator was a religious fundamentalist, which was fine with us. But one day we were entering a rescue area along the northern Ho Chi Minh Trail and the aircraft commander suspected we were getting into an area of heavy AAA and SAM activity and he asked the navigator about it. "The lord will protect us," the navigator replied. That he was relying on faith rather than intel frankly scared the shit out of us. He caught hell from all of us about that.

*Spc5 **Bernie Wright**, Wireman/Switchboard Repair*

At times we would pull our money and buy a pig down in Saigon. We had a guy from Hawaii who knew how to cook it but first the pig had to be inspected by one of our veterinarians to determine if it was safe to eat. There was a lot of paperwork involved.

*SSgt. **Jack Stroud**, Commo Chief*

I was tasked to set up a beer joint for the troops. I guess they thought I had more time on my hands than I had. Anyway they gave me a building and told me to turn it into an EM Club. So we had an EM Club for two months before we left. That was fun and I was glad that I did that for the guys. In fact those are the only pictures I have of Vietnam. Once it was set up I handed the keys to a lieutenant and I never had much to do with running the operation. I'd scrounge things up for them, ice or beer or whatever. I scrounged up an old pool table with no legs and I got them a ping pong table.

*SSgt **Allen Thomas Jr.**, 4th Infantry Division*

On my first tour in the mid 60's, we were dealing with a lot of professionals. The younger kids were still draftees but you had a core of trained officers and nco's. By the time the early 70's came around we were dealing with six-month warriors. They were sent to leadership school after basic and they'd come out of there sergeants or staff sergeants with barely six months in the army; same with the officers; thirty months after leaving OCS the guy would be a company commander -- a captain.

*Spc4 **Les Daulton**, Truck Driver*

They were really strict with us in the closing months. That one run we made to Duk Pho was the only time they let us lock and load. That time we had our rifles, helmets and bandoliers.

The Sergeant Major told me I deserved a promotion to Spec5 and he gave it to me a week before I left. That promotion allowed me to earn an extra $800, ship my refrigerator home, and move my wife from New Mexico to Cincinnati at government expense.

*Lt. Cdr. **Paul Gesswein**, Deputy Commander*

The guy who wrote my fitness reports from my Operation Giant Slingshot tour was Captain Crowe, who later became Chief of Staff. He was a prince to work for. I really liked the guy.

In June of 1972 General Fred Weyand replaced General Creighton Abrams. U.S. troop strength dropped to 157,000 as 1972 began. The ARVN had 1.1 million troops and the "free world" 69,000.

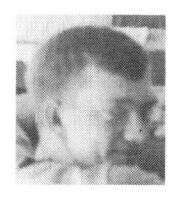

*Sgt. **Don Wilson**, Aviation Supply*

We had a crazy CO we were transporting once. The rule was to not lock and load on the chopper until we were almost to the drop off point, but he did. We did have a few accidental discharges now and then.

*Electricians Mate/Fireman **Bob Miller***

They pay you in cash but most of us took pay in postal chits. Once we were in port and the pay envelope flew out of my hands and over the side. I took off my shoes and jumped. They said I looked like Johnny Weissmuller. It was about thirty-five feet down to the water. And the XO says get that man. In my record, it says JUMPING SHIP IN A WAR

ZONE. PUNISHABLE BY DEATH. The captain called me in and asked what happened. I said I was retching and lost my grip reaching for my check. I was confined to my quarters for 30 days but we were in a combat zone anyway.

The reason the XO wanted to get at me was we had a run-in about a month prior. He came below decks and I was hooking up the fire and flushing pump (about the size of a Volkswagen). They had to cut the deck to lower it down when it was brought on board. This pump worked on three-phase electrical power. There are no ground wires; it is all electrical power. It's naturally grounded. The XO (I was 21 and he was about 23) says "Son, what are you doing here?" I told him and he said he knew a lot about electrical, and one wire has to be the ground wire. I told him that they were all three power leads. He didn't believe this. "Son, don't back talk me." At that point I lost my cool and started calling him lots of names. He's writing me up for everything. I asked him which one he thought was ground. He said the red was ground. I told him to pick out a bolt and I'll ground it. I hooked up that motor, put the sound powered phone on his head, and I was going back to the power board. Had I put power to it he would have blown up. I'm still yelling at him and he's threatening to put me up for captain's mast, and I wasn't worried about it because he wouldn't be around. My first class heard the commotion and as I was going up the ladder he grabbed me and pulled the pockets off the back of my pants. And he looked at the motor and asked me why I did it that way, and I told him "he wants it that way and he's an officer." He went to the captain's mast with me and explained that I was right and the captain agreed and confined me to the ship for 30 days. The XO complained but the captain waved him off knowing I was right.

*Sgt **Bill McGonigal**, Fuel Handling Specialist*

I had trouble sometimes getting guys to do things. I had some guys that helped me out but some that sat on their butts waiting for their tours to end. I had some ex-grunts whose units had been disbanded, and since they weren't finished with their tours they were sent to me. One guy refused to clean a truck but another guy volunteered. When he finished I gave him the rest of the day off. The first guy glared but I just shrugged my shoulders. Years later at Fort Hood I walked into the mess hall and the guy who had said no was sitting there wearing sergeant's stripes. I walked up to him and tapped him on the collar and said "Where did they come from?" He told me that after I left everybody got sergeant stripes. I had been the first. The little extra effort I had made paid off. They thought I was crazy for making the extra effort.

Toward the end of my tour they put stationary pumps in. At the time we had little rubber-tired 350 gpm pumps in the fuel station with and they installed 500 gpm which were great if you were fueling fourteen choppers at the same time -- they really put out the fuel -- but if you were fueling just one the pressure was enormous. I had tried everything I could think of to reduce the pressure on those pumps but due to their design I couldn't do a thing with them.

Near the end of Tet (1971), I was told to set up some auxiliary station in case our main one got hit. I was sent to the AirCav and they had some equipment which I borrowed. I set up these stations and one of the filters wasn't working. I went back to my co and told him I thought I could get it going but the formula wasn't in the book. He said "You know more about this than I do. Go ahead." This surprised me.

*Spc5 **Bernie Wright**, Wireman/Switchboard Repair*

In 1970 the guys worked well together. We were a team. By 1972, guys were lazy and didn't want to do anything.

BBQ
Courtesy: Bernie Wright

U.S. troop levels dropped to 69,000 by May 1.

CHAPTER THIRTY-SIX

THE LAST HURRAH

1971 - 1975

U.S. troop strength declined to 44,000 by mid-August of 1972.

Sgt ***Bill McGonigal****, Fuel Handling Specialist*

One night we had nine mortar rounds come in. Three of them went off. The second night three more came in; one of them went off. They were one for three. Maybe their ammo was getting wet. I was on my way out to our fuel station when I spotted an unexploded mortar round on the airstrip. I asked somebody about it and he said it came from the nine-round attack from the previous night. I had slept through that attack! The second night I slept through the next three. That just proved how sound a sleeper I am. Or was.

SSgt ***Allen Thomas Jr.****, Americal Division*

They had guard towers around the side of the mountain at our Chu Lai camp. That mountain was covered with monkeys. The Americal had harassed these monkeys so much that periodically the monkeys would come down and retaliate. The first time I experienced this we had an alert and I heard all this screaming, and everybody's locking and loading and it turned out a monkey had attacked one of these guard posts. When we found out what had happened we were all rolling with laughter.

When my tour ended in April of 1968 I was at Cam Ranh Bay waiting to board my flight. The MP's told a bunch of us NCO's that each of us would be required to "escort" a prisoner – an American GI – back to the states. We were each issued a .45 and a set of handcuffs. My prisoner was a twenty-year old Army guy who had gone AWOL and was living in a village of like-minded soldiers in Saigon. There were about 3,000 GI's like him on the run at the village. I got his hair cut and took him to the club where we had a steak and danced with the girls. I told him to be ready to board the plane at 0600. He asked me if I would shoot him. I told him I'd been away from home for a long time and was anxious to get home. He understood and he was ready at 0600.

SSgt. **Jack Stroud**, *Commo Chief*

We had some random mortar attacks and we had occasional satchel charge attempts to blow up our helicopters, but nothing ever hit close to me. But these were scary moments; one time they caught one of the sappers within our lines.

Spc5 **Bernie Wright**, *Wireman/Switchboard Repair*

We were out on the perimeter one day inspecting the phone lines, and I was taking a break and napping on a bunker. I woke up to the sound of my fellow troops laughing at me. They knew I was afraid of snakes and there was a cobra a few feet away from me. I killed the snake; I was going to be at that bunker that night on guard duty.

Sometime in 1971 I received a message from the Red Cross that my sister had died. I was authorized thirty days leave and I came home right away. When I reached my house it was locked. I went to the neighborhood bar where my dad sometimes worked. He wasn't there but one of the customers recognized me and asked me what I was doing home. I told him and he said "Nita isn't dead. The surgeon saved her. Your dad is at the hospital visiting her right now." Local military authorities told me to just stay home for the thirty days, so I did. Nita pulled through that scare and lived until 1986.

During my first year I received the Army Commendation Medal. On another occasion I was able to meet General Westmoreland. He was coming to Long Binh around his birthday so we prepared an elaborate meal with cake and everything. It was the best meal I had in two years over there. Each company sent one man to participate in the ceremony. As I was the person with the most time in Vietnam, I was selected. After the party I was able to speak with him and we went out on a PT boat with him, down the river to Saigon. That was a great day. He had been replaced by General Abrams by that time. I think he was a helluva man.

One of our Spc5's received a letter from his wife saying she wanted a divorce. He seemed to be taking it okay but then he shot himself on guard duty that night.

I used to attend church regularly in Vietnam. They provided orange juice each Sunday and I used to mix the OJ with vodka. The chaplain finally noticed and told me to take a ride with him. He took me to a local orphanage and showed me around. After a bit I started to do some visual measurements of the size of the place and tried to determine what they would need. I asked the chaplain's forgiveness for what I was about to do to get the materials. When I was doing carpentry work on the orphanage I was able to trade extra phones, and my ability to wire them, for plywood and other construction materials. I had gone to vocational school before the military and had learned some carpentry skills; once my unit found out about that I did a lot of carpentry projects in whatever spare time I had.

Courtesy: Bernie Wright

Lt. Cdr. **Paul Gesswein,** *Deputy Commander*

One day the Vietnamese PBR's came into the pier returning from a mission. They are supposed to clear their guns before they get to the pier. The guy in the trailing boat cleared his .50 caliber as they arrived at the pier by shooting a guy in the lead boat in the head.

A few of us were bored one time and we went out in one of the whaleboats. We had heard about some spider holes up one of the rivers so we went out there and blasted the holes. The holes were empty at the time; the VC would occupy them at night to ambush the PBR's on patrol.

One of our sailors was bitten by a dog. In hopes of avoiding the painful but necessary rabies shots, the corpsman suggested we find the dog to determine if it was rabid. We were unable to determine if the dog was rabid because the Vietnamese at the base had cooked the dog and ate it.

Petty Officer 3rd Class **Vince Malaterra**, *Seabees*

So many officers seemed to be oblivious to what was going on. They were so busy telling us what to do they didn't notice the futility; they blow it up, we rebuild it, etc.

It was on my second tour that I felt all the things we thought we were accomplishing, helping the Vietnamese, was just bullshit. At one point they asked for volunteers to help unload some stuff from a Korean ship. I chose not to volunteer but the guys who went told us that they were offloading oil drilling equipment for exploration out there in the South China Sea someplace. They said they were doing it for a guy named Bush.

2ndLt. **Jane McCarthy,** *Nurse*

Any time one of us rotated home we would have a party. Keep in mind that most of our group were either draftees or were tired of seeing all the boys hurt. None of us believed in this war. Anyway we'd end each party with the James Taylor song about "If You Were My Friend," or something, and we'd be stomping on the floor. One of the guys had a movie camera. On one of these occasions there were a lot of FTA signs and signs about peace and that sort of thing. This particular party had gravitated toward the top of the bunker and the XO found out about it and called Saigon. They decided to do an investigation of us. They flew the Chief Nurse up from Saigon. Our helicopter pilots tried to avoid letting her see the top of the Officer's Club, which had FTA written on it. Although I wasn't at this party (I was working), I was interviewed too. This whole experience just reinforced for me how wrong the war was.

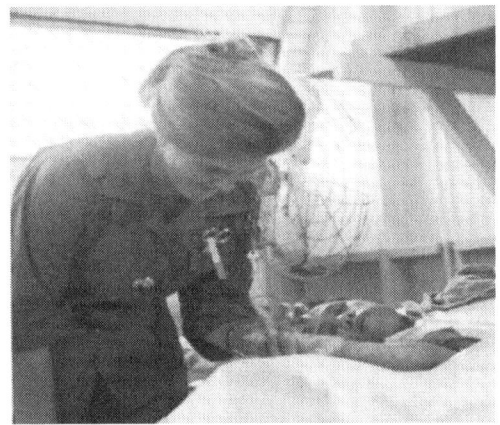

Courtesy: Jane McCarthy

If I had night duty there would be a radioman nearby, and two corpsmen, an X-ray person, a Blood bank person, a physician; and they could all go off and go to sleep. I had to stay up all night and if that radioman went to sleep sometimes I would hear a chopper and I would have to go and tell them. The way we usually found out about incoming was when the helicopter pilot called in to our radioman, which gave us time to get ready.

*Spc4 **Rich "Saw" Negich**, MP*

A friend and I decided to go to the chapel that they had there on the base at Phu Bai. The preacher is up there talking about war and my buddy stood and yelled "what the hell are you talking about war for? You should be talking about Christmas!" Of course we were both loaded. It ended up they called the MP's and our buddies came and got us!

Another time, at Camp Eagle they called our entire MP Company out. The commanding general had received a death threat. So the MP's surrounded his hooch. We figured the guy who threatened the general wouldn't do anything under these circumstances. But what he did was drive a deuce-and-a-half into the water tower that was near the general's quarters in hopes that it would fall into the general's place. I don't know if the general was even there at the time. The guy was crazy; he may have been on drugs, I don't know. Anyway the water tower plan didn't work and the guy was hauled away.

**Pohl Bridge
Courtesy Robert Negich**

We were about twelve miles from the A Shau Valley. There was a bridge, the Pohl, that was always blown up and we had to cross the river on a ferry built by the engineers. The ferry would hold two tanks and a jeep at one time, or two deuce-and-a-half and a jeep, or whatever. Anybody in that area was bad! There was always stuff going on. You were an easy target when you were in the middle of the river on that slow-moving ferry. There were always two MP's on each side of the river. We got shot at there. At this time the war was winding down and as the firebases were being closed we would line up the traffic to cross the ferry. The engineers used to go fishing there with hand grenades.

There was a time we were taking civilians across the Perfume River on that ferry. There was a Montangard and his wife. We weren't supposed to do this but we'd take them across. A GI started groping this Montagnard's wife and the Montagnard shot him right in the chest with a crossbow. The guy -- I'll never forget the look in his eyes as he looked down at the arrow in his chest -- and he shot that Montagnard to pieces. And then he collapsed and we had to call a medevac. Of course we never learned what happened to people after they left us. Many times I wondered if we could have avoided that incident by telling the guy to just take it easy.

Ferry over the Perfume River
Courtesy: Robert Negich

I lived in a four-man hooch with a tin roof. We had roaches and rats there. We had an albino rat at one of the bunkers we manned. We used to feed this rat. It got so the rat would recognize the sound of our vehicle nearing the bunker; it was his dinner gong! It was like a trained dog. Trained rat!

The monsoon changed our temperature from over 100 at one point, to 38 degrees, according to the radio. You could see your breath. We also had to cope with mosquitoes. Then a typhoon hit during the monsoon. Double trouble. There was furniture and government equipment flying around, sand hitting you in the face. The sand felt like shotgun pellets.

*1stLt **Claude Roberts**, Rescue Pilot,*

Previous occupants of our Quonset hut had built a little wooden deck on the roof of the hut with stairs going up to it. The routine when I got there was when the base loudspeaker (The Giant Voice) and the siren went off; despite the explosions in the area everybody would grab the beer and go to the deck to watch the show. The show was always the same; rocket fire would be coming into the base from nearby, heavily-forested Huk Mountain. This happened every week or ten days. The army would send counter-battery fire toward the mountain and the Air Force would scramble a few alert planes, and Puff the Magic Dragon would exhale in the direction of the mountain. It was quite a spectacular show. And we would drink beer. I had done some research and learned the VC 80-something mm rocket did not have the range to hit us at our hut so I knew we were safe. Then one night a rocket whooshed over our heads and landed about a half block away. They were now using a Russian-made 122mm Katusha rocket. That night marked our last visit to the deck!

Many missions failed. We might go through all the efforts and steps to save a downed pilot but sometimes they were either captured or killed. Another frustration was our isolation from The World for a year. Communications (letters) were so slow and you just kind of felt the world passing you by.

The monsoon slowed combat operations which in turn, slowed rescue operations. Unfortunately it didn't slow the movement of men and materiel down the Ho Chi Minh Trail.

We kept a very detailed computer book on the locations of enemy AAA (anti-aircraft) and SAM (surface to air missiles) sites. Our navigator was responsible for keeping us away from the heavy concentrations of AAA and SAM activity. And we flew too high for small arms fire. We did keep an eye out for enemy Migs, but our system kept us away from harm most of the time except when we went down to 4,000 feet to refuel; then we were subject to ground fire. Our plane was never hit but some of our other planes did take a round or two. One of the planes did get hit with a 12.5 which knocked a hole in it. We also had to leave the area a couple of times because a Mig was approaching.

Bosun Mate Chief **Don McMurray**

In the Delta we were close to Cambodia, where we weren't supposed to be. We got a call from an outpost that needed twelve engines. We had just finished working on these engines. This outpost was nineteen miles west into enemy territory. Along the way I found out that I didn't have a qualified coxswain when the ammis we were towing started taking on water. Then I'm told there would be an escort waiting for us, two Vietnamese and two American advisors. We met them and started our trip up the river. We got into the free fire zone and tested our weapons. All we had were .30 caliber machine guns. One of the Vietnamese wanted to get a drink of water. We had two jugs sitting there, one for water and one battery acid. Of course he drank the acid so he and his American had to split, leaving us with one escort. The other guy said his Vietnamese came down sick so that left us with no escort. We went seventeen miles with no escort, the enemy on both sides.

Coming back we left at 0400. We followed a lights-out freighter back down the river. I had to follow right behind them, following their wake since they had no lights on. I was six feet behind their stern. By the time daylight arrived I was beat. My eyes were all red. We returned safely and our XO, who was on the trip and had been drinking, fell into the river as he debarked. Somehow he was awarded a Purple Heart for this mission.

North Vietnam "formally" invaded South Vietnam on March 30, 1972.

Petty Officer 3rd Class **Charlie McDonald**, *Gunner's Mate*

The communists launched the 1972 Easter Offensive and it was our gunfire support in many cases that kept guys alive. We were considered one of the most reliable gunships there. The *Buchanon* was there with us at first but within a few weeks there were twenty destroyers providing support.

*Spc4 **Les Daulton**, Truck Driver*

We had problems with the road between Danang and Chu Lai. There was a pass where we used to get held up all the time. I asked one of the drivers why we were stopped. He said they ran over something. "What?" I asked. He said we have to wait until we pay the bounty and then they let us go. What was happening is the Vietnamese would concentrate around this narrow pass and then one of them would throw one of their little kids out under the tires of a vehicle. They demanded we pay for the loss of life to their child. It was even worse if you hit one of their water buffalo!

I was responsible for setting up the stage for the Bob Hope Danang Show in December of 1971. It took a week to get everything ready. I met Mr. Hope and the girls in the show and they were pleasant and down to earth. Then I had my seven day leave. I flew to Hong Kong, then to Texas. I had to pay my own way for the flight. This is where fate intervened. One of the friends at the base invited me to join their crap game. I told them I'd never played craps so they were most anxious to have me join in! But beginner's luck was with me and I won $1,000 which paid for the flight.

I went to Hawaii for my R&R to marry my wife in October of 1971. When I returned to Chu Lai the base was empty. Prior to leaving guys told us to be sure to take care of our dogs before we leave for Danang because the Vietnamese eat them! Everybody had a pet dog; one guy had a pet monkey. Well I see these 55-gallon drums being used for stew pots and they're filled with dogs. One guy pulled a dog out of the drum and I was just . . . I couldn't believe it. The drums were full of dogs.

Dressed in civvies, William Westmoreland saw the Hope crew off from Van Nuys, California. The tour's first stop was for 18,000 troops at Schofield barracks, in Waikiki, for the 25th Infantry Division. The last time Hope saw this unit they were at Cu Chi; still no mention of the tunnels. Then they visited Wake Island and Okinawa.

Next stop: U-Tapao, in Thailand, a familiar stop. Hope said his tour was going half way round the world. "You remember the world; you used to be part of it." The next Thailand stop was Ubon, for the eighth time, and then on to Danang, where it was raining again. Hope said it was a pleasure to be "working for you leftovers." There was another sarcastic remark about the Paris Peace talks. The tour tried to visit the USS Coral Sea next, but couldn't land on the carrier due to fog; Hope's first missed show in thirteen years.

The tour went to Vientiane, Laos, and then Camp Eagle. Hope noted all the signs in the audience and asked "what do you guys do all day, sit around and paint?" The Christmas Day show was at Long Binh, where Bob said "there's so much big brass here the GI's sleep at attention." Bob also observed that "you haven't lived until you've tasted C-rats in brandy sauce." "The 24-hour Christmas truce gives us a war with a commercial break."

The tour visited Tehran, to refuel, then Rota (Spain), where Bob commented that "the rain in Spain falls mainly on the Hope show." Then they hit Madrid, Guantanamo Bay, in Cuba, and did their last show at the Air Force Academy, in Colorado. About this tour Bob concluded that the empty seats in Vietnam were a good sign that things were winding down.

Ship fitter 3rd Class Diver 2nd Class **Steve Doak**

We were going to rescue a Zippo boat that had hit a mine next to one of our firebases. We had some support gunboats and started down this straight canal. There were six or seven boats and we also had helicopter support. It was easy to become complacent with all this firepower and we did! We started off with our helmets and flak jackets on and our fingers on the triggers of various machine guns. After about thirty minutes we started to relax. After thirty minutes more the helmets and flak jackets came off. A couple hours later there were four or five of us sitting on the top deck playing cards! When we reached the firebase a guy on the radio tells the choppers and duster planes overhead that they can go home. He thanks them and tells them this is the first time we've come up this way in over a month that we hadn't been hit! The card players just looked at each other!

Electricians Mate/Fireman **Bob Miller**

While we were escorting the cruiser *Chicago* we followed an enemy freighter from the Canary Islands. The *Chicago* received orders to sink it. I thought it was a routine bang-bang but we got caught in a cross fire between the *Chicago* and the beach. The loudspeaker barked "Tempest (our call sign). Tempest. You are expendable. Draw fire." I don't ever want to hear that again.

**USS Chicago at work
Courtesy: Bob Miller**

There was one time the Engineering Officer didn't tell the captain that he had shut down the after turret. So the *Mackenzie* started in on a gun run without the aft gun. They jury-rigged everything to bypass the electrical problem and pulled it off.

We were shot at all the time. A 5" gun shoots seven miles. We were near the shore and we would sit there for eight to ten hours lobbing shells. The spotter would say "there are tanks on the beach." We'd fire from the forward mount going in, then we'd turn, and the aft mount would kick in. And the boiler technicians would put in extra oil to create a smokescreen as we pulled away. And we'd zigzag. Their shells would walk up our wake. They were smart. I'm unsure whether this was North or South Vietnam. I was never told where we were; all we knew was that we were on the Gun Line.

*CWO **"Woody" Woodruff**, Pilot*

One of my assignments as a helicopter pilot on this tour was to drop excess religious books and manuals into the ocean.

On April 19, 1972, the USS Higbee DD-806, the first American warship named for a female member of the USN, became the first ship to be bombed during the Vietnam War. Two MIG-17's from the 923rd Fighter Bomber attacked and pilot Le Xuan Di dropped a 500lb bomb onto the Higbee's rear 5" gun mount, destroying it. The gun crew had been outside the mount due to a previous misfire and four sailors were wounded. The second MIG bombed the light cruiser USS Oklahoma City CLG-5, causing minor damage. The USS Sterett DLG-31 claimed a direct Terrier surface-to-air missile hit on one of the MIGs.

*Petty Officer 3rd Class **Charlie McDonald**, Gunner's Mate*

We were in port working on the *Strauss* gun mounts after we hit the mines, and the *USS Higbee* took our mission up to North Vietnam. Our missile guys were really upset after the *Higbee* was bombed by a North Vietnamese MIG because the *Higbee* had no missiles and we did. The *Higbee* was a WW II tin can.

Hull Technician Chief Jim Sooy

We were steaming from Yokosuka to Subic Bay ending a seven-month deployment but en route we were diverted back to Danang. The emergency was the *USS Higbee* (DD-806). The armor piercing MIG bomb had started the ship listing by the stern. The *Gompers* sent an emergency crew to patch it so it could be towed to meet Fat Sam at Danang.

The *Higbee* may or may not have been carrying nuclear weapons, (only the captain, XO, and the weapons officer, and maybe the chief in charge of the weapons locker would know for sure) and they are not supposed to send a ship into a harbor under those conditions. Our ship DID carry nuclear weapons since we supplied destroyers that carried anti-submarine weapons. You are dealing with some Top Secret equipment here. No one can say because it's so damn classified.

The first thing the morons on the *Gompers* did when they reached Danang, they convinced their division officer that they should have a beer party on the pier. So later that afternoon they go ashore to have two beers on the pier. Now you can see rocket and mortar holes on the pier which didn't get there from old age, they got there from attacks. Somebody finally decides that this is a bad situation and they better get back aboard the *Gompers*. You can't have 100 unarmed sailors running around the pier with a beer in their hands in a potentially hostile environment.

The *Higbee* is nested to the *Gompers* for two or three days, and the sailors finally realize that when red flares come up at night, Charlie is in the area. And they did not want a ship with the *Gompers* capability to get a hit because you don't know what kind of catastrophic result there might be. A warhead shot from a Mark 48 torpedo carries 500 pounds and in plain English, it's known as a cow hit bomb. It's made of manure and it's an explosive force.

So they decide it is wise to deport and come back during daytime. On their return it's not so safe either because the VC do have frogmen. They're not very good but they do blow themselves up! I don't recall what time of day it was (it was daytime), but I heard the explosion. We sent a diver and a corpsman to investigate. They determined that the frogman had carried at least a 40-pound satchel charge. They found part of his foot in his flip flop and part of a fin. They couldn't find his breathing apparatus. Their usual plan was to take a tree bush and float it down the river, and hide within the bush.

Looking back, the enemy to be aware of the weaponry aboard the *Gompers*. Their intelligence was so superb. The VC wanted badly to hit ole Fat Sam as the value on our ship was in the billions of dollars. Fat Sam was not meant to go in harm's way. The *Higbee* departed again for safety sake and returned later figuring that nothing more was going to happen. And of course that night as they were preparing to get under way a rocket attack started. Both ships got under way and that was the end of that. Or was it? Repair work finished, the *Gompers* got out in the Gulf of Tonkin and the engines went dead. One of the boilers died. We maintained radio silence until repairs were made.

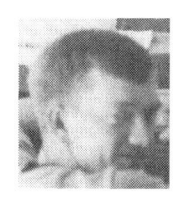

Sgt. **Don Wilson**, *Aviation Supply*

The ARVN had a habit of leaving heavy equipment behind them when we dropped them off at the LZ's. Once they were off the chopper I'd notice claymore mines, LAW's (Light Anti-Tank Weapons) and things like that. They'd leave half their ammo on the chopper.

I regularly flew to Danang for supplies. Supply guys there worked a 9 to 5 schedule. Nothing was done without the proper paperwork

We were shot at a lot when we inserted the patrols into the LZ's. We were shot down once and the co-pilot broke his leg in the crash. This happened in a dangerous location but there were four helicopters with us and they picked us up very quickly.

Spc4 **Rich "Saw" Negich**, *MP*

Some of the American guys we had to arrest were pretty wacky. At Phu Bai we got a call to proceed to a certain area. We pull up and this captain tells us they have a guy in this hooch and he's nuts. Just as he says that tracers start flying out of the roof. The shooter had already wounded one guy. The captain says "Go get him." We said "Fuck you. You go get him. We don't want to get shot." He told us it was our job. So two of us inched up toward the hooch -- and tracers are still flying out all over the place -- and when we heard the guy changing magazines we rushed into the hooch and tackled him. He was pretty nuts. We trussed him up and took him to the provost marshal. He was swearing at us and real belligerent. I finally had enough and I beat the hell out of him. This bothers me to this day. He just would not cooperate. I kicked him right in the solar plexus; I could see his eyes turn. So the next day CID comes to get me and I'm getting irritated, and they told me to cool down, that they were on my side. I never heard anything more on that.

Camp Eagle was mortared a few times while I was there. One of these attacks, at Phu Bai in January, 1972, wounded fourteen men.

Mortar Attack at Phu Bai
Courtesy: Robert Negich

The Easter (March 1972) offensive was going on and the NVA were overrunning some of the bases. They moved us down to Saigon. There simply weren't enough troops there to do much of anything. We never reclaimed much of that lost ground but our pilots really did a job on the NVA. That's the only reason they stopped them.

Being required to call for permission to return fire was immensely frustrating, and damned dangerous. Our attackers at the main gate knew they were safe and that's where they would plunk their mortars from.

In May, 1972, Nixon ordered the mining of North Vietnamese waters.

Petty Officer 3rd Class **Charlie McDonald**, *Gunner's Mate*

We were fired at many times from North Vietnamese shore batteries. I was on the *Strauss* when we hit two mines. This was outside of Haiphong Harbor, at night. What happened was we had seeded the waters off the harbor with mines but the North Vietnamese had towed the mines further out to sea and we ran into one, and then another soon after the first one. Five or six of our ships hit mines; one, a World War II tin can, was so badly damaged it was de-commissioned right there. We suffered no casualties and there was no damage to the ship, although we checked our gyroscopes in dry dock once we got back to Subic Bay. What saved us from real damage was we were in deep water when we hit the mines.

There were a lot of frustrations. Being at sea for months at a time is difficult. Getting replacement parts was a serious problem for us. It was an exceedingly serious problem; not only getting the parts but getting the time to do the repairs. We were so busy firing; there was no down time for maintenance. On the 1972 tour we fired 25,000 rounds.

Since we were not allowed to open the doors to the gun mounts at night, eventually our gas ejection air system broke down. Depending on how the wind was blowing we might get a lot of smoke right back into the gun mount. We tried to rotate our positions to give each guy a chance to stick his head out of our vent and we even tried wearing gas masks. What it took for them to finally acknowledge this need for maintenance and repair was the time we were busy firing and the smoke got so bad I started to have seizures. I could not control my muscles. I had to go outside the gun mount to get fresh air and someone else took over. They finally seemed to realize that this kind of situation could kill somebody. We also had two extra guys in the gun mount and one of them would have to pry the round out of the cradle into the transfer tray because one of the mechanisms was not working right. The other extra guy was beating on the projectiles with a mallet to get them to seat correctly due to yet another mechanical problem.

When the *Strauss* was new in the early 1960's, we could fire forty 5" rounds per minute. By 1972, we were firing about thirty rounds per minute. The constant firing took a toll. There were two trays in the lower part of the magazine, each holding twenty rounds loaded electronically. Once those twenty were fired the rate of fire was cut in half as the crew loaded each round into the tray.

We went up north one time to try to rescue a couple of pilots that had gone down. A helicopter picked up one of the pilots but the other one was grabbed by the North Vietnamese. We could have moved on them by force but they would have shot the pilot.

We did a lot of cruising up and down the North Vietnamese coast shelling the SAM sites to protect the flyboys. I worked for a short, wiry gunner's mate on Mount 51. He was very high strung. You could see this when you fired the 5" gun. When you fire the gun there are some gasses that come out before the powder gets kicked out and sometimes, when the oxygen gets in there it can re-combust, and there is a small flame. This guy would always jump back and say "Whoa." Well we were steaming along at general quarters waiting for our next fire mission and the first mine goes off. I reach down for the phones and I notice that the door to the gun mount is open. This guy is gone! I close the door which we were required to do and report that we've been hit on the starboard side forward of the gun mount. Seconds later, WHAM, we hit the second mine. The door opens and there's the gunner's mate coming back in, soaked from head to foot. He had been soaked by the wave from the second explosion. After the first explosion he headed for the life raft station. He was on his way back to the gun mount when he got soaked from the second explosion.

We had some white phosphorous shells that needed to be returned to the ammo ship, probably because their expiration date had been reached. These are potent shells and they have to be stocked vertically. The box we had these shells in caught on the lip of the rail on the way to the ammo ship. The shells fell down to the main deck, a distance of about ten feet. They're normally good for about six feet. We had to grab these shells and throw them over the side. Each shell weighs seventy-two pounds. Most of the guys scattered when this happened; only one or two guys were up to the task of throwing these live shells overboard.

Spc4 **Les Daulton**, *Truck Driver*

Since my friends knew I wasn't on drugs, they told me I had to do their urine tests. Guys were coming to me with tears in their eyes telling me I had to help them. I told them they should just turn themselves in for treatment to get the help they needed. I was in this testing area for about ten days. I finally went behind a tree and peed in this cup, but they ended up grabbing the guy and leading him away. They were just watching too closely.

We were sent to a firebase beyond Duk Pho. This was actually an American base in Cambodia where we weren't supposed to be. They had a sheet metal runway and about five or six tents and that was it. We took bombs, artillery shells and Agent Orange to that base.

A guy I came to know volunteered the two of us to close down Duk Pho. When we turned it over to the ARVN the American guys there below the rank of sergeant had to get rid of their refrigerators. They were not allowed to ship them home (when I made sergeant I shipped mine home and it still works fine!). The guys there said they would rather destroy them than leave them for the ARVN. We loaded them on my flat bed trailer and I took them back to our base. At one time I had three or four refrigerators. On the way back it grew dark. My friend suggested a firebase he knew for us to spend the night.

At Chu Lai by the end of 1971, most Americans had already left the base. The guy I was replacing was checking out (turning in his rifle, web gear, etc.) and a rocket came in and made a direct hit on him. He was on this one-story high porch going through the checkout process and bam! I never wanted to know people's names after that! It shook me up pretty bad.

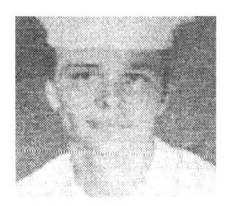

Electricians Mate/Fireman **Bob Miller**

On my second tour we were doing a gun run, and the enemy was walking shells up our wake. They knocked out our steering so control of the ship went over to the After Steering compartment. I had to hold the guy steering up by the waist due to the difficulty of steering the ship manually. Thank God for the dual steering capacity of the old WW II destroyers.

Bosun Mate Chief **Don McMurray**

The *Lawrence* 116 high speed attacks with our 5" 54 on Haiphong Harbor. We'd go up there every night and hit it, and they'd rebuild it. Coming back we would give support to infantry units on land. We got this one call; they were surrounded but they had spotters and we got them enough relief that they got out of there.

In our early days on the *Lawrence* we were stationed in the waters off Danang. We had a lot of what we called rice paddy duty; the enemy would float one-man sampans full of rice into shore to supply their troops. Our job was to prevent this; it was boring duty. While on this rice paddy duty at night we would encounter high speed aircraft overhead. Procedures called for us to exchange recognition signals with this plane. Often each of us accused the other of not always following procedures, which was important since any boat or plane in this area could be ours or theirs. The next time we signaled a plane and received no reply our captain did what the captain of a guided missile destroyer should do. We prepared to launch a missile. When the plane, which was one of ours, saw that we had "locked on" him, he quickly squawked his recognition signal.

One time on the rice paddy patrol the CO was in the Combat Information Center and the XO was on the bridge. The XO is jerking the ship right to left. The captain storms up to the bridge wanting to know why we were swerving. "I was dodging all the sampans," the XO responded. "Just ram them" the captain ordered.

Spc4 **Bernie Wright**, *Wireman/Switchboard Repair*

We took a lot of mortar fire but none of it landed real close to me. I guess they spent most of their time shooting at the air strip at Bien Hoa.

In my second year – this would be late 1971 or early 1972 – we had fewer people to do the work. They sent us a warrant officer to run things and he really didn't want the responsibility, so he pretty much let me run things. For about six weeks I was the company commander of our unit.

It was difficult to get the spare parts especially for the switchboards. And the monsoon really created some problems for switchboards. The rains filled the six or eight-foot ditches around the compound. We had little bridges inside the compound and some of those would wash away during the rains. We did a lot of cannibalizing to keep things running.

1stLt **Claude Roberts**, *Rescue Pilot*

The only time I really felt fear was a couple of times on the ground at Cam Ranh Bay. In the first case a sapper came through the wire and blew up the ammo dump. I was awakened by a huge concussion, my windows blew out and I found myself on the floor. I couldn't see out due to the walls around the Quonset hut so I didn't know what was going on. Large, secondary explosions kept going off and I wondered if we were being attacked or what. We finally realized what was going on but the noise was continuous. The explosions continued for 36 hours; 500 lb. and 1,000 lb. bombs going off one after another.

Bosun Mate Chief **Don McMurray**

We were providing gunfire support to some action in-country in January of 1973, just prior to my return home. When we started to send in rounds I saw the flash of return fire and my job was to take a bearing. Just as I did that I heard bing, bing, bing, as shrapnel was hitting right behind me. A lookout was standing beside me. I told him to get inside. I felt like I was indestructible. They didn't hurt me in two other tours . . . . and they aren't going to get me now! The ship got a Purple Heart for that.

My proudest moment was giving fire support to our infantry at the DMZ when they were surrounded. Some people stayed in Vietnam another year in return for a field promotion. I was never that lucky.

*Petty Officer 3rd Class **Charlie McDonald**, Gunner's Mate*

On my second tour (January – August 1973) we hardly fired at all. We played more cards than anything. We did a lot of picket duty providing coverage for the carriers. This tour was more relaxed to the point of boredom. There was some marijuana use. We fired 25,000 rounds in 1972, and none in 1973. We returned to Pearl Harbor on December 7, 1973.

Per the Paris Peace Accords a ceasefire went into effect on 1/27/73. Operation Homecoming returned 591 POW's from Hanoi and occurred simultaneously with the dismantling of U.S. military bases in the South

*SSgt **Bill Roy**, Environmental/Occupational Medicine*

Flying out of Clark AFB in the Philippine Islands in 1973 I was a crewmember of the first planeload of POW's out of Hanoi. We had no idea what to expect, what shape these guys might be in both physically and mentally, so we had a supply of strait jackets, just in case. We also had a large complement of doctors, nurses, medics, etc. Hanoi had the POW's ready and waiting for us; we were not on the ground long.

We remembered from the prisoner exchange at the end of the Korean War in 1953 that they did all they could to make things unpleasant including filling the plane with mosquitoes so I was well-armed with bug sprays when we landed. All but two of the POW's were ambulatory and could proudly return the salutes of welcoming officers; Shortly after takeoff we heard a dog barking! Our higher-ups were furious; one of the POW's had smuggled a dog aboard. Lots of examinations would be necessary! Lots of paperwork. But the guys were home!

CHAPTER THIRTY-SEVEN

WELCOME HOME!

So after a tour – or two or three – we came home. Over there we created over twenty-one million bomb craters but built hundreds of churches and schools. We sprayed eighteen million gallons of herbicide and erected thousands of kilometers of roads. Between us and our enemy we injured thousands of civilians and treated them all. It was that kind of war. And now we were home.

Don Campbell

After getting out of the green machine, I received a letter from my buddy who worked in the message center. He told me of the number of Headquarters Company guys killed during Operation Starlite (the first nighttime helicopter assault in history). I had been attached to this unit during their training exercises and field competitions back on Hawaii. He also told me that some marines we knew were killed in a plane crash on return from their first liberty on Japan. To this day I think about why I survived and they didn't, and the what-ifs, though it has abated somewhat over the years.

Bruce Quinlan

On my return in August of 1969 I heard no marching bands or cheers. I was greeted by a lot of robe-wearing cowards. This was within twenty-fours of being in a combat zone and I felt like I had entered a different kind of combat zone. They were chanting. For years afterward I was reluctant to say I was a Vietnam veteran because of those people that greeted the plane. Every day I was in Vietnam I was proud of what I did. I realized that even though I wasn't in combat I was making a difference to those that were. I still get choked up thinking about that. I have four flags on my porch right now: the Stars and Stripes, a POW flag, an Air Force flag, and, since I have a son in the Coast Guard for eighteen years, a Coast Guard flag.

Larry Rock

In early September, 1966, I flew on a C130 with thirty or forty others whose time in Vietnam was up, going from Okinawa, stopping at Midway to refuel, and then over Catalina Island to southern California. After a couple of wasted hours we paid a marine to drive us to LAX. I flew from there thru Chicago to Pittsburgh. I took a cab to the house where my sister helped carry my bags into the house. My mother cried. I had been flying and had not eaten for twenty-four hours but I wasn't hungry. My dad took me to his favorite watering hole. He knew I wasn't one for beer and he offered a Coke, but I drank a beer. One of his friends asked me how we were doing over there. After a year of ninety hour work-weeks, and watching South Vietnamese pilots strafing their own troops, longshoremen strikes on the dock at Danang, and the overriding lack of clarity on the rules of war, all I could say to the room full of World War II vets, some of whom had wrested the two islands I had been on earlier that day (Okinawa and Midway) from the Japanese, was that we were working hard.

Cpl Larry Rock on Midway Island Stopover Going Home – Sept. 1966

Gary Nunn

I returned to California in spring of 1967 after my tour and they wanted me to become a highway patrolman. They were recruiting from the military. But I had accrued some seniority at my job back home while I was in the service and I returned to that. I appreciate the police but I feel that they really don't get enough respect for the tough job they do. Naturally the Army offered me another stripe to stay six more months but I told them they could make me a general and I wouldn't stay.

Chuck Glazerman

I didn't get much involved with the politics of the moment as I did my job over there but being largely ignored after my return from Vietnam was pretty frustrating. There weren't many people who had much interest at all in what you had been exposed to.

Garry Ramsey

We flew into Seattle on our return in October, 1969, and a colonel boarded the plane when we landed and told us to exit the plane and walk through the airport in a straight line and refrain from talking to anybody.

Allen Thomas Jr.

I returned from Asia three times. The first and last times nothing memorable happened. On the second return in the Spring of 1968 we ran into a roadblock leaving our base outside the San Francisco airport. One of the master sergeants on the bus had a rock thrown at him as he attempted to talk to the protestors. Finally, since many of us had planes to catch, a colonel led us off the bus and we dismantled the roadblock, forcibly. The bus driver was laughing as we re-boarded the bus.

Dick Immes

I came back to Columbus AFB in Mississippi in 1970. It was a rural community and I think the South does a better job of respecting the military than other regions. After Vietnam the Army lobbied for a good close-support plane and the A10 (Warthog) was the result. The A10 is almost ugly enough to be a navy plane! The A10 is not as well powered as the A37. It's almost impossible to stall the A37. We thought the A37 was the answer. It carries a lot of ordnance, a lot of fuel, and it is accurate.

E. Jane McCarthy

I don't remember any particular frustrations while I was there. Over the years however, watching my friends die from Agent Orange-related leukemia and things like that have been hard to take.

When the guys started coming back they started to recognize PTSD. And we as nurses said "Oh, that's for the soldiers. That's not for us." But looking back on it I can see that I had classic PTSD symptoms where I had nightmares; I only slept every other night and the night I slept I had nightmares. I wasn't eating, I was depressed, and this went on for several months. As I thought about it I realized that some soldiers maybe only saw combat once or twice. We were seeing these wounded every day. We had to cut off their clothing. Chrissie and I were exposed to Agent Orange from the clothes of the wounded.

There was a group of about ten or twelve of us that stayed friends for years. We really cared about each other. I think our feelings for each other became more apparent after we returned home. I'm still in touch with some. Last year was a tough year because my friend Chrissie that I worked with died of leukemia. One of the other nurses married an officer over there and he died about four or five years ago of the same leukemia.

Coming home was the tougher time. How do you relate to the world after what you've seen? How do you live the rest of your life? I remember thinking the rest of my life would be anti-climactic; nothing that could surpass that. But we all kept on going. We helped each other afterwards.

Vic Griguoli

When I returned to the United States a guy spit on me and called me a baby killer at the Greyhound Station in San Francisco.

Bernie Wright

I returned through the San Francisco airport. I saw six young girls approaching me. I stopped them and told them what a pretty sight they were and how I hadn't seen round-eyed full-breasted girls in a long time. They were flattered and pulled up their tops. The waiting passengers nearby applauded.

Tom Petersen

I left the Army in April, 1970, and graduated with "high honors" with a B.S. in Biology from Michigan State. Most of the returning vets I knew did very well in college after their time in the service.

Jack Stroud

I returned to the United States in April, 1971. Coming home was different; there were more protestors at the gate, screaming and spitting. That hurt me more than anything. Not being welcomed. Go on back, we don't want you here. That's okay. I did my job. I put on my uniform at Oakland Army Terminal and I got me a steak dinner. Like most guys coming back I thought I could handle all the stuff going on; people calling us baby-killers and things like that. But it was difficult putting the memories of lost comrades to rest. Those memories never go away. Eventually everyone has to deal with those demons. I felt like my life was so riddled with emotional wounds then that I doubted if I would ever be normal again. But I'm still hanging in there.

Edie Meeks

When I got near my time to go home other nurses advised me to take a civilian outfit with me and change as soon as I could. When my time came I took off my uniform and threw it in the trash; that's how I felt about all the waste! When I got home I didn't even try to explain to anyone what I saw and most people didn't want to hear it anyway. I just shut down. Years later they did a story about me in the local paper and someone came up to me in the supermarket and said "Edie, I've known you for twenty-five years and I didn't know you served." My anger came back with the Iraq War and my kid told me to go get help. Luckily I talked to a psychologist who did help. I went to an art show once and there was this painting of Vietnam and the grunts in the painting looked like they had spider webs all over them; like they were broken and shattered, and they all shattered differently, and it said PTSD. I showed this to the psychologist and told him this is what I felt like. He hung the painting and later told me a lot of the guys that came in to talk to him said that was how they felt too. Until I got help I didn't know how shut down I was. I thought I was doing okay but I was really just holding on.

Garry Ramsey

Years after Vietnam I was attending a Veteran's reunion in Las Vegas. A friend and I had our Veteran's caps on. Two Vietnamese ladies came up and thanked us for our service to their country. They were both doctors who left Vietnam in the late 60's, and worked in Cleveland. They ended up living in Miami. It was the best Welcome Home I ever received.

Jim Sooy

The crew of the *Gompers* was not prepared for Vietnam.

Dave Cass

My journey home from Vietnam started at 10:00 AM on a Sunday morning, September 22, 1968 when Hershel Gossett, from Athens, Tennessee and I were blown off a steel telephone pole by a concussion grenade thrown by a VC off a nearby roof top. Hershel fell over 40 feet and was killed instantly. His name is found on Panel 43W, Line 62 engraved on the Viet Nam Veterans Memorial Wall in Washington, D. C. I broke a few tiles on the roof of a nearby Vietnamese guard-shack with my face on the way to the ground. I hit on the back of my head when I landed. I felt certain that I had broken my neck. It hurt much worse than a high school football injury and I couldn't move my arms or legs. Most of my body was protected by the guard-shack but my head was exposed to fire from the VC shooting from the rooftop at me. The ARVN soldiers in the guard-shack heard the commotion and rushed into the street. They exchanged fire with the VC but two of them were hit in the legs as they protected me. The wounded ARVN's were brought to the 24th Evacuation Hospital in Long Binh.

An American Med Cap medic was down the street holding a clinic for the local Vietnamese and he rushed to the scene when he heard the shooting. He put me on a stretcher and stabilized my head with sandbags. I never lost consciousness. As they placed me on the medevac chopper I saw rainbow colors reflected on the visor of the door gunner. I asked him if there was a person behind those colors and he raised his visor and smiled like the pot of gold at the end of the rainbow. I thought I might just make it back alive now.

I was flown to the 24th Evac Hospital at Long Binh. A Neuro-surgeon kept pricking me with a pin to see if I felt anything but I didn't. They shaved my head and drilled two holes into my skull. A device known as Krutchfield Tongs became my new head gear and I was placed in a Stryker frame. A ten pound weight was attached to the Tongs and ran through a pulley and hung by gravity to help stretch my neck to minimize the damage to the nerves branching out between the vertebrae. I thought I was going to survive until a Catholic Priest came in. I asked him if he was administering the Last Rites. He said no, he was giving me the Sacrament of the Sick but now I was worried. My Battalion Commander -- Lieutenant-Colonel Jordan -- also arrived wanting to know what happened. I wasn't sure myself at that point; were we electrocuted or hit by a grenade? I had suffered severe trauma to the back of my head where I made contact with the road. I wore a donut to keep pressure off the wounded area. Every two hours I was sandwiched and strapped in with three straps between a front and back panel of the Stryker frame. Then locking pins on each end were released and I was rotated 180 degrees from face up to face down. Then the straps and back part of the bed frame were removed to air out my back after the locking pins were re-engaged. Two hours later it was back the other way again. As I remember it took three people to safely affect this maneuver.

My best friend in Viet Nam, Captain Daryl Solomonson with the 720th MP's came to visit often and met one my two favorite nurses -- Cathy Hendersen. They dated, later got married and have two wonderful sons. We are still good friends.

I slowly stabilized at the 24th in Long Binh, VN. A Physical Therapist named Major Victory came in every day to "break my arms" to help in the healing process. I had a Foley Catheter and had to be hand fed. The toes in my left foot moved first. On October 1, 1968 I was awarded the purple-heart on my way into an ambulance, but soon lost the orders accompanying it.

 My ten pound weight was replaced by a tension-pull. Still in my Stryker-Frame they took me by ambulance to Ton Son Nhut air base in Saigon for transfer to Japan. As the Medevac plane was being readied on the tarmac we came under fire and the VC shot the out some of the tires. Everyone hit the dirt but me. I was the highest target around strapped into my Stryker-frame. I asked if maybe I could be moved back into the air conditioned depot while they fixed this problem. Finally with new tires, I was loaded and locked into my Freedom bird and we were off to the 249th General Hospital, Camp Drake, Asaka, Japan.

At Camp Drake, in Japan, they told me my disks were pulverized and they couldn't be fused back together. They had me completely immobilized in a fancier Circle-electric striker frame and I was still rotated every two hours but I could be partially vertical. When an earthquake hit two nurses held onto me so I wouldn't fall off while still attached by head. It would have been fatal. Other patients had fallen out of their beds and breaking casts and hanging by their traction.

Courtesy: Dave Cass

Also there were student riots that threatened the hospital. At one point during the stay in Japan I saw a lieutenant – the guy who had once stolen my jeep's trailer in Vietnam -- hobbling to the men's room. We had a good laugh over that.

While in the critical ward in Japan I awoke to a shower of blood from the patient next to me. This man died. A day later the guy on the other side of me died. The priest told me that this was an unlucky section of the ward; the next day he was in bed next to me with a ruptured appendix! About this time I had my first erection since I was wounded. The nurses laughed about it and they told me it was good news/bad news. The bad news was the tape in that area was now inside me. The good news was everything was working again.

After two weeks in Japan I was flown home. We refueled in Elmendorf AFB, still with the metal apparatus sticking out of my head. Some of the wives of the higher-ranked officers at Elmendorf entered the plane to cheer up the patients but they were reticent to approach me with all the head stuff. The guy in the bunk above me was smoking and his ashes kept falling on me but I was unable to move out of the way.

After the refueling, we flew to Washington, D.C. I was put on a smaller plane and flown to Bedford Air Base in Massachusetts; I ended up in Chelsea Naval Hospital. My right side was still not working. Late one night I was awoken by a patient who up to this time appeared comatose from a head injury. I could see him in my mirror sitting upright in his bed uncommunicative day after day. However he watched me being turned day in and day out. He had released the locking pin at the foot of my bed while mumbling "time to turn you." I yelled for help but the radio was on and the duty nurse couldn't hear me. My left leg had become very strong. I used it to hook on the overhead bed frame to pick myself up for bedpan use. I told the patient to unstrap my other side. When he moved over there I clobbered him with a strong leg kick. The nurse heard the commotion and rescued me. The patient graduated to Section 8 and I never saw him again.

After three months at Chelsea I was walking, eating and writing with my left-hand. I was assigned to Post Engineers at Fort Dix, New Jersey in February, 1969 with a limited profile. I was working mainly with civilians doing various construction jobs and I enjoyed it. In early April I saluted the Post Commanding General with my left hand. He stopped me and I explained my right arm wasn't working yet. I thought that was the end of it but I was called in by my boss, an Engineer Colonel and informed that I was being put in for a medial discharge. They told me that Ft. Dix was a Basic Training Post and walking wounded might have an adverse effect on the new trainees. In April my promotion for a captaincy came through which was later denied because I was still on a medical-hold status. I was sent home. I was put on a temporary disability status for the next ten years and finally discharged. I really enjoyed the Army and would have been a career Engineer officer. With my wife's help I was finally awarded a Purple Heart forty years after the fact. My right hand never regained its full use but I'm glad to have it. I wear a prosthetic brace on both legs to compensate for foot drop and I developed syringomyelia (cavity in my spinal cord) which is slowly impairing all my sensory functions. I have a loving wife, four wonderful children and am active in the VVA and VFW with my other VN wounded veterans.

Bob Hope's 1972 tour included his final stop in Vietnam. They visited bases in Japan, Korea, Thailand ("Udorn is a native word for "keep the motor running") and U-Tapao, then Tan Son Nhut, near Saigon, on Christmas Eve, Bob's ninth and last trip to Vietnam. "This has to be my final trip. The last chicken with my blood type died." Bob final jibe on the Paris Peace talks: "Not only did the talks fail. Now they're fighting over the hotel bill."

Hope's tour also stopped at Nam Phong, in Thailand, Singapore ("It's been 22 years since the Road to Singapore movie – I'm back here to apologize"), the USS Midway, including sailors from the USS Cleveland, then Subic Bay and on Christmas Day they entertained 1,200 Seabees on Diego Garcia, in the Indian Ocean. The last show was on Guam.

Over the years Bob Hope made twenty-two Christmas trips, beginning in 1941 in California, including nine trips to Vietnam. Any man that could bring laughter to a place like Vietnam deserves the Road to Heaven.

CHAPTER THIRTY-EIGHT

1975

PEACE WITH HONOR

Military Assistance Command Vietnam (MACV) was dis-established in April 1973 by the Paris Peace Accords. This agreement also permitted 100,000 NVA soldiers to remain in South Vietnam. Sort of a Lose-Lose deal!

Aid to the South Vietnamese was cut dramatically in 1974; the ARVN were consigned to fight "a poor man's war" thereafter.

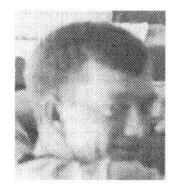

Sgt. **Don Wilson***, Aviation Supply, USS Tripoli LPH-10*

After two years of working off the LPH's I started to do some things at Group Supply, on Okinawa. Early in 1975 one of the helicopter captains who was privy to the upcoming evacuation of Saigon asked me to come back to his unit. I joined this unit late in March, 1975, and we finished this mission in April.

The reason we used helicopters for the Evac rather than the much larger transport planes is that some of the deserting South Vietnamese bombed Tan Son Nhut airfield, putting it out of business. For some reason, when the Evac began we were about 3 ½ hours late getting started; somebody couldn't figure out the time zone changes or something. When we got started in the afternoon we flew straight through until the next morning. So our part of the final Evac lasted just under 24 hours. The Marine helicopters made 530 trips during this period; I personally did nine trips. Our trips all involved Tan Son Nhut and the American Embassy; other units may have been involved in other Saigon locations, but we just did those two. Maybe four choppers went in at a time at Tan Son Nhut and two choppers could land at a time at the embassy, one on the roof and one in the courtyard.

One of the hardest parts of this job was trying to maintain order. Many of the Vietnamese had converted all their assets into gold; I had one Vietnamese who stood about 4' 9", but he weighed about 250 pounds with all the gold he was carrying. We had to throw a lot of people off the choppers. I carried a .45 and a .38 on this job.

We landed in the courtyard one time and I had brought a magnet with me because I had seen a lot of weapons in the swimming pool. We wouldn't allow anyone on the helicopter with a weapon so Americans and Vietnamese alike were discarding their handguns in the pool. I fished a couple of them out on this trip.

We had at least thirty people on each trip in my chopper. The CH-53's could take about 45 people. The pilots had some concerns about the weight on the choppers but the biggest fear was flying in there during the dark. My chopper was not fired upon during the Evac that I am aware of but some South Vietnamese did fire on a few other choppers. They fired on their own people. The South Vietnamese army had turned into rabble at this point. They took off their uniforms and ran around naked until they found some civilian clothes.

Those that were rescued were kept on the hangar deck of the LPH. Eventually we took them back to Okinawa, and ultimately back to the United States. I was back in the U.S. by May 12 and I got back there just in time to be assigned as a guard for the refugees when they arrived at Camp Pendleton. I met Vice President Ky there. I felt proud that the captain asked me to join him for the final trips into Saigon. He remembered me from my earlier tour.

My major frustration was during the Evac. President Ford stopped us from making the final trip that would have rescued the last remaining people. I have never seen so many grown men cry, including myself. The last trip plucked the American Ambassador off the roof -- the ambassador was the second to last to leave -- and we left eleven Marines there. We did go back and get those Marines; I was on that last flight. The NVA were knocking down the gate at the South Vietnamese President's house. It could have been a lot worse. We lost one CH-46 during the Evac. I don't know what happened to it.

During the Evac in 1975, I thought the guys were very professional. The pilots had all served in country before this event, and the junior enlisted men could see how important this was from the atmosphere around the carrier. We'd wasted almost fifteen years. And a bunch of American lives.

6,000 Americans and 50,000 Vietnamese were evacuated. Marine helicopters evacuated the final Americans from Cambodia on April 12, 1975.

NVA troops under General Nguyen Huu An captured the presidential palace in Saigon. General Nguyen Huu An had led the NVA troops in the Ia Drang battle in November, 1965, nearly ten years earlier. [xc] *The NVA did not use a twelve-month tour of duty program.*

Paul Gesswein

One of the most disappointing things to me was to see the ladder going up to the helicopters at the American Embassy in 1975, and we just gave up. That to me was a sad, sad day in American history.

Vince Malaterra

After I got home, I'm sitting in a bar with a beer in front of me, and the TV is showing the fall of Saigon. All those guys died for this crap?

On April 30, 1975, the day Saigon fell to the communists, by then retired William Westmoreland was recovering from a recent heart attack at his home in Charleston, South Carolina. On this day he wrote to the Veterans Administration about the possibility that his retirement disability be upgraded to reflect a "possible heart malfunction" at the time of his separation from active duty.[xci]

Cambodia's five-year war was ended in 1975 as the capital Phnom Penh fell to the Khmer Rouge, which instituted radical policies that claimed an estimated 1.7 million lives – a high cost for playing dominoes -- until the regime was overthrown in 1979.

EPILOGUE

997 soldiers were killed on their first day in Vietnam, 1,448 on their last day. Thirty-one sets of brothers are on the wall together. Eight women are also on the wall. As in most wars, West Virginia had the highest per capita casualty rate – 711West Virginians died.

The USS Higbee earned one battle star in WW II and seven in Korea before her service in Vietnam. She was sunk as a target ship 130 miles west of San Diego on April 24, 1986, missing by five days the fourteenth anniversary of her bombing by a Mig off the coast of Vietnam.

The Joseph D. Strauss won ten medals/commendations and was de-commissioned on February 1, 1990. The Strauss was transferred to Greece on October 1, 1992. Greece sold the ship for scrap in 2004.

The USS Cleveland first saw action during Tet. She was de-commissioned on September 30, 2011 after forty-four years of service and nearly four dozen awards and ribbons. She is currently on inactive reserve status.

Our riverine navy was given to the South Vietnamese as part of Vietnamization. When Saigon fell the NVA inherited the largest and most sophisticated brown water fleet in the world, including hundreds of riverine vessels.

Jim Sooy

The first harpoon missile to strike the *Gompers* on July 22, 2003 was fired by the *USS Cole* which would later gain notoriety in the Middle East. Fat Sam took sixteen missiles and 40,000 pounds of ordnance to put her to rest at 32 28' 04" north   119 58' 07" west.

The Navy has changed immensely over the years. There are no such things as steam-powered boilers anymore; it's jet turbines now. The days of the tender are history. There's no longer a need. Now the technicians can fly to the disabled ship. Now the upper superstructure is aluminum, not steel. The old days of using an oxygen acetylene torch are history because they have electronic torches that will cut finer than gas torches. You no longer twist wrenches; you're in a soundproof booth with a computer. The old days are gone; it's a different era.

The ships wore out before the men who manned them. Likewise the planes. Veterans of Vietnam returned home unsung but not unworthy. Belated attempts to give these veterans the welcome they deserve may do more to assuage leftover civic guilt than to embrace the veterans. Support troops and combat troops mingle now in the camaraderie of veterans groups. There is, to me, a surprising lack of bitterness for the job they were asked to do, and the thanks they received for doing it.

In the last analysis it was a different war for everyone; the Early Years were certainly different from the Later Years, there were differences across the branches of the service and differences across each job description. What was common to everyone, combat and support troops alike, was abiding faith in the short-timer's calendar, and a hope that This Too Shall Pass.

Support troops are team players. While proud of their individual and unit accomplishments – roads and bridges built, communications maintained, supplies delivered, lives saved – the bottom line for support troops is the same as combat troops -- the success of the mission. Vietnam cannot be judged a success but since the combat troops won most of their battles and no engagement was ever cancelled due to lack of supplies or support, the explanation for the lack of success must lie elsewhere.

ACKNOWLEDGEMENTS

The idea for this book was mine. From that point the final product had many fathers, not the least of which are the voices of the 150 men and women interviewed. I began the interview process early in 2010 with my friend Tom Emmons. I knew I could count on my brothers, the guys I grew up with in Pittsburgh and my friends and neighbors in Kentucky. After that I attended parades and picnics, wearing my Vietnam Veteran cap. It appeared after a few months that the interview process could take quite a long time. But my brother Bobby suggested I contact Vietnam Veterans Inc., in Pittsburgh. Butchie Burke of VVI suggested I attend their picnic in June of 2010. I did and collected twenty names. Butchie then suggested I attend a reunion of his 46th Engineer Battalion in Memphis, in September. I did and got another twenty names. Some of those guys provided a name or two, so about a third of my 150 target came from Butchie. Thank you my friend.

Two other contacts suggested I attend their reunions, so I met with the men of the *USS Joseph Strauss* (in Cincinnati) at the invitation of Ted Harris, and the *USS Cleveland* (in Chattanooga) at Rick Dolinar's suggestion. Each of these meetings yielded a handful of participants. At some point I began contacting some of the Vietnam Veterans groups and several of the chapter presidents provided a few contributors. Dave Fuchs, Drew Vargo, Steve Doak, Steve Newsom, Jimmie Johnson, and others were a big help. Other veterans that provided a name or two were Allen Thomas Jr., Dave Warman, Garry Ramsey, Tom Emmons, Tom Petersen and others. Floyd Hastings, Tom Cole, Marilyn Calto, Vicki Herper and other friends also gave me names.

Between the interviewing, editing and finding a publisher, the last task proved to be the most difficult. As a few of them told me, "we pass up dozens of good books every year." I invested over a year in this process but along the way I received some guidance for which I am grateful. Gary Smailes of Bubblecow, Stephen Wrinn of University Press – Kentucky, Demond Jefferson, Bobby Clark and Sherry Welch were helpful at one time or another. In the end, Create Space (Amazon.com) proved to be the best solution.

My sister-in-law Charlotte Clark worked tirelessly to help me remember, or learn, some of the rules of punctuation. I, don't, think,; it, worked.!;

My family was supportive. My wife Carol has read this book more than anyone but myself. I'm sure she earned a Campaign Ribbon. At one time she finished Book One and said she liked it. "Did you remember each guy from chapter to chapter," I asked. She said she didn't, but she still liked the stories. I believe it is important for the reader to be able to connect each story with the right guy so I decided to use the "head shot" pictures in each chapter. It added more space than I wanted but I really believe that to be important. My daughter Regan helped with computer questions, and my youngest daughter Caitlin helped a ton with the picture insertion, as did Tom Emmons. Caitlin turned out to be the publisher. The help with picture insertion was vital. Tom Emmons was my first interview; fittingly, he was there at the beginning and there at the end.

My final and most heart-felt thanks go to the 150 veterans with whom I spoke. I think they recognized that the support troop story needed to be told. Most of the participants provided their stories during taped phone conversations. Although the passage of time has undoubtedly blurred some recollections, I think the participating veterans did a fine job in describing their role in Vietnam. It was my honor and privilege to help fill in this piece of the history of the Vietnam War and to help tell the story that never was told.

GLOSSARY OF ACRONYMS AND ABBREVIATIONS

AFB	Air Force Base
AIT	Advanced Infantry Training
Amtrac	Amphibious Tractor used by USMC
APC	Armored Personnel Carrier
Arty	Artillery
BOQ	Bachelor Officer's Quarters
C-4	Explosives in Play Do form
Chieu Hoi	Amnesty Program for VC
Chinook	Helicopter Used Mainly for Hauling Big Loads
HQ	Headquarters
LAM	Light Anti-aircraft Missile
LPH	Landing Platform Helicopter (ship)
LST	Landing Ship Tank; a supply ship
LZ	Landing Zone
MEDCAP	Medical Civic Action Program
Medevac	Air rescue of wounded troops
MGYSgt	Master Gunnery Sergeant (E-8) USMC
NCO	Non-commissioned officer, i.e. Corporal, Sergeant
P	Piaster – Vietnamese currency
ROTC	Reserve Officer Training Corps
SAR	Search and Rescue
Tender	Repair Ship

SELECTED BIBLIOGRAPHY

Books

Karnow, Stanley. *Vietnam: A History*. New York: The Viking Press, 1983

Dillion, Noah B. Surviving Vietnam: Tales of a Narcoleptic Hangar Rat. Lakewood, California: Avid Readers Publishing Group, 2011

Bellardo, Joseph M. Sr., Dusterman. Jacksonville, Texas: SamPat Press, 2010

Sheehan, Neil. A Bright Shining Lie. New York: Random House, 1988

Summers, Harry G. Jr. Historical Atlas of the Vietnam War. New York: Houghton Mifflin Co., 1995

Westheider, James E. The Vietnam War. Westport, CT, The Greenwood Press, 2007

Carrico, John M. Vietnam Ironclads.

Heiser, Lt. Gen. Joseph M. Logistics Support. Washington, D.C., Dept. of the Army, 1974

Mason, Robert. *Chickenhawk*. New York, Viking Penguin Inc., 1983.

Maurer, Harry. *Strange Ground*, New York, Da Capo Press, 1998.

Halberstam, David, *The Best And The Brightest*, New York, Random House, 1969.

Karnow, Stanley, *Vietnam A History*, New York, The Viking Press, 1983.

Fall, Bernard B., *Hell in a Very Small Place*, Philadelphia, Lippincott, 1967.

Gibson, James William, *The Perfect War*, New York, The Atlantic Monthly Press, 1986.

Moore, Harold G. and Galloway, Joseph L., *We Were Soldiers Once...And Young*, New York, Random House, 1992.

Nalty, Bernard C., *The Vietnam War*, New York, Barnes & Noble Books, 1998.

Sheehan, Neil, *A Bright Shining Lie*, New York, Random House, 1988.

Westheider, James E., *The Vietnam War*, Westport, Greenwood Press, 2007.

Other Sources

A Pocket Guide to Vietnam, Department of Defense

Military Sea Transportation Service Society History

NOTES

[i] Military Sea Transportation Service Society History
[ii] James E. Westheider, *The Vietnam War*, (Westport, CT: Greenwood Press) p. xx.
[iii] Stanley Karnow, *Vietnam: A History*, (New York: Viking Press) p.341.
[iv] David Halberstam, *The Best and the Brightest*, (New York: Ballantine Books) p. 143.
[v] Bernard C. Nalty, *The Vietnam War*, (New York: Barnes & Noble Books) p.146.
[vi] Lt. Gen. Joseph M. Heiser, Jr., Logistic Support (Washington, D.C. Dept. of the Army), p. 37.
[vii] Ibid.
[viii] Ibid., p. 22.
[ix] Ibid., p. 110.
[x] Ibid., p. 8.
[xi] Ibid., p. 194.
[xii] Ibid., p. 197.
[xiii] Maj. Gen. Robert R. Ploger, U.S. Army Engineers 1965 – 1970 (Washington, D.C. Dept. of the Army), p. 108.
[xiv] Ibid.
[xv] Heiser, Logistic Support, p. 212.
[xvi] Ibid., p. 214.
[xvii] Ibid.
[xviii] Ibid., p.35.
[xix] Ibid., p.9.
[xx] Ibid., p. 17.
[xxi] Halberstam, p. 167.
[xxii] Lewis Sorley, *Westmoreland*, (New York: Houghton Mifflin Harcourt) p. 95-6.
[xxiii] Hornfischer, p. 283.
[xxiv] Dept. of Defense, A Pocket Guide to Viet-Nam (Armed Forces Information and Education), p. 5.
[xxv] John M. Carrico, *Vietnam Ironclads* p. 10.
[xxvi] Neil Sheehan, *A Bright Shining Lie*, (New York: Random House) p. 639.
[xxvii] Westheider, p. 32.
[xxviii] Ibid.
[xxix] Harry G. Summers, Jr., Atlas of the Vietnam War, (Boston/ New York: Houghton Mifflin), p. 92.
[xxx] Sheehan, p. 621-623.
[xxxi] Ploger, p. 116.
[xxxii] Heiser, p. 26.
[xxxiii] Ibid., p. 164.
[xxxiv] Ploger, p. 46.
[xxxv] Ploger, p. 106.
[xxxvi] Heiser, p. 164.

[xxxvii] James William Gibson, *The Perfect War* (New York: Atlantic Monthly Press), p. 78.
[xxxviii] Heiser, pgs. 31, 61.
[xxxix] Ploger, p. 163.
[xl] Summers, p. 70.
[xli] Ibid.
[xlii] Nalty, p. 139.
[xliii] Summers, p. 86.
[xliv] Westheider, p. 20.
[xlv] Summers, p. 12.
[xlvi] Karnow, p. 334.
[xlvii] Heiser, Pgs. 34, 35.
[xlviii] Ibid., p. 35.
[xlix] Summers, p. 70.
[l] Heiser, p. 153.
[li] Summers, p. 92.
[lii] Nalty, p. 169.
[liii] Ibid., p. 208-9.
[liv] Westheider, p. 31 – 33.
[lv] Heiser, p. 58.
[lvi] Ibid., p. 61.
[lvii] Ibid., p. 148.
[lviii] Ibid., p. 147.
[lix] Ibid., p. 145.
[lx] Summers, p. 92.
[lxi] Carrico, p. 14.
[lxii] Karnow, p. 437.
[lxiii] Ploger, p. 172.
[lxiv] Summers, p. 150.
[lxv] Ibid., p. 117.
[lxvi] Ibid. p. 138.
[lxvii] Ibid., p. 122.
[lxviii] Walter Geer, *Campaigns of the Civil War*, (Old Saybrook, CT: Konecky & Konecky), p. 13.
[lxix] Karnow, p. 436.
[lxx] Heiser, p. 37.
[lxxi] Ibid., p. 25.
[lxxii] Ibid., p. 276.
[lxxiii] Ibid., p. 167.
[lxxiv] Ibid., p. 194.
[lxxv] Ibid., p. 197.
[lxxvi] Ibid., p. 213.
[lxxvii] Harry Maurer, *Strange Ground*, (New York: Da Capo Press), p. 269.
[lxxviii] Ploger, p. 145-6.
[lxxix] Heiser, p. 43.
[lxxx] Ibid., p. 183.
[lxxxi] Heiser, p. 204.

[lxxxii] Ploger, p. 172.
[lxxxiii] Ibid., p. 118.
[lxxxiv] Ibid., p. 120.
[lxxxv] Ibid., p. 176.
[lxxxvi] Heiser, p. 71.
[lxxxvii] Karnow, p. 426.
[lxxxviii] Ploger, p. 176.
[lxxxix] Summers, p. 172.
[xc] John Prados, *In Country*, (Lanham, MD: Ivan R. Dee), p. 32.
[xci] Lewis Sorley, *Westmoreland,* (Boston New York: Houghton Mifflin Harcourt), p. 258.

Made in the USA
Charleston, SC
29 October 2012